Museum Public Relations

**AASLH Management Series
Volume 2**

This book is the second in a series of handbooks on
the varied aspects of management encountered by
administrators in museums and historical agencies.

Museum Public Relations

G. Donald Adams

The American Association for State and Local History
Nashville, Tennessee

Library of Congress Cataloging in Publication Data

Adams, G. Donald.
 Museum public relations.

 (AASLH management series ; v. 2)
 Bibliography: p.
 Includes index.
 1. Public relations—Museums.   2. Public Relations.
I. Title. II. Series.
AM124.A33   1983   069'.68   83-3708
ISBN 0-910050-65-1

Publication of this book was made possible in part by funds from the sale of the Bicentennial State Histories, which were supported by the National Endowment for the Humanities.

Designed by Gary Gore

to my parents

Contents

Preface

———————◆●◆———————

During my several years in higher education as a one-person public relations department, I could often have used a reference book that addressed my specific needs. When I moved to an office in a museum and began to conduct workshops throughout the country, I met many individuals who were working alone, part time, and with no special training in public relations. In writing, I have tried to answer their questions and to speak to museums large and small, to veteran publicists as well as to beginners. After all, no museum should feel exempt from a concern with public relations.

This book is intended to serve as a basic reference for any type of public relations activity, whether volunteer, part time, or full time. Although many program examples relate to history museums, the concepts, procedures, and policy recommendations apply equally to institutions concerned with art, natural history, and science; to historic homes, parks, and preservation organizations; to aquariums and planetariums; to company, university, and state museums and archives; to performing arts organizations; and to botanical gardens and zoological parks, regardless of size, budget, or staff. I have emphasized basic programs that can be conducted with small budgets and with services contributed by professionals, but I have also discussed more advanced programs involving specialists and larger budgets. Because advanced marketing concepts are employed most effectively in conjunction with advertising campaigns that are more extensive than many museums can afford, I have discussed only basics that are useful to the majority of museums that rely heavily on free publicity, sound public relations, and limited advertising. These marketing basics include audience research and segmentation, targeted communication, and ongoing evaluation of message feedback. How these basics are being used at many American museums was summarized in the September 1982 issue of *Advertising Age*.[1] Whether programs are managed by a well-assisted director or by a volunteer is less important than a museum's commitment to meeting both its professional standards and its public responsibilities.

ix

I offer my suggestions on the assumption that they can and should be modified to fit individual circumstances. Readers may find it helpful to keep certain questions in mind when evaluating my ideas. What is your museum's purpose? How is it being expressed? Do people know how to use the institution? Do programs perhaps answer questions that no one is asking? If the media were the public's sole source of information, what would people think about your museum? Does the museum believe it is communicating one message when it is really communicating another? Try to look at your institution from the perspective of people beyond its doors. These individuals form the constituency on which the survival of your museum—any museum—depends.

I am grateful to all the many people who helped with my research and writing. I regret that it is possible to recognize only a few. Foremost I wish to thank the American Association for State and Local History, which recognized the need for such a book, and particularly Betty Doak Elder, who provided excellent advice throughout the project. Donald Friary (Historic Deerfield), Albert O. Louer (Colonial Williamsburg), Larry Morrison (Old Sturbridge Village), and John Sheppard (The Brandywine River Museum), are colleagues who were especially helpful. Robert Dawson, Sharon Blagdon-Smart, Craig Brosch, Peter Logan, David DeVore, Will Lawson, Charles Sena, Jan Sherbin, Geoffrey Upward, and David Wojack are members of the public affairs, publications, and development departments at Henry Ford Museum who reviewed copy and made important suggestions. Carl Malotka, Rudolph Ruzicska, and Tim Hunter, of Henry Ford Museum's photography staff, and Mark Gordon, at Chacma, Inc., made significant contributions to the section on photography.

Finally I owe special thanks to my wife, Jane, who survived living with me through this project and reviewed every page, and to Monica Valant, who typed the manuscript.

G. *Donald Adams*

Introduction

Successful public relations today means a relationship with, rather than simply to, the public—an exchange of information and ideas. Such was not always the case. The nineteenth-century advertisements by which Phineas T. Barnum initially enticed people to his American Museum are filled with exaggerated claims and promises that show scant awareness of the public being addressed. They can have done little to allay the growing skepticism of publicity among warier members of society, including museum directors. Still, Barnum profited in about 1883 from the example set by the American Telephone Company, which began testing programs that involved two-way communication. Further development of the publicist's profession resulted from allegations of corporate irresponsibility in the first quarter of the twentieth century: the emerging concept of public relations meant that firms needed to listen to and communicate with their publics and be genuinely responsive to public needs. Early practitioners of public relations as we know it were corporations, educational institutions, and religious and health organizations. PR has become important to other groups in society, including museums, somewhat more recently.

Why has it become of greater concern to museums? A few of the simpler reasons will suffice. Only by understanding its publics can a museum hope to attract visitors in increasing numbers, to satisfy them, to expand and improve its programs, and to prosper. In addition, public relations serves to educate society in the use and enjoyment of museums and, as consultant Frances Koestler has noted,

> When used to optimum advantage, public relations thinking contributes an essential viewpoint to virtually every kind of policy and management decision: a viewpoint that reflects existing public attitudes, predicts the decision's impact on those attitudes, and proposes appropriate communication methods and channels to make it understandable and acceptable.[1]

That museums increasingly agree has been apparent from several developments. At its 1980 national conference, the American Association of Museums unanimously endorsed goals that emphasized the

1

need for a museum to retain its intellectual independence. The association noted, however, that "the vitality of museums depends upon their ability to adapt their programs and their operations to reflect the changing standards and characteristics of the public they serve."[2] Furthermore, although of 317 museums which answered the AAM's 1980 position qualification study only 80 respondents described themselves as engaged in public relations,[3] it is noteworthy that more than 500 association members in that year indicated an interest in joining the organization's newly formed standing Committee on Public Relations and Communications Management.

When the AAM established a Commission on Museums for a New Century in 1981, its two major objectives were to assess the direction museums must take during the next twenty years and to increase public visibility of museums. In a synopsis of the key issues that are important to the future of museums, an AAM report to the commission noted that "The educational role of the museum is firmly established. Since World War II museums have been increasingly aware of their public and of their duty to that public." As stated by AAM President Thomas W. Leavitt, one of the important questions confronting museums today is "How are museums viewed by the public, and are those views in accord with our images of ourselves?" [4] When the commission report is completed in 1984 it will identify new needs to be met by people in public relations. Meanwhile, the responsibilities enumerated by part- and full-time respondents to a questionnaire sent out by the AAM Public Relations Committee in 1980 include, in order of frequency:

1. print media publicity;
2. management of public relations programs;
3. radio and television publicity;
4. publications;
5. fund raising and membership development;
6. attendance development;
7. mailing list development and maintenance;
8. advertising;
9. community relations;
10. special events;
11. marketing;
12. handling emergencies;
13. maintaining relations with professional organizations;
14. working with outside public relations counsel;

15. photography;
16. legislative relations;
17. development of tourism;
18. volunteer relations.

The nature of the work varies greatly, but in any given institution the public relations efforts of different individuals ideally combine to form a coherent program with a coherent purpose. Successful public relations requires:

- a thorough understanding of the museum's programs, collections, and publics served;
- a mechanism for the continuous recording and evaluation of public opinion about the museum;
- a policy-forming procedure that considers public reactions and the museum's needs, balancing the two interests within the framework of professional standards, goals, and objectives;
- a public relations plan that defines needs, sets goals, and provides for evaluation of performance;
- a purposeful communication program that uses the most appropriate media to reach specific publics;
- a long-range view that permits the institution to anticipate opportunities and problems and to deal with them effectively.

Communication may be regarded as the primary task of public relations staff.

People receive messages not only from the museum, but also from friends who have visited the museum. Word-of-mouth communication is the basis for many museum visits and has a strong influence in obtaining support of all types.

Figure 1 illustrates how word-of-mouth communication is produced continuously. Along with other messages, it can generate expectations and a desire to visit. During the visit, on-site messages create an impression that may or may not meet expectations. Later that impression is communicated to friends, creating a new previsit message and influencing their expectations.

Although their emphases will vary, publicists, interpreters, educators, and other museum employees should develop their messages from the same basic information to assure that previsit, on-site, and postvisit messages will be consistent and that expectations created by word-of-mouth communication can be fulfilled. To achieve this objective, it is

△ THE WORD-OF-MOUTH MESSAGE CHAIN

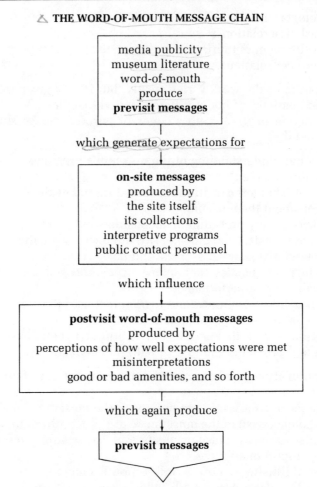

Figure 1. *The word-of-mouth message chain*

helpful to have a message base. It may be written by the public relations department but should be shared with the staff. It can be a simple statement that establishes:

△
- the nature of the collections (fine art, folk art, technology, local history, agriculture, etc.);
- The scope of the collections and programs (what is the geo-

graphical focus? which collections are the most complete and of highest quality?);

- the facilities (is the museum a farm, a house, or open air?);
- the point of view (does the museum wish to represent the cultural contributions of a minority group, to legitimize a community's claim as a historically important manufacturing center, to interpret a specific time period?);
- the emphasis, as expressed by educational classes, special events, permanent and special exhibits, labels, sales and entertainment offerings, and publications (does the museum present itself as a park for family relaxation? does it encourage visitors to feel awe when viewing the collections? does it emphasize educational aspects of the visitor's experience?);
- interpretation (is it living history, presented in the third person or the first person?);
- dependence (does the museum depend for its funding upon government agencies, corporations, foundations, or a few wealthy individuals? from what region and from what groups must it draw audiences for its programs?).

Many of these questions may be answered by the museum's written statement of purpose or mission. If one is not available, a specially prepared message base statement such as the following is a useful substitute.

△ XYZ is an open air regional farm museum, a nonprofit educational institution supported by paid attendance primarily from the eastern United States and by private and government grants. XYZ emphasizes nineteenth-century cultural and technological changes as they were experienced by rural farm families in New England. Living history interpretation and specialized collections stress dairying and the production of feed crops.

Once it has been written and approved, the message base serves as a foundation for many types of communication between the museum and its publics. Since effective communication depends upon an understanding of certain principles, I will consider them briefly before discussing the nature of work in public relations and the qualifications necessary to perform the task.

Whether it takes place in informal conversation or through the medium of a printed brochure, communication involves a process with △ certain distinct stages. Initially an event of some sort is interpreted, or decoded, by a person. To express his or her understanding, that person must then encode it and transmit it, perhaps by simply speaking aloud but equally possibly by writing and mailing it or by broadcasting it. The message sent constitutes an event for the recipient, who must then decode for understanding. This process is depicted in figure 2. The diagram may seem to complicate our view of a brief conversation unnecessarily, but it is useful in showing what all forms of communication have in common and in indicating the points—encoding, decoding, and transmission—at which the message may become garbled.

Effective communication thus has several prerequisites. A sender must skillfully encode his or her understanding of a situation, producing a message that is both accurate and comprehensible to the intended receiver(s). Whether or not the message is understood will depend on its decoders, and the sender must therefore identify and understand them. Finally, to learn whether or not the message accomplished its objective, the sender needs feedback.

If we translate our abstract model into the specific context of a museum, several points immediately become clear. First, the com-

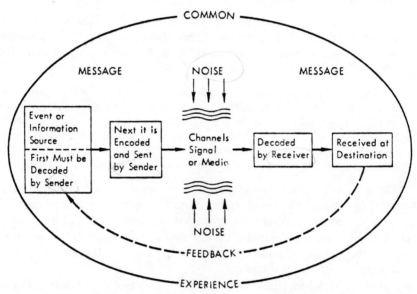

Figure 2. The communication process. Source: *Scott M. Cutlip/Allen H. Center, Effective Public Relations, 5th ed. © 1978, p. 191. Reprinted by permission of Prentice-Hall, Inc., Englewood Cliffs, N.J.*

municator must comprehend the message before he or she can send it, which broadly construed in an institutional setting means understanding the museum—its needs, goals, and activities (and anything that affects them) as well as the specific purpose that the message is intended to serve. It is also important to know the most appropriate channels of communication—those that will most effectively relay the message to the target audience. Bearing in mind the word-of-mouth communication model, the message base, and the basic communication process, let us now consider public relations and its place in museum management.

1

Preparing for Public Relations

Because public relations forms such a vital link between an institution and its publics, the PR director, whether a volunteer, a part-time practitioner, or a full-time specialist, must be regarded as part of management. Only at this level can he or she incorporate public needs and concerns into decisions about policy and procedure while at the same time remaining informed about the rationale for the museum's actions and ready to interpret them. Even the public relations director who is a volunteer must participate in meetings to plan policy.

The person chosen for the job must be loyal to the museum and its objectives, respected by the staff and the community, and known to show good judgment in making decisions and handling information. If the position is part time, extra efforts may be needed to keep the staff member informed and involved at the policy level. A very special person may be required, someone who can perform dual functions, perhaps serving as a curator, educator, or librarian while at the same time remaining sensitive to the public's point of view. In most cases when budgetary considerations mean that a PR person will work less than full time, someone who is employed in public relations elsewhere and has specialized training and experience will be best qualified.

Regardless of institutional differences in the position, however, it must be filled by a person who routinely helps determine the museum's responses to matters of public concern. PR staff must have input into operating procedures and policy decisions, and the public relations director must therefore learn early about all problems, emergencies, and new developments. He or she must also have direct access to the executive director and must be involved in preparing any messages that the museum communicates to the public, whether they are news releases, publications, or signs.

How best to staff, budget, and organize a public relations department obviously depends on the size and objectives of the museum. It is important to evaluate needs carefully before making these important decisions.

Trustee and Advisory Committees

Trustees continuously assess museum operations and may produce policy changes that will change public relations objectives, plans, and programs. The trustees' own role in PR will depend upon the museum's organizational structure. Active trustee committees may include one for public relations that is chaired by a trustee and includes a museum staff member and board members with relevant expertise. Such a committee will usually review public relations budget recommendations with the executive director and will take the budget to the full board for approval. The committee may also present periodic reports on public relations performance to the board at large. Whether or not such a committee exists at your institution, the staff member with the greatest responsibility for public relations should attend trustees' meetings. That person could be the chief executive officer, a vice president to whom the public relations person reports, or the public relations director (whether volunteer, part time, or full time).

In every case, the museum's executive director is responsible for informing and counseling the trustees on public relations needs. In addition the executive director participates in the development of promotional policies and keeps the public relations director generally informed, making certain that that person is represented on committees and in all activities involving relationships with the museum's publics.

An institution may also have nontrustee public relations committees. Public relations counselor Arthur C. Frantzreb suggests, however, that public relations persons inexperienced in volunteer work should not create institutional relations advisory committees too early in their professional careers, because such groups of volunteers can be overzealous, volatile, and difficult to handle.[1] He explains that if such a committee is established, its function must be to advise in the early rather than the final stages of planning. A second problem may arise if the advisory committee's members include persons employed in the management of print and broadcast media. The vested interests of these individuals may bring offers of special treatment in their media that interfere with in-house promotional plans and cause media not represented on the committee to suspect favoritism.

It is safer to use volunteers on a reactor rather than advisory panel, to evaluate completed public relations programs and to recommend corrections in mid-course. Such a panel, including representatives from the media, from an opinion research agency, and from important local government offices can be helpful in objectively reviewing programs.

Departmental Staff

The public relations functions required at a museum depend upon its objectives. The columns of table 1.1 show some common specific ways in which museums often seek to increase their attendance and financial support. The rows indicate public relations functions often brought to bear on these objectives. Table 1.2 describes how responsibilities might change as a museum's public relations staff increases.

One highly qualified PR person working part time and assisted by volunteers can be very effective if the museum is small and has

- adequate and assured financial support that does not vary with annual fluctuations in the size and breadth of the museum's audiences;
- collection and program offerings of primary interest to visitors from a local area or to a small special interest group;
- a respected position in the community that is unlikely to be eroded by other agencies competing for a portion of the museum's financial support base;
- a small staff, a small physical facility, and a limited budget.

A staff consisting of one or more full-time public relations specialists is recommended when the museum:

- depends heavily upon outside financial support from several sources, at least some of which use the size and breadth of audience as important criteria for awarding funds;
- must use admission fees to help meet operating costs;
- has collection, program, and staff resources that can be used to appeal to new interest groups and to attract visitors from a broader region;
- has competition for financial support from other local nonprofit organizations;
- has a sizable operating budget and large overhead.

A public relations office staffed with professionals in several areas of expertise is recommended when the museum has:

TABLE 1.1   A FUNCTIONAL ANALYSIS OF PUBLIC RELATIONS

Public relations function	Increased paid admission	Increased membership	More effective annual giving programs	More individual and corporate gift income	More government grants	More productive employees	More productive volunteer programs
Informal public opinion research	•	•	•	•	•		•
Formal public opinion research	•	•	•	•			
Long-range and strategic public relations planning	•	•	•	•	•	•	•
Factoring public opinion into policy decisions	•	•	•	•	•	•	•
Public relations operating plan	•	•	•	•	•	•	•
Media relations and publicity program	•	•	•	•	•		•
Publications	•	•	•	•	•	•	•
Employee relations	•		•	•		•	•
Donor relations		•	•	•	•		
Volunteer relations	•	•	•	•		•	•
Community relations	•	•	•	•	•	•	•
Special events	•	•					

TABLE 1.2. AN ANALYSIS OF PUBLIC RELATIONS STAFF NEEDS

Public relations responsibility	None	One (half time)	Public relations employees			
			One (full time)	Two	Three or more
Informal public opinion research	Work is coordinated by executive director, involves all employees in conversations with visitors	Same	Coordinated by PR, involves employees	Same	Same
Formal public opinion research	Donated professional service from agency or university or contracted for a fee if budget permits; supervised by executive director	Same	Same except PR is liaison with professional service	Same	Same except PR implements simple research programs on continuous basis
Long-range and strategic public relations planning	Executive director in liaison with trustee or volunteer pr committee does research, prepares plan	Same	PR works with executive director and with any advisory committee to prepare plan	Same	Same
Transmitting public opinion into policy decisions	Executive director	PR on informal basis	PR on systematic basis	Same	Same
Public relations operating plan	Executive director and trustee or volunteer PR committee	Same but with PR input	PR	Same	Same

Table 1.2 (continued)

	None	One (half time)	One (full time)	Two	Three or more
Media relations and publicity program	Executive director and designated members of staff or volunteers	PR person with free-lance or volunteer help	PR	Same	Same
Publications preparation	Executive director and outside service	Same	PR	Same	Same
Employee relations	Executive director and personnel manager	Same	Personnel manager with PR input	Same	Same
Donor relations	Executive director and trustees and development director, if any	Same	Same, with assistance from PR	Same	Same
Volunteer relations	Executive director and designated member of staff	Same	Same with input from PR	Activities such as recognition programs by PR	Same
Community relations	Executive director and all employees	Same	Systematic program by PR	Same	Same
Special events management	Executive director and all employees	PR supported by appropriate departments	Same	Same	Same

- collections and programs of sufficient importance to attract visitors from throughout the nation, in a region of several states, or in a densely populated metropolitan area;
- high operating costs reflecting a large staff, major facilities, and numerous programs;
- financial support dependent upon cultivation of many diversified publics.

The museum may meet its public relations staffing needs by

- making public relations the responsibility of the museum's chief executive officer;
- adding public relations to the existing responsibilities of a presently employed member of the professional staff;
- hiring a part-time public relations specialist;
- employing one or more full-time public relations specialists;
- combining volunteers, volunteer advisory counsels, and reactor panels with any of the preceding suggestions;
- using a professional public relations counseling firm if there is an appropriate staff person to oversee its activities.

Each of these possibilities has drawbacks as well as advantages. Although executive directors necessarily act as museums' chief liaison with the public, they seldom have the time to implement and to maintain a public relations program and still attend to other important tasks. Trustees should be aware of this fact.

It is only slightly more advisable to add public relations to the existing duties of a presently employed staff member. Such a person is not usually trained for public relations and will view the job from a limited perspective.

Volunteers trained and experienced in public relations may succeed if they are well acquainted with the museum. Inexperienced volunteers can also be effective if they are supervised by someone more knowledgeable.

The Part-Time Specialist

The part-time public relations specialist should possess the following requirements at a minimum:

- an ability to write, speak, and listen well;
- a good attitude toward the museum, its employees, and the people who support it;

- tact and an initiative that make it easy to develop working relationships with internal and external publics;
- creativity and an ability to identify and exploit the interesting, novel, and significant aspects of situations.

If possible, the part-time public relations candidate should have these additional qualifications:

- a bachelor's degree, preferably in public relations, journalism, or communications;
- public relations experience in a nonprofit institution or organization, such as a college or university;
- an interest in subjects corresponding to the museum's principal focus.

The Full-Time Specialist

According to a 1980 AAM report: "The public relations officer's function is to establish useful relationships between a museum's substance and goals and the perceived needs and interests of its various publics. The public relations officer establishes community relations for the museum and monitors specific interests and issues so a museum can participate in the development of issues affecting it." [2]

The museum public relations person should have:

1. a sound knowledge of the collections and the desire and willingness to learn continually about the museum's operation;
2. typing, copyediting, and proofreading skills, sound judgment, and knowledge of all the media and how they work;
3. a fetish for accuracy and a preoccupation with meeting media needs in a professional manner;
4. an inquisitive mind, a compulsion for listening, and a consciousness that automatically asks regarding every event, "Is there a story in it?"
5. an ability to manage and understand people and budgets;
6. a sensitivity to human motivation and an ability to develop cooperative relationships;
7. an ability to be supportive of other departments without interfering in their work;
8. an ability to work on many projects simultaneously, taking the most direct route to the accomplishment of each;
9. an ability to be objective about evaluating and correcting his or

her own work and to take criticism and disappointment constructively;

10. a sense of graphic design and good taste.

Museums occasionally recruit reporters and editors to fill public relations positions. Such persons often need training. There is the risk that they will view the position too narrowly, perhaps as merely publicity, and that their background in one area will limit their initiative and skill in others. Celebrities from the local media may identify so strongly with their former place of employment that their former colleagues and the general public have difficulty associating them with the museum.

Museum public relations salaries should be comparable to those paid for similar management positions at colleges and universities. Members of the public relations staff should not be allowed to accept outside payment for articles, films, or photos when the museum is the subject.

Effective outlets in which to advertise for full-time public relations specialists include the *AVISO* (published by the American Association of Museums), *History News* (American Association for State and Local History, or AASLH), *Preservation News* (National Trust for Historic Preservation), and *Editor and Publisher* magazine. Mailing addresses appear in the sources section of this book.

Training the Public Relations Person

With the exception of the executive director, no one in the museum's employ needs a broader grasp of its operations than the staff member responsible for public relations. In addition to reading everything available on the museum, this person should complete any interpreter's training program that the institution offers and, with the help of curators, should become aware of the contents of all collections. A knowledge of the entire institution and of the demands made of it is essential before PR staff can understand the nature of the available resources and plan for their appropriate use. Visits to representatives of key media and acquaintances with printers and other suppliers should also be high priorities.

The PR person may wish to apply for accreditation by the Public Relations Society of America, which requires a minimum of five years' experience in public relations. Membership in the Standing Professional Committee for Public Relations and Communication Management of the AAM is also helpful. AAM and AASLH publications offer useful ideas and inspiration, as do regional and national conferences, workshops, and seminars. The Smithsonian Institution; George Washington University; the Museums Collaborative associated with Columbia University Graduate School of Business and the State University of New York; New York University School of Continuing Education; and the Association of College, University, and Community Arts Administrators all sponsor public relations and marketing training workshops. See the sources at the end of this book for addresses.

It is always useful to learn how others have resolved the types of public relations problems that confront your museum. Exchanging experiences and ideas at professional meetings, workshops, and seminars prepares you to make sound judgments and to plan successful programs. Professional associations offer opportunities to write papers for publication and to participate on panels. This improves the practice of public relations at all museums, strengthening them to better compete with other nonprofit organizations for support.

Public Relations Staff and the Curator

Even the most seasoned public relations practitioners need to be aware of the problems that can be encountered in working with colleagues in other museum departments. Conflict between curators and public relations personnel, for example, may arise from differences in perspective; public relations is still relatively new at museums, and museum professionals sometimes view it as lying beyond the museum's proper sphere of interest.

The public relations person must act as a source of information for the media, but the curator constitutes a source of information as well. Conflict may begin when the PR staff member answers questions about specific items in a collection without consulting the appropriate curator. If incorrect information is published, the mistake will reflect badly on the publicist, the curator, and the museum. Tension may also result when curators approached directly by reporters do not inform the public relations person, who needs to be aware immediately of all museum information that is being considered for publication.

Public relations people should always rely upon information prepared or approved by curators and should check with curators when answering questions related to artifacts. A simple "I'll get back to you" in response to a writer's telephone request makes possible contact with the appropriate curator that will forestall difficulties. If the curator does not know the answer and cannot find it quickly, the best approach is to advise the writer accordingly and to suggest that he or she call the public relations person at a museum likely to have the information desired. An awareness of other museums' resources allows PR staff to serve the media better and helps museums in general serve the public.

Differences in perspective may also become apparent when the public relations person contacts the curator for a brief answer to a writer's question. Uppermost in the public relations person's mind is a concern with meeting media needs as fully as possible so that writers will continue to contact the museum, confident that they will receive prompt and helpful service. Writers often have a story in their typewriters and call as they are approaching the completion deadline. They frequently want only a short, interesting, immediate answer that will add color and impact to the copy.

Curators, however, are likely to see themselves as sources of precise information that is researched over a long period of time and is developed from a historical perspective that is consistent with their professional concerns. Development specialist Michael Radock, referring to differences in perspective among university faculty members and public relations people, notes that academic professionals are inclined to be concerned with detail, whereas public relations staff are more concerned with broad impact.[3]

Although situations vary with the personalities involved, certain basic guidelines will help PR personnel maintain productive relationships with the museum's curators and other important information sources, including educators, registrars, and conservators.

- Understand the different perspectives from which others operate, and be as cooperative as possible.
- Be certain the curator is the source of factual information about collection items and is credited as the source.
- Be sure the person responsible for a collection or area of operation that is in a story written by the museum checks the copy, but only for the correctness of facts. Explain that the publicist must write the material so that it meets the requirements of the target media.
- Suggest that the employee manual explain the purpose of the public relations program in terms such that everyone will understand its objectives and the support it needs. Suggest that curators' job descriptions include the responsibility of providing collections information to the public relations office for use by the media;[4] parti-

cipation in publicity efforts will give curators the opportunity to interpret their collections beyond the physical confines of the museum.

- Make a point of introducing curators to representatives of the media. As acquaintances develop, curators will see that reporters share their concern for the correctness of facts, and they will learn firsthand why journalists use certain writing styles and must work with short deadlines.
- Because sessions that require a curator to accompany media visitors can be lengthy, particularly when film crews are involved, be sure to notify curators in advance as to when and for about how long they will be needed; demands upon their time should be as minimal as possible.[5]
- If you are asked questions about collections or artifacts during talk show interviews and on other occasions when a curator is not present, confine yourself to general information derived from fact sheets and backgrounders written jointly by the public relations person and the curator (samples appear in the appendix.)
- Make curators aware that publicity for their specific collection can stimulate public interest in it, which can lead to increased attendance at their exhibits and perhaps also to donations of needed artifacts. Furthermore, publicity can build the curator's professional visibility, with the result that his or her desires for exhibit space and accessions receive greater consideration by the museum.
- Become an integral part of daily operations by attending lectures and gallery tours, enrolling in adult education enrichment courses, and participating on committees. The less you are an outsider, the better you can interpret the museum on the basis of firsthand knowledge, can judge your work continuously in relation to that of other staff, and can work to improve relationships with museum colleagues and with the public.

The Counseling Firm

Association with a public relations counseling firm may result when the firm is hired by the sponsor of a traveling exhibit hosted by the museum or by the donor of a collection gift. The museum itself may occasionally contract for a specific short-term project or may retain an agency on a continuing basis.

When an agency is engaged by an outside organization for a single project, such as publicity for a traveling exhibit, the in-house public relations person may be at a disadvantage. Because the museum wants to display the exhibit and wants to see it promoted, permanent staff may be viewed as obstructionist if the two sets of plans conflict. To avoid such difficulties, museum departments that are booking traveling shows should delegate publicity management to the in-house public relations person before contracts are signed. The museum PR office would do well to discuss the counseling firm's operating procedures with colleagues at museums where the exhibit has already appeared. Some firms that are retained to promote exhibits sponsored by corporations are accustomed to a more commercial approach than is customary or perhaps even desirable for a museum. The museum and the firm may bring entirely different backgrounds to the relationship and may have different views of the agency's function.

Corporations may also involve their public relations counsel when they present a museum with a gift in the form of an early version of a product still being manufactured. In such cases the prestige from the museum's acceptance and exhibition of the gift serves as a subtle testimonial for the firm's current products, and the company naturally seeks to publicize the occasion of presentation. Before the gift is accepted, extreme care must be exercised to prevent the public relations agency from using the museum as a sales arm for the corporate client.

Retaining Public Relations Counsel

A public relations counseling firm is not a substitute for in-house staff. Someone in the museum must always provide liaison with the firm and keep it on track. Public relations counsel and assistance can be used most effectively by museums when specific short-term projects call for extra help. It is best to delegate to the counseling firm those programs for which the museum public relations department does not have the necessary staff, expertise, contacts, or equipment. For example, if your institution plans to begin in two years its first major capital gift campaign in a three-state region, a counseling firm might develop a series of one-minute television public service spots for that region's key stations and might book selected museum employees on television talk shows. Meanwhile the museum's public relations department could produce supportive print media publicity and campaign mailers.

A recent issue of *Museum News* published a checklist of questions that you should ask when entering into a contract with a consultant.[6]

1. Have you fully examined your motives for hiring the outside adviser?
2. Do you have the intention, resources, and will to implement the agent's advice?
3. Have you allowed enough time to choose the right firm or individual?
4. Did you check the right resources to identify the field of available consultants?
5. Did you cover all necessary aspects of your agreement in the written contract?
6. Were you too quickly charmed by techniques designed to impress you as a client and to win your business?

Familiarize yourself with the particular strengths of each firm being considered. Not all are skilled at producing film for television, for example, and some firms will be costly because they offer expensive services that the museum does not need.

Counseling firms often claim to offer:

- a fresh outlook on problems;
- objectivity and open-mindedness;
- a variety of special skills that can be brought to bear upon a museum's problems;
- regional offices with media contacts that are personal and therefore more effective for broad campaigns;
- mailing lists, graphic design, and photographic and other services;
- knowledge gained through experience with other accounts.

Although each of these qualifications may hold appeal for a museum, equally satisfactory results can often be achieved in other ways at less cost. Properly administered volunteer reactor panels can give a fresh outlook on problems, and in-house research studies can provide reliable and objective information. Special talents are almost always available on an hourly or single-fee free-lance basis. Seldom are a museum's public relations programs broad enough in scope to require public relations offices in several regions. Finally, because the counseling firm is not privy to a museum's operations every day year round, the consultant will inevitably be less informed than you about the museum's work and needs. At worst, the outsiders may prove insensitive to the precarious balance that must be maintained between the museum's professional standards and the needs of its publics.

Fee Structures

When you contract with a counseling firm for a specific short-term project, you will probably be charged a fee for services plus out-of-pocket expenses. The basic fee will include the firm's overhead expenses and staff time.

Ongoing contracts, for continuing services, involve a fixed monthly retainer, a retainer plus monthly billing for staff time on an hourly or per diem basis, or a base fee billed monthly, to which increments are added for extra services performed. Out-of-pocket expenses are usually billed at cost and are not included in the basic fee.

Budgeting

The public relations budget is the museum's public relations plan expressed in terms of cost.

Many public relations people dislike budgeting and are afraid of it. Don Bates notes in *Channels*, published by the Public Relations Society of America, "As a result, [PR staff] leave important decisions about their activities in the hands of accounting or other executives with little interest or understanding of the public relations function." [7]

When developing the budget, be aware of the total operating funds available to the museum, and be prepared to establish and defend a reasonable percentage for public relations. A public relations plan that is approved by the trustees and has operating and contingency cost estimates is important in securing adequate budget allocations. The nature and urgency of the public relations problems with regard to the museum's key publics and their priorities in the public relations plan are important considerations in establishing budget needs. Checking the percentage of total operating costs allocated to public relations by similar museums and hospitals, colleges, and universities that have successful programs may be helpful. Public relations performance measured in terms of increases in paid attendance, gift income, and other results can help persuade the executive director to make adequate budget allocations.

It is important to determine if the services that public relations provides to other museum departments, such as the writing of publications for the education department, will be in the PR budget. You should also consider any overtime labor charges and packaging, handling, and postage costs and should make allowances for any contingencies. In allowing for annual inflation, be particularly attentive to changes in the costs of materials used in services such as printing. If the proposed budget has to be reduced, the public relations person should have the authority to reallocate funds within the budget so that programs of the highest priority can be retained.

Preparing a cash flow analysis for the twelve months of the fiscal year based on accurate cost estimates will be helpful in monitoring expenditures. Because most museums' business is seasonal, cash flow problems are a common occurrence. Linear budgeting, in which one-twelfth of the total is allocated to each month, does not work well. If a major expenditure is scheduled for a month when income is expected to be lean, it is best to advise the comptroller of this fact at the time when the proposed budget is submitted.

Accurate and frequent disbursement reports, coded so that they correspond to budget entries, are essential. Assign a separate departmental code number to each public relations administrative function. When authorizing each expenditure, assign it the proper number. Because public relations is so broadly involved in museum operations, precautions are necessary to ensure that the PR department does not pay for items and services included in other departments' budgets.

Constructing the Budget

Functional budgets state the costs of resources in terms of what they accomplish. Administrative budgets describe the nature of expenditures rather than their specific function. The administrative budget shows the code numbers assigned to each line item, which can be matched to invoices, thus permitting changes to be monitored. Cash flow budgets realistically appraise anticipated expenditures for each month of the fiscal year.

Below are portions of a hypothetical museum public relations budget expressed in functional, administrative, and cash flow terms. All costs except staff salaries and benefits are included.

Functional budget

Fund-raisir support	
Annual report	$ 5,000
50% of community leader list development	150
25% of publicity costs	200
50% of production of motion picture	10,000
Attendance support	
75% of publicity costs	600
50% of production of motion picture	10,000
Volunteer relations	
50% of community leader list development	150
Volunteer Newsletter	250
Total	$26,350

Administrative budget

(Public relations code number 300 followed by numbers indicating categories within that budget)

Printing (300–001)	$ 5,250
List Development (300–002)	300
Publicity (300–003)	800
Film Production	20,000
Total	$26,350

Cash flow budget

Month	Fund-raising support	Attendance support	Volunteer relations	Total
Jan.	$ 50.00	$ 25.00	$ 20.00	$ 95.00
Feb.	5,000.00	25.00	20.00	5,045.00
March	50.00	50.00	20.00	120.00
April	50.00	50.00	20.00	120.00
May	50.00	150.00	20.00	220.00
June	1,000.00	100.00	20.00	1,120.00
July	2,500.00	75.00	20.00	2,595.00
Aug.	2,500.00	1,025.00	20.00	3,545.00
Sept.	4,000.00	4,025.00	20.00	8,045.00
Oct.	150.00	2,025.00	170.00	2,345.00
Nov.	—	2,025.00	20.00	2,045.00
Dec.	—	1,025.00	30.00	1,055.00
Total	$15,350.00	$10,600.00	$400.00	$26,350.00

The following is a sample list of items to remember in budget planning. You will undoubtedly want to extend and alter this list to fit your museum's special needs and situation.

Checklist of items to remember in budget preparation

Research
Questionnaire forms
Contracting outside research services
Media directories
Clippings services
Subscription fees
Memberships, workshops, seminars

Cultivation
Name badges
Business cards
Food, lodging, travel reimbursements for visiting writers
Receptions
Staff travel and entertainment of media visitors

Production
Release stock and imprints
Photography, prints, modeling fees
Free-lance writing fees
Telephone charges
Motion picture film or videotape stock
Production and talent fees, television film, radio tapes and records
Publications design, graphics services, printing
Contingency reserves
Equipment

Distribution
Addressing, handling, and postage
Computerized distribution service fees
Multiple prints of motion pictures or videotapes
Radio tape dubs or records
Press kit folders and imprints

Although preliminary public relations plans will be affected by budgetary considerations, budgetary decisions will also need to be influenced by public relations plans. Once you have defined the overall scope of your efforts, you will want to compare plans and budgets repeatedly in the course of the year, adjusting as necessary to accommodate unexpected contingencies. Flexibility can help you make the most of public relations opportunities.

2

Approaches to Research and Planning

The first step in communicating with the public is identifying and learning about its members. This chapter will consider ways of doing that by using research to plan and establish PR priorities. The publics audit defines groups of people in relation to the museum, analyzes the institution's present and future dependence on them, and records existing and potential problems in each category of relationship. To make a publics audit, first prepare a list of all the sorts of people who are involved with or participate in the museum. Some individuals may be in more than one public at a time, like the donor who is also a volunteer and a student in museum classes.

The publics list should be as comprehensive as possible and probably will include:

employees;
trustees;
volunteers;
participants in special events;
neighbors;
community residents;
members;
major donor individuals;
major donor corporations;
major donor foundations;
local, state, and federal government officials;
local opinion leaders, such as teachers and ministers;

national opinion leaders associated with museum and travel industry associations;

regulatory bodies such as the Occupational Safety and Health Administration (OSHA);

municipal services such as police and fire departments;

commercial services, such as vendors and private contractors;

businesses benefiting from the museum, such as lodging and eating
establishments;

participants in ongoing museum activities, including craft dem-
onstrators and speakers;

professional peers;

individual visitors (youngsters, teens, and seniors) and visitor groups
(schools, churches, scouts, motor coach, and charter group tours).

When you are satisfied that all publics have been listed, consider
each from several perspectives. The publics audit shown in table 2.1
can be used as a guide for such an examination. Each audit entry described in table 2.1 should be factual, complete, and specific. Office
records and people in other departments at the museum may help you
research this information. Table 2.2 illustrates publics audit entries for
a hypothetical museum's major donors. The entries in the "resources"
column should include not only obvious forms of support but also the
goodwill of important publics, membership in associations that advance the interests of the museum, and alliances with organizations
whose goals coincide with those of the museum and whose support
enhances the museum's message. Existing programs that link the
museum with its publics, even though they may not be conducted by
the public relations department, should also be listed as resources. For
example, a volunteer newsletter published by and for volunteers independent of the museum, is a resource that maintains communication
with an important public.

TABLE 2.1. THE PUBLICS AUDIT

Col. 1	Col. 2	Col. 3	Col. 4	Col. 5	Col. 6	Col. 7
Public	Existing dependence upon this public	Potential dependence upon this public in next two years	Existing problems with this dependence	Potential problems with this dependence in next two years	Needs existing and potential	Existing resources, strengths, and weaknesses

TABLE 2.2. A SAMPLE PUBLICS AUDIT

PUBLIC: MAJOR DONORS

Existing dependence upon this public	Potential dependence upon this public	Existing problems with this dependence
Enable the museum to fulfill its basic purpose of collecting. Provide incentives for pursuit of matching gift possibilities. Provide the largest percentage of the total goal of any fund-raising program. Lend credibility and prestige to the museum through their association with it. Provide valuable word-of-mouth support with influential publics.	More involvement in such roles as team captains in possible future fund drives. More involvement in encouraging peers to become donors.	Diminished giving potential due to reduction in the earning power of donors' investments. Disapproval of museum's unwillingness to accept some gifts of artifacts that in the donor's opinion (but not the museum's) fit with the collections. Disapproval of some deaccessioning of artifacts that the director and board of trustees consider unneeded.

Potential problems with this dependence	Needs	Existing resources
The changing thrust of the museum to become more oriented to public needs could cause some donors to disapprove and thus to disassociate themselves. Collection scope may become more confined in future as museum better defines its purpose, resulting in the acceptance of fewer major collection gifts.	To communicate better and to defend the museum's changing collection philosophy and policy. To involve major donors in the museum's work and to find ways for them to experience firsthand the programs that are broadening the museum's base of support.	Strengths Reputation of museum that makes association with it socially desirable. Benefits to major donors consisting of free admission and sales item discounts, both of which are frequently used.

Table 2.2 (*continued*)

Potential problems with this dependence	Needs	Existing resources
As the museum becomes more aggressive in courting donors, they could seek to exert greater influence on policies and operation.	To help them understand their new roles as helpers in the museum's advancement. To help them develop an awareness of specific gift opportunities that are in their self-interest in dealing with tax problems and inflation.	*Weaknesses* Lack of ways of giving public recognition to major donors. Exhibit space for new accessions that is inadequate for prompt exhibition of collection gifts from major donors. Lack of opportunity for personal contact to explain changes in museum policy and to gauge reactions.

Research

The publics audit, then, is useful for identifying key groups of people and for analyzing their roles in the life of the museum. To understand how these groups view the institution, it is important first of all to listen to them talk about it. What are visitors saying to on-site interpreters and to their friends in the community? Are there museum staff members who attend meetings of local service clubs and other functions where they hear opinions expressed about the museum? Informal conversations can yield much information about the layman's understanding of the museum and its purpose. Curators who participate in seminars, volunteers, and staff people—all have the opportunity to listen to various publics. Also ask people outside the museum, such as those who represent area businesses at travel shows, to report comments about the museum.

Do letters received indicate negative opinions or misunderstandings? Especially important are complaints. Incoming correspondence over a period of several years should indicate whether a problem is generating repeated complaints. Notes from telephone calls may yield clues to misunderstandings. You might also scan internal memoranda and reports. Have public relations needs been discussed in the past, perhaps repeatedly, without actually being addressed? The person responsible for public relations should have access to documents reflecting those discussions and should call the executive director's attention to needs that are going unmet.

By examining the annual report, museum magazine, visitor promotion and fund-raising literature, and publicity clippings, you can develop an understanding of the information base upon which some publics are forming their impressions. A content analysis of museum publications will also permit you to judge whether the message being communicated is accurate, coherent, and in line with institutional objectives.

Newspapers and news magazines offer broader information about the institution's social and cultural surroundings—for example, trends in public attitudes regarding financial support, legislative issues affecting nonprofit institutions, and the uses to which people are putting their leisure time. Harris, Roper, and Gallup survey results, often published in newspapers, frequently present revealing data about the museum's environment.

Record-keeping reports can supply valuable specific details, although here it is important to remember that the information-gathering process is secondary to the interpretation and intelligent use of findings.

Attendance Studies

The attendance study is a record-keeping report which should be kept by even the smallest museum. It involves simply noting the number of visitors each day. Figures may be compared with those from previous years for the purpose of estimating the anticipated number of visitors or to determine whether a special event or exhibit had a measurable effect on attendance. It may also be useful to analyze the figures. By isolating admissions of children, for example, comparisons can be made to assess attendance at events and exhibits that were designed to attract them. Variables may need to be recorded as well. For example, you might wish to take into account events outside the museum that competed for visitors when you compare attendance at events held in various years.

Point-of-Origin Studies

The point-of-origin study is a record-keeping report useful to museums that draw visitors from a broad geographic area. Arrange for volunteers to be at the museum exit with a clipboard for two hours a day, two days a week, for two or three weeks during each season of the year, and ask a random sampling of visitors for their zipcodes. Using a zipcode directory, determine where your visitors are coming from. You will obtain precise information that can help you target publicity and advertising where they can be most useful in increasing attendance. You might also discover new visitor markets that could be developed.

Visitor Comment Cards

Place comment cards and pencils conveniently near exits, and make it known that they are available for visitors to use. Responses on the cards will provide the museum with valuable feedback. The sample shown in figure 2.1 invites visitors to record positive or negative im-

```
Please print
                        VISITOR COMMENT CARD
   DATE _____
   VISITOR'S COMMENT:




   LOCATION: _____
   TIME: _____
   NAME OF PERSON OR EMPLOYEE CONCERNED: _____
   SUGGESTION:




   VISITOR'S NAME AND ADDRESS: _____
                              _____
                              _____

   This information will be forwarded to the appropriate department for immediate action.
   Attention will be given to all suggestions.
```

Figure 2.1. A visitor comment card

pressions. Simple questionnaires of this type given only when a visitor asks for them are reliable indicators of significant problems, and also can bring to light favorable comments that can be published in an in-house newsletter to encourage good employee-visitor relations. With the visitor's permission, favorable comments may also be used as testimonials in the museum's advertising.

All cards should be acknowledged. If a complaint reflects a misunderstanding or mistaken information, the matter should be explained and clarified in the written response. If the complaint identifies an actual problem, the reply should outline plans being made to correct it or explain why corrective action cannot be taken because of the budget or other reasons. The public relations person should bring such problems to people who can solve them and should encourage their immediate resolution.

Opinion Surveys

Opinion surveys can be costly but are useful in understanding and evaluating the museum's relationships with its publics. Through pretests conducted by research specialists you can determine whether the questions are eliciting the information you want. Established procedures will permit you to select a statistically reliable sample that is manageable in size, and the survey can be administered repeatedly over a period of years, thus indicating long-term trends.

Opinion surveys may detect new problems or may indicate whether suspected problems exist. Surveys can also determine what people mean when they say they like or dislike the museum and can supply answers to questions when other forms of research do not. For example, before introducing an evening program for adult education, one museum surveyed people who had participated in weekend daytime classes. It found that fear of being out after dark in the neighborhood would have made the proposed courses a failure. Guided by its findings, the museum directed its attention to expanding weekend offerings during daylight hours.

"Cross-section" surveys may use any of three techniques to obtain a representative sample:

1. Probability sampling involves selecting subjects at random, such as every fifth visitor or every tenth name on a list.
2. Area sampling is probability sampling confined to a single geographic area, such as a certain neighborhood.

3. Quota sample subjects are not selected on a probability basis. Rather the interviewer chooses them by known characteristics, such as age and sex. The number of subjects with each characteristic is determined by the proportion of people with that characteristic in the whole population. For example, if you were surveying a community in which 35 percent of the residents were unmarried black women, 35 percent of your quota sample would have those characteristics. This sample recreates in microcosm the total population under study.

Questionnaires distributed in person or by mail, or read over the telephone, may be used in conducting surveys. They may be distributed randomly or sent to a whole population, perhaps everyone with a street address within a four-mile radius of the museum. Unless a cross-section sampling is used, however, there is no assurance that responses to the questionnaire sent through the mail will represent the whole population being surveyed. Telephone surveys use a sample that is biased because it is limited to people who have telephones and listed numbers.

Survey panels involve selection of a cross section of subjects who are interviewed by research professionals more than once over a period of time. Although they are often difficult to administer, survey panels can be useful in measuring awareness of a museum or the effectiveness of programs created for the purpose of changing opinions. "Depth" interviews involve subjects selected randomly or on the basis of characteristics pertinent to the study. Depth studies are difficult to evaluate and require a professional interviewer to probe for and analyze factors underlying an expressed opinion.

"Focus interviews" use a group of about twelve people selected on the basis of characteristics such as frequency of visits to the museum and size of family. They can determine benefits that people seek during a visit so the museum can focus on them in its offerings and publicity. They may also be used to test the appeal of completed ads. Focus interviews should be conducted by professionals and are expensive.

The "semantic differential" is a technique that may be incorporated into a written survey. Subjects answer each question by selecting one of a fixed number of predefined, graded responses (usually seven). For example, an XYZ Museum survey might ask the subject to indicate whether its stamp exhibit was uninteresting, moderately uninteresting, slightly uninteresting, neutral, slightly interesting, moderately interesting, or extremely interesting. Many bipolar adjectives could be used in a museum survey; possibilities include attractive/unattractive, superior/inferior, pleasant/unpleasant, informative/uninformative, and good/bad. The semantic differential establishes not only the direction of the opinion but also its intensity. It can be administered to a representative sample and is usually relatively easy to interpret.

Although the public relations person is encouraged to consult a research specialist in writing questions for use in visitor surveys, it is helpful to understand the following basic points.

- Do not try to persuade people to change their opinions.
- Make questions easy to comprehend.
- Do not reveal the survey's objectives.
- Allow the respondent to be anonymous.
- Test the questionnaire before it is administered.
- Be prepared to take whatever actions are indicated by the survey results.

The Edison Institute's visitor survey (see the appendix) is distributed to a random sample of departing adult visitors in varying frequency throughout the year. Visitors are asked to complete it at home and to mail it back in the postage-paid envelope provided. Subjects need identify themselves by name and address only if they want to receive a souvenir booklet. Reports are prepared summarizing the survey findings, are circulated to management, and are used to monitor opinions and to define problems and needs.

Although survey research can be costly when contracted out, there are ways of making it affordable for even the smallest museum.

1. Contract with college students to design and conduct the study.
2. Ask a local advertising, marketing, or research agency to donate services in preparing the questions and evaluating the results.
3. Develop a joint survey with costs shared by several participating institutions.
4. Apply for a grant to fund the cost of contracting with a professional survey agency.
5. Determine whether surveys are contemplated by fast-food chains or other companies that are considering moving into the community or region. If so, the firms may be willing to include a few questions for the museum or may permit the museum to review their own pertinent findings.

6. Position a survey specialist on the board of trustees. Ask that he or she donate a service, such as managing a survey carried out by volunteers.

However formal or informal your research procedures—and their nature will almost certainly be dictated by considerations of budget and staff capabilities—you will at some point need to put your findings to work. Before proceeding, consider whether your information is accurate, whether it is broad enough to sustain interpretation, and whether you have assessed it objectively. If you are satisfied, ask yourself:

1. Do I know who the museum's publics are, how the museum's programs relate to them, what the museum expects from them, what they expect from the museum, which publics are most important to the museum in achieving its objectives, and why?
2. Do I know where problems lie in the museum's relationships with its publics, which publics are involved, what the problems are, what resources are available or are needed to solve them, whether the problems warrant the expenditure of resources in the required amounts?
3. Do I have ways of keeping abreast of trends and issues that may affect the museum? Is my information adequate to enable me to counsel the museum's executive director and trustees on contingency plans that should be developed to deal with future problems?

When these questions have been answered, public relations planning can begin.

Planning

Planning organizes, allocates, controls, and establishes priorities in the use of a museum's public relations resources. Properly specified, plans also provide a basis for defining individual or departmental accountability and for controlling overall museum operations. To be effective, planning must be ongoing. Too often, however, budgeting takes precedence, locking public relations into a program that lacks objectives. The publics audit supplies a list of the problems, needs, and resources corresponding to each public. Based upon the varying degrees to which your museum depends upon each of its publics and the anticipated problems and changes in these relationships, you can number your publics list in priority order and use it as an important aid in setting public relations program priorities.

Developing Goals and Objectives

One definition of a goal states that it is a long-range guideline, spanning five years or more, that might never be accomplished and is not measured.[1] *Publicity Craft* defines public relations goals as "the specific opinions you decide to try to inculcate [in] specific publics." [2] Whereas goals are general, objectives are more specific—measurable, short range, and time limited. They can be accomplished by assigning specific responsibilities to individuals. An objective should be explicit enough to guide action and to support alternative plans. Museum public relations objectives should:

- be supported by the museum's operating philosophy and by the information that is available on trends and other factors in the museum's environment;
- be based on the museum's strengths and resources;
- reflect collection scope and quality;
- be ambitious enough to be challenging.

For example, if a high-priority need were to attract more repeat visitors, one goal might be to persuade visitors that the museum provides a worthwhile experience. Achievement of this goal might involve such objectives as improving visitor orientation and developing new special programs that involve visitors. In turn, each objective might involve several subobjectives. For example, to improve visitor orientation you might create a slide show or produce a guide book. Defined in specifics, these subobjectives are easily translated into programs. Each program should:

- have a specific purpose and a built-in mechanism by which its performance can be measured;
- be carefully analyzed to assure that it will stay within budget, staff time, and facilities allocations;
- be flexible enough so it can be changed if it fails to perform adequately or if the problems and needs change.

Returning to the example of the slide show, we might ask the following questions to measure its effectiveness in fulfilling its purpose:

1. Do the script and photos fulfill those information needs of visitors that have been identified through research? Is the script supportive of the museum's purpose? Is it persuasive in emphasizing the worthwhile aspects of visitors' experience?
2. Have arrangements for shooting and processing the slides, writing the script, and acquiring, maintaining, and monitoring the equipment taken into account staff and budget resources? Where will the slides be shown; how will the show's location affect the flow of visitor traffic; how will the light level be controlled without creating safety hazards? Will visitors be seated or standing? If visitors stand, how will children and people in wheelchairs see the film?
3. Will the slide show require changes in the room that prevent it from being easily returned to its former arrangement should the show not serve its purpose?
4. How will one decide whether the orientation slide show achieved its goal of influencing visitors to believe that the museum offers a worthwhile experience?

Long-Range Planning

Some plans will be dictated by necessity. Obviously a publicity campaign to attract money to repair a building's leaking roof is of higher priority than a plan to develop a folder describing that building. Long-range plans are usually based on anticipated operating needs in areas such as facilities, staffing, and budget.

In long-range planning, consider the amount of time that will be required to realize an objective. Many objectives, such as improving visitors' experience by instituting a slide show that will orient them, can be met in the course of a year. Other objectives, such as increasing the museum's educational visibility by producing a motion picture to be shown in schools by volunteers, would require greater time for implementation.

Because programs involving long-range effort are often costly, they require a strong commitment from the museum's management. Long-range programs can be dropped or modified as problems and opportunities change, however, and should therefore by considered more speculative than short-range projects. Enough flexibility must always be allowed to accommodate unanticipated problems or opportunities, which even in the best-planned programs can demand a great deal of attention. Long-range planning can be particularly valuable for the small museum. Important public relations programs can be made feasible by spreading the work and cost over a period of years. For example, if a fund-raising film would fulfill a high-priority need, it could be researched one year, written and produced the second, and distributed the third.

Strategic Planning

Compared with long-range planning, which focuses on changes in the museum's internal operation, strategic planning is concerned with long-range changes in the museum's external environment and the museum's ability to deal with them. "Museums must look around and look ahead if they are to succeed in a changing environment," says Larry Morrison of Old Sturbridge Village.[3] Strategic planning enables them to do so.

Alice McHugh of Arthur D. Little, Inc., maintains that strategic planning is grounded in the belief that factors in the museum's external environment affect its success in achieving its objectives more than do the desired goals or expressed intentions of the museum itself.[4]

Strategic planning involves:

1. identifying long-term environmental variables affecting the museum;
2. developing different sets of assumptions based upon the best available information on the future environment;
3. analyzing possible interaction between key variables and assumptions;
4. measuring the feasibility of the strategies against the museum's resources and its purpose;
5. developing written scenarios which are brief descriptions of possible strategies.

Most museums probably develop strategies for responding to environmental factors affecting only two areas, fund raising and attendance. For example, the following variables could affect fund raising:

the overall economic climate;
government grant programs;
changes in visitor demographics and attitudes;
media exposures.

The following abbreviated scenario is based on the economic climate variable.

Assumption. A national trend of declining automotive sales could eventually result in layoffs of employees at local plants that produce parts for vehicles. Forty percent of the museum's membership is employed in the auto industry. Membership renewals from this high-dependency public will decline.

Strategies. Solicit memberships from publics not previously approached. Retain interest and involvement of laid-off publics by encouraging them to function as membership solicitors.

Alternate plans. Reallocate or eliminate programs funded by memberships. Raise dues for upper-level members who will be relatively unaffected by the layoffs.

Strategic planning, because it is time consuming, is usually limited to only a few well-developed scenarios concentrating on the most important factors affecting the museum's future. Although strategies can often be budgeted, a contingency fund should ideally be reserved to cover the possible implementation of key strategies necessitated by uncontrollable circumstances. If a fund cannot be set aside, budget allocations should be requested as soon as it becomes apparent that conditions are going to call for a new strategy. The process of monitoring the external environment for variables that will affect the museum's future forms part of the larger topic of issues management.

Issues Management

Larry Morrison has observed, "Issues themselves are not susceptible to management, but the organization's response to them must be." [5] Issues management differs from strategic planning in only two ways, according to Raymond P. Ewing, director of issues management at Allstate Insurance Company. "First, issues management is concerned with near-term emerging issues—18 to 36 months out; strategic planning is more concerned with longer-range issues emerging three, five or twenty years out. Second, issues management is concerned with the 'plans' the sociopolitical environment—the public policy process—would make for the institution." [6] In contrast, strategic planning involves future plans that the museum has made for itself in response to its changing environment. Ewing describes the "public policy process" as the mechanism by which public feelings evolve into laws and regulations that can affect the institution's operation.

The process begins when people feel dissatisfied because of a real or imagined wrong or because they believe that a right is being ignored. Eventually the issue in question assumes a name or label, such as "displacement," the process by which residents are moved out of historic homes. Now the media begin to pay attention. Otto Lerbinger, the public relations department chairman at Boston University, notes that newspapers tend to determine through their coverage the items occupying the public agenda for debate and that television in its coverage tends to rank at least the top items.[7] Next, according to Ewing, a pressure group places the issue on its agenda, hoping to mobilize a political force extending beyond its membership. If sufficient interest is generated, government officials become concerned, because of their legislative responsibilities. Elected representatives weigh the issue to determine how voters feel. Observing this process, issues managers often express concern that too often an issue receives insufficient attention until it reaches the legislative stage, when the course of events can no longer be influenced.[8]

Issues-based legislation that could affect museums includes energy rationing, tax credits for gifts, minimum-wage laws for part-time employees, measures regarding consumerism and equipment safety, and Internal Revenue Service regulations involving nonprofit institutions.

Concern with issues is becoming more important, as is demonstrated by the new interest of large corporations in focusing their communication on specific issues rather than simply at target publics. Because of the complexity of a changing environment, big business increasingly believes that decisions based on present environmental considerations are likely to be obsolete as soon as they are made. Major issues of the 1960s and 1970s that have caused corporate public relations people to become more issues oriented and less publics oriented, according to Robert O. Carlson, dean of the School of Business Administration at Adelphi University, include:

- a concern with protecting and improving our physical environment;
- consumerism, including concern about protecting investors;
- demands for upgrading the career opportunities for women and disadvantaged ethnic and racial groups.[9]

Ewing notes that policy analysts at the Human Resources Network, Inc., and the Library of Congress have found that issues emerging in public consciousness require about six years to be enacted into law at the federal level. "Thus," he concludes, "a careful scanning for emerging issues, plus consistent monitoring of them thereafter, affords ample opportunity for a concerned organization to develop policy and supporting programs in time for it to participate in the process well before the issues reach their final legislative stages." [10]

At present, issues management for museum public relations staff usually consists simply of monitoring available professional and general reading materials, television programs, and various forms of popular entertainment for indications of environmental variables that are developing in ways that could affect museums. In the future it is likely that associations of museum professionals will become more involved with issues studies so that they can make environmental forecasts for their member institutions.

3

Publics within the Museum and Just Beyond

In museum public relations, the assessment of public opinion, participation in policymaking, and coordination of communications efforts take place continuously. Additionally, special employee, volunteer, visitor, donor, governmental, and community relations programs are usually conducted to establish and maintain productive relationships with these key publics.

Employees

Personnel departments share with public relations staff the responsibility for facilitating two-way communication between employees and management.

Employees need to understand the museum's purposes and goals and must know how their work relates to that of others in the museum. Since they communicate daily with the museum's publics, they also need correct information and a mechanism for registering suggestions and complaints.

Handbooks, orientation "backgrounders," newsletters, bulletin boards, and directories are commonly used to communicate with museum employees. The employee handbook, which is usually prepared by the personnel office, contains rules, regulations, and benefits. Public relations should recommend that it also include the general objectives of each department, expressed in a way that makes plain how the work of each department contributes to the fulfillment of the museum's overall purpose and goals. Also important is a statement explaining why a friendly and helpful attitude in contacts with the public is crucial for the museum's success. Orientation backgrounders that familiarize new employees with highlights from the museum's history, its collections, and its programs—should be prepared jointly by the public relations person and the appropriate departments. The printed material should include a list of individuals who can answer questions in specific subject areas.

Internal newsletters keep in-house staff up to date on museum events, interpret programs, explain policies, recognize employee achievements, and provide an opportunity for the executive director to answer questions of general concern. The newsletter's editor must be allowed to develop stories that speak fully and truthfully to subjects of general interest to employees, such as operating policies, wages and benefits, and future plans. As Joseph Varilla of Xerox Corporation suggests, "If employees understand and accept the policies and plans of the company, it is likely that those policies and plans can be carried out; if they oppose them, success is unlikely." [1]

Sources of copy and topics for a newsletter are many. A column by the executive director could be published in each issue and might include answers to employees' questions. Other columns could help employees become better acqainted with one another (especially useful when there is a large staff). News items might report on employee awards, promotions, interaction with the community, and recognition of special services performed for the museum. Some institutions publish copy naming employees who have been mentioned favorably by visitors. The newsletter might also recognize individuals who have served on community committees and have participated in media interviews. Occasionally employee stories, poems, and art or photographs are published. If material from the museum's news releases is used, it should be rewritten to address employees or to focus on information of special interest to them. To save time and expense, most museums use a simple format and print the employee newsletter internally. Some favor mailing it to the employee's home, particularly if the copy includes information of interest to families.

Bulletins, which often are single page memoranda, also relay information to employees, especially regarding urgent matters. Bulletins may alert employees to special plans for an unanticipated visit by a VIP or may advise of changes in holiday schedules. In the absence of a personnel department, the production and distribution of bulletins may be the responsibility of public relations, which may also create staff telephone directories and lists of employees' home addresses.

Bulletin boards or display cases in employee areas such as office corridors offer another means of communicating with employees. Displays may include clippings of interest to staff and should be changed frequently.

Without infringing upon personnel department responsibilities, the PR director should always advocate and support programs that will help build good employee relations. For example, public relations functions may include advising the executive director to send thank you, congratulatory, or get well messages to staff members. Sometimes a party to recognize special employee efforts is in order.

Volunteers

Although public relations departments are not usually expected to manage volunteer programs, PR staff should help create a climate that will encourage people to offer their time and energies. Arthur C. Frantzreb, a public relations and development counselor, notes, "Most volunteers give of their time and talent in proportion to their estimate of their value to the institution, their confidence in the management, and their loyalty, faith and gratitude for benefits received by themselves and society." [2]

In every community many worthwhile nonprofit organizations and causes are competing for volunteers. Individuals choose institutions to serve on the basis of their experiences with the organization in question, information received from friends and/or the media, and their personal needs. By persuasively communicating a clear sense of purpose and by identifying, encouraging, and working continuously with each of its publics, the museum can successfully compete for volunteers who will fulfill its needs for personal contact with the community, for specialized knowledge and experience, for advice and counsel, and for services such as ushering at performances and preparing outgoing direct mail. Volunteers who are docents or who are in other positions with public contact are major links in the word-of-mouth communication network that keeps publics informed about the institution and its programs.

Foremost among the volunteers are the members of the board of trustees, whose responsibility is not unlike that of the governing board of a college or university. In addition to setting overall policy, according to Frantzreb, their responsibilities include:

1. the selection, appointment, or dismissal of the chief administrative officer;
2. the acquisition, conservation and management of the institution's physical and financial resources; and
3. the oversight of the type and quality of education and services offered by the institution.[3]

PR staff may be asked to help strengthen the museum's links with its trustees by:

- producing orientation materials to acquaint new trustees with the museum's purposes, goals and objectives, facilities, collections, programs, and staff;
- keeping trustees regularly informed, perhaps through bulletins carrying the executive director's signature;
- distributing museum news releases and publications that interpret policy to trustees;
- working with a trustee public relations committee;
- providing materials such as attendance summaries and audiovisual presentations for trustee meetings;
- assisting the chief officer of the board with the research and writing of speeches, annual reports, and fund-raising letters.

People engaged in the professions form another important category of volunteers. Their offers of free service should be accepted with many thanks. Unless the museum is operated almost entirely by a volunteer staff, however, one must be cautious about expecting professionals to provide anything more than advice free of charge. Awkward problems can develop if some people are paid for services and others are not.

Public relations staff can help generate volunteer workers for fund-raising programs. Most funding campaigns are successful only when a great deal of work is performed by a large number of volunteers. Because workers should be enlisted from among the groups they are expected to influence, the public relations person's knowledge of the museum's publics can be useful. However, simply knowing of potential volunteer fund raisers is not enough. Before an effective team can be recruited, a public relations program must link the volunteers' interests with those of the museum.

Perhaps most important of all volunteers are those who provide the services—from running docent programs to stuffing envelopes—that keep many American museums in operation. Appreciation of their work should be expressed at every opportunity, and paid staff should be instructed to make every effort to maintain good working relationships with them.

Volunteer Management

A good relationship with volunteers is important to a museum's public relations; thus you will be concerned with volunteer management even though you may not be responsible for it. Volunteers expect to have assignments clearly defined, to be properly trained, to have the materials and staff assistance necessary to do the job, and to have a realistic work load and deadline. A supervisor must therefore be able to explain clearly how to do the job and why it is necessary.

Noting that volunteers fail to perform as expected chiefly when they are ineffectively managed, Frantzreb suggests several guidelines for supervisors.

1. Be able to plan and delineate specific steps toward the achievement of volunteers' goals and objectives.
2. Be able to delegate tasks and follow up on them.
3. Have patience and sensitivity in dealing with people.
4. Like people, respect their desire to help, and help them achieve.
5. Be personally accountable, honest, fair, and objective in evaluating people's successes and disappointments.
6. Develop skills in administrative techniques.[4]

Frantzreb also suggests that problems in working with volunteers are likely to arise when their role is overstated or understated, when they lack confidence in staff management, when busy people are not used properly and productively, when a conflict of interest exists, and when volunteers' efforts do not receive staff support.[5]

A volunteer manual printed inexpensively and describing the program's importance and any special privileges or awards that recognize various levels of volunteer service can contribute to sound volunteer relations. The manual should clearly differentiate between volunteer and employee areas of operation so that employees will not feel threatened. Volunteers should also be told how they may advance to positions of volunteer leadership, and office procedures—including those relating to reimbursement for out-of-pocket expenses—should be explained. In 1976 Congress passed a resolution urging all public and private businesses to recognize volunteer experience when reviewing job applications. Records kept by the museum (and they should be kept) can be important credentials for job seekers.

Volunteers at some museums publish their own newsletters that include stories about projects and mention exceptional numbers of hours served by individuals. Public relations department assistance should be provided if it is requested. Publicizing the accomplishments of volunteers and helping plan an occasional social event for them are additional ways to build sound public relations.

Recruiting Speakers for the Museum

The Volunteer Speakers' Bureau

A well-informed and enthusiastic volunteer speaking about the museum and answering audience's questions can be a very effective communicator and a persuasive representative of the museum.

One may manage the speakers' bureau through a coordinator who reports to the public relations person and whose duties, performed on a volunteer basis, include:

- keeping a file on each speaker, listing times when he or she is available, travel restrictions, foreign language and other special skills, and previous speaking engagements;
- receiving requests, assigning speakers, providing program chairpersons with background information on the speakers; publicizing speeches in coordination with the host organization's publicity chairperson;
- developing booking sheets on which are recorded the speaker's name, date of speech, directions to the speaking location, description of the room in which the speech will be given, time of meeting, name and nature of organization, name and telephone number of the contact person in the organization, nature and size of the audience expected, and equipment needed. Copies of these sheets should be sent to the speaker and the program chairperson and should be kept in a public relations office file. The day before the engagement, the volunteer coordinator should reconfirm all arrangements with the speakers.
- calling local residents and checking the chambers of commerce and local media to develop a list of organizations' program chairper-

sons or presidents. Names and addresses should be kept up to date
and may be used for publicity mailings.

A promotional flyer may be needed if media publicity does not
generate adequate interest in the bureau. It would describe available
programs and would tell people wishing to engage speakers to contact
the bureau coordinator directly.

Select a number of volunteers equal to about twice the expected
number of monthly requests for speakers. Bureau participants should
be available during lunch hours and evenings and should be articulate,
knowledgeable about the museum, and interested in it. Speakers
should advise the coordinator of any special interests they have de-
tected among members of their audiences. When interest warrants,
several programs could be developed on a variety of museum-related
subjects. At a minimum there should be separate programs for adults
and for children of school age. Other topics might involve fund raising,
collections interpretation, special exhibits and events and educational
programs.

The slide show with script or audiotape is usually the basis for the
speaker's presentation. If a volunteer photographer prepared the slides,
the museum should retain the rights to their use. For variety the presentation should include closeups; panoramas; day, night, and seasonal pictures; and unusual angles on familiar subjects. The slides should
show the museum being used by people with whom the viewer can
identify.

Beginning with a title slide, the show should advance from an atten-
tion-arresting opening to a fast-moving narration to a brief summary of
what has been seen and said. The narration should explore the subject
in ways that relate to the interests of the viewers. Most organizations
allow twenty minutes for programs. The slide show should not require
more than fifteen minutes, with one minute for introducing it and four
minutes at the end for questions. Speakers need to be equipped with a
properly operating projector which they are experienced in using as
well as with extension cords and extra bulbs. The host organization
should be asked to provide a screen.

If budget permits, a tape-slide unit that automatically advances
slides synchronized with a recorded sound tape can be used. This
machine is easy for the volunteer to transport and operate and has the
advantage of giving the museum complete control over the message.
Taped sound effects and a professionally voiced narration make the

show dramatically more appealing but eliminate the spontaneity and enthusiasm of the personally delivered presentation. Most slide show narrations are delivered live from the front of the room using a remote focus and slide advance control. The narration should be based on a script prepared by the public relations department.

The use of two projectors with a dissolve unit permitting one picture to fade into the next makes the presentation appear more professional but adds costly equipment that can be difficult for volunteers to transport and operate. If the museum has produced 16mm television public service announcements, they could be edited into a short movie with a taped audio accompaniment. Television public service announcements on videotape could be transferred onto 16mm film. Super-8mm films or home videotape recorders using one-quarter-inch tape are not of professional quality and are not suitable for speakers' bureau use.

Opaque projectors make it possible to cast the image of a small collection artifact, such as a piece of jewelry, on a large screen in a darkened room. The item can be seen by the audience without being handled. Flannel boards allow speakers to attach flat visuals with felt, adhesive, or Velcro backs to a felt-covered board to illustrate how a given situation can be changed by adding or subtracting elements. Overhead projectors enlarge on a screen an image of any material produced on a transparency. The speaker can mark the transparency while it is being projected, and the marks can be erased later. It is possible to focus the audience's attention on different parts of the image by placing a plain sheet of paper over the transparency and moving it down or from side to side to uncover different areas selectively.

Filmstrips are a series of individual still pictures vertically placed on rolls of 35mm film. They are generally inexpensive, especially when they are produced in large quantities for distribution with a script to schools or other audiences. The script and pictures are numbered so that the operator can keep the presentation synchronized. There is usually an audible chime that signals the operator to advance to the next picture. The strip can also be synchronized with a record or cassette tape.

Volunteers should receive instruction on how to introduce the program and should carry a fact sheet for use in answering questions following the slide show. Key dates in the history of the museum, principal collections and notable artifacts, admission prices and fees, including any special discounts, hours of operation, and dates of future special events and exhibits, should all be included. Speaker training should be continuous, and speakers should receive all the museum's informational mailings. The names, addresses, and telephone numbers of people in the audience who asked questions that the speaker was unable to answer should be relayed through the coordinator to the public relations person, who should respond promptly.

Speakers' bureau costs can be kept to a minimum by requiring the host to pay travel expenses and to provide meals when appropriate. Equipment costs can be reduced if organizations are asked to provide a projector, an operator, and a screen. News releases and publicity stories can make bureau engagements known to the public. A flyer describing the service and mailed to organization chairpersons could be funded by selling advertisements to local businesses.

The Executive Director's Speech

The public relations person should seek appropriate speaking opportunities for the executive director, should assist in recommending topics, and should write the speeches if asked to do so. Engagements that would be appropriate for the executive director and useful to the museum might include:

- meetings and conferences of business and civic organizations and clubs whose members are representative of the museum's high-priority publics;
- college and university audiences, parent-teacher associations, conferences of Junior Achievement, 4-H, Boy and Girl Scouts, YMCA, and similar youth organizations whose involvement helps position the museum as an educational institution, a factor that can be important in fund-raising efforts;
- conferences of travel associations such as the American Society of Travel Agents.

The effectiveness of the executive director's speech as a communication device for the museum can be strengthened if one observes the following guidelines:

- Match the speaker to the audience. Sometimes the professional staff member cannot satisfy a major donor or other high-priority group that expects to hear the museum's chief executive officer even though the staff member is more knowledgeable about the subject.

- Know in advance the expected size of the audience and the key people who will be present, how long the executive director is expected to speak, and what will precede and follow his or her speech. Find out who will be speaking before the director and what that person will be talking about. Provide the person introducing the speakers with a summary of those aspects of the director's credentials that apply to the subject of the speech.
- Determine what the organization expects the museum executive director to talk about. The director should speak to a topic that builds upon the museum's greatest strengths and is appropriate to the interests of the audience.
- Link the speech with the personal needs and interests of the audience. Address the subject using layers of facts sandwiched between supportive human interest anecdotes and examples and conclude with a clear statement of the action the audience is to take—visit the museum, vote for helpful legislation, volunteer to work in a fund drive. The speech will be most effective if it develops one major point. The most important material should be covered in the first few minutes, when the audience's attention is greatest.
- If the speech involves the explanation of complex material such as a budget, flip charts can be effective. Charts should break down the concept into simplified segments each of which is clearly illustrated in bold lettering or illustrations that can be seen by everyone in the audience. When the audience is large, the same material can be projected on a screen via an overhead projector.
- Major speeches by the executive director should be preceded by telephoned or written tips to the appropriate media, with an invitation to attend. A summary of the presentation and a photo of the executive director could also be provided in advance. Television and radio stations need to know before the speech begins when the most important statements will be made so that they can be ready to record. They may also want to interview the speaker following the address. The interview room should be nearby, equipped with 110-volt outlets and large enough so that each reporter can talk with the speaker individually. (It is nice to provide coffee and tea in the media room.) Media not in attendance should be given speech summaries immediately afterward.
- You may wish to tape-record the director's speeches for later use. Tapes can be kept on file for reference if questions arise as to what actually was said. If the speech involved any new announcements

of specific interest to museum employees, they should receive summaries immediately.

Professional Staff Speakers

By handling bookings and publicity for curators, conservators, historians, and other staff professionals, you can encourage them to pursue speaking engagements that are beneficial to them and to the museum.

Existing collection photographs and other museum material should be made available to staff speakers free of charge. However, it is usually their responsibility to do their own preparation, either on their own time or during working hours, depending on museum policy. Professional staff members should set their own fees on the basis of their credentials and the amount of preparation time required.

Visitors

In recent years museum personnel have become increasingly uneasy regarding their relationship to the general public. We have come, increasingly, to want to understand the lasting effects, not measured in attendance figures and popularity, but in terms of the heightened awareness—aesthetic, historical, scientific, humanistic—which is supposed to accompany our unique institutional role. In a word, education has become the preoccupation and business of many museum professionals.[6]

So says Nelson Graburn, curator of the Lowie Museum of Anthropology at the University of California in Berkeley. He suggests that visitors have three types of needs: the reverential, the associational, and the educational.

Graburn applies the word "reverential" to the visitor's need for a personal experience with something out of the ordinary, for a place of peace where fantasy is possible. Some museums offer visitors the freedom to think and to dream without interference from security guards or from visual or other noise. Graburn suggests that reverential visitors are more likely to be found in art or basic science museums than in museums of history and technology.

"Associational" visitors use the museum as a place to socialize with family or friends. They are looking not for a great deal of intellectual challenge but rather for a comfortable environment that provides a pleasant contrast to school and employment, according to Graburn.

When a museum wishes to be a tourist destination, it must be well known, he explains, so that when the visit is talked about back home it will be a key symbol, "marking the achievement of the tourist, as proof of having been to say San Francisco, London, or Paris." [7]

Visitors also appeal to museums for education, to interpret the world. "Many people look upon the world as a 'museum,' a model of itself, something to be studied and understood, rather than to be participated in unselfconsciously," Graburn notes. In this sense museums become events in a string of events that are incorporated into a search for meaning in life. If, following Graburn, we view visitors as possessing these three characteristics in varying degrees, we can better understand the role of public relations in helping the museum relate to them effectively.

Public relations involvement with visitors includes sharing with other museum departments responsibility for encouraging a favorable attitude toward visitors on the part of museum staff, for orienting the visitor to the museum, for creating a pleasant environment, for clearly interpreting the collections, and for establishing interesting exhibits and events.

Employees and Visitors

The process of making employees sensitive to the importance of satisfying visitors begins with the job interview and requires training, reminding, and a firm policy that puts first priority on serving visitors' needs. The executive director and PR staff should regularly call attention to this policy in the employee newsletter. The public relations person can assist in training docents to be effective communicators. Most museums have the greatest number of visitors on weekends, making it necessary to adapt public contact employees' work schedules to a weekend operation.

For most museums, favorable word-of-mouth publicity by satisfied visitors chiefly determines attendance. Friendly, courteous, and thoughtful parking lot and ticket attendants will make favorable first impressions, and maintenance workers, security guards, sales clerks, curators, and others should take an active interest in making sure that the visitor is having a worthwhile and enjoyable experience. The importance of such staff contacts has been documented in studies at Henry Ford Museum and Greenfield Village; visitors frequently mentioned friendly and helpful employees when describing the most pleasant aspects of their experience. PR staff should try to set a good example and should personally commend an employee when it is known that he or she has been particularly considerate of a visitor's needs.

Orienting the Visitor

Interpretation of the museum begins when the prospective visitor learns of the institution for the first time, often during casual conversation with a friend. The content of such spontaneous messages cannot be controlled but will inevitably reflect personal impressions, both positive and negative. Thus flaws in individual experiences—surly guides, for example—tend to become widely known. Partly to justify their own reluctance to visit the museum, people are likely to relate to their friends the negative comments that they have heard about it.

Visitors can also be dissatisfied if the public relations department creates unrealistic expectations through inaccurate and exaggerated promotion. Although the word of a friend is most credible and persuasive, prospective visitors see a museum's publication as a statement of its own point of view. The following guidelines will help assure that a publication does not misrepresent the visitor experience:

- Present the museum as it is and not as something that you or others might like it to be. Take care to balance the entertaining and educational aspects of the visit. Museums are not theme parks, nor are they dusty attics.
- Emphasize the museum's special qualities and strengths. Simply throwing the door open is not enough. The promotional publication should establish the nature and importance of the experience that the visitor can expect to receive.
- Do not publish pictures of people doing things that museum policy does not allow, such as sitting on collection furniture. Do show the museum's collections and facilities being enjoyed by visitors.
- Do not picture artifacts that are not on exhibit. The likelihood that collectors will travel great distances expecting to see particular items of interest to them makes the museum responsible for showing what it promotes.
- Information that the visitor needs should not be overlooked: give details about days and hours of operation; holiday closings; dates of special events and exhibits; the museum's location relative to principal routes of travel; shopping, restaurant, lodging, and camp-

ing facilities; all admission fees, including those for senior citizens
or other special groups; provisions for handicapped visitors and
pets; acceptable credit cards; and the museum telephone number.

The visitor's sense of expectation peaks upon arrival at the
museum. Well-executed directional signs at points where people enter
town, property that appears well tended, and a clean, well-organized
parking lot convenient to the entrance make a reassuring first impression. A sign that appears professional should be placed near the
entrance to describe any special events of the day and to show the
location of major exhibits, helping visitors organize their limited time.

Every effort should be made to prevent waiting lines at the entrance.
If lines are unavoidable, try stationing a volunteer nearby to describe
major attractions and to answer questions. The purchase of a ticket
should be a simple transaction that does not require the visitor to read
large quantities of information beforehand. It is important, however, for
each visitor to learn of any special discounts before buying a ticket.

When they stand on the threshold of the exhibit area, visitors will
not want to read or to listen to a lengthy orientation talk. Yet some
communication at this point is critical if people are to know how best
to use their time. If they discover after they leave for home that they
missed something because they did not know of it, they will feel
cheated and may form a negative impression of the museum as a result.
Strong graphics help emphasize the thematic and/or sequential nature
of exhibits and activities, making them more easily appreciated by
visitors and therefore more effective. Signs are visually disruptive,
however, and should be kept to a minimum. Use them with discretion
so that they do not detract from or overpower the exhibit. Rules pro-
hibiting touching objects or smoking should be expressed politely, using "please" and perhaps also including a few words explaining why
the rule is enforced. Expressions such as "keep out" or "visitors not
allowed," should be rephrased to be less harsh, less negative, and more
polite. Visitors expect immaculate restrooms that are convenient to the
entrance. Foldup wheelchairs should also be available, along with
information about handicapped accessibility to exhibits, programs, and
facilities.

If access to the collections is by guided tour only, a comfortable
public waiting area should be provided with a host or hostess who will
discuss the museum and will answer questions. All museum employees who have contact with the public should carry a list of area

restaurants, nearby gas stations, and automotive repair shops, with notations as to which ones are open on weekends. Such staff should also be able to give directions for driving or walking to other points of interest in the area. Finally, employees in contact with visitors should be trained to give basic first aid and to respond properly in the event of a medical emergency.

Sometimes museums prohibit photography even when their collections could not possibly be damaged by a flashbulb. An alternative policy of value to the museum is to encourage people to take pictures that might persuade friends back home to visit. Whatever the decision, visitors should plainly not be allowed to obstruct aisles with tripods.

Creating a Pleasant Environment

Once in the museum, visitors' expectations may quickly turn to frustration. According to Graburn, "After half an hour or an hour of what is supposed to be a pleasant experience, the visitor gets turned off, develops headaches and feels tired." He suggests that unlike hours spent in "a church or school, the tempo of the [museum] experience is controlled not by the person orchestrating the event, but by the visitor himself; and thus a heavy burden of decision making falls upon the visitor, who must decide to move on or to stay, to avoid the crowd or be pushed on at a difficult pace, to read or not to read the labels, to glance at or study the exhibit." [8] Sore feet, an aching back and shoulders, and a sense of listlessness can overcome even the most dedicated museum goer.

There is no way to eliminate "museum ache"; however, PR staff should consider whether any factors contribute to it unnecessarily.

* Although public relations personnel are seldom responsible for writing artifact labels, as communications specialists they should consider whether labels have been placed at the best height and angle for easy reading by both children and adults. Is label copy organized consistently throughout the museum so that visitors can locate at a glance the information they are looking for? People are not accustomed to reading while standing and will not do so unless they are keenly interested in the subject. Are the labels interesting? Do they describe the object in terms that relate to people, perhaps telling how it was created and used? Is the operation of a complicated artifact illustrated by a line drawing or by other graphics? Is

the copy concise, set in a type size large enough for readability, and devoid of jargon?

- Are there adequate public seating places, water fountains, and rest-rooms strategically located throughout the museum? Is the eating area conveniently located and attractively furnished, with food reasonably priced? Is the quality of the food acceptable?
- Are vacuuming, floor polishing, lawn mowing, and other disrup-tive chores performed during hours when visitors are not present?

Interpreting the Collections

In a sense the public relations person is responsible for interpreting the museum to the public before it visits and in a way that encourages people to visit. The previsit message should be consistent with reality and should prepare people to perceive the museum in ways consistent with the institution's intentions. For example, it would be inappropri-ate for an open air museum's publicity releases and publications to emphasize a return to the good old days if its guided tours focused on nineteenth-century hardships. In any case such cliches as "good old days" are incorrect from a historical perspective, make the museum experience seem trivial, and should be avoided.

Special Events and Exhibits

By comparison with banks and grocery stores, which people visit daily or at least very frequently, museums are low-use institutions of which the public has relatively little awareness. Some visitors come to a museum in response to a special need; others are attracted when they are somehow made to take notice. The problem of maintaining con-tinuous visibility is rendered more difficult because many visitors feel that one visit is enough (the museum does not change) or that a trip to see it may as well be put off until next month or next year (the museum will always be there).

Institutions often use special events and exhibits to add variety and to encourage attendance during lean periods. By restricting a special program to a given time span, museums discourage people from defer-ring their visits. Scheduled events also provide the media with news to cover and thereby maintain both their interest and the museum's visibility.

Art museums have demonstrated the extent to which special exhibits can produce a surging tide of visitors. To broaden their own appeal, history museums have been challenged to attract groups ranging from tractor-seat aficionados to Chippendale chair collectors, from school classes to corporate managers on outings. Special events and exhibits are opportunities for the museum to engage its many publics in personal ways.

The selection of special offerings should be based foremost on the ways in which they advance the museum's purpose, goals, and objectives. Although a steam festival sponsored by a museum of art could attract throngs of paying visitors, the event might well seem unrelated to the institution's main purpose and might therefore inspire confusion among donors and other key publics that outweighs the advantages of the increased ticket revenue.

The following list indicates some ways in which public relations staff might involve themselves in special exhibits:

- The exhibit's title. Does it mean anything to the public? For example, the title "Warp and Weft" for a weaving exhibit would have little meaning for most prospective visitors.
- Do surveys, or even one's own instincts, indicate that there will be enough public interest to support the exhibit? How will the exhibit be promoted?
- How will visitors be oriented to the exhibit at its entrance? Will there be adequate ventilation and seating space in the exhibit area to assure visitors' comfort? Will labels and other graphics be readable by both youngsters and adults? Will handicapped visitors be provided for? Can publicity, publications, labels, and graphics convey the importance of the exhibit?

Plans for special events, particularly at history museums, may be delegated to the public relations department. The following recommendations apply to many of the tasks involved.

1. Review, probably with a group representing education, curatorial, and crafts areas, the types of events that would support the museum's purpose.
2. Check with local authorities for any fire, traffic, or other restrictions.
3. Determine how much historical research, what sorts of special equipment, and how many volunteer participants would be required to stage the event, and consider their potential availabil-

ity. Special events can divert the museum staff from fulfilling its ongoing responsibilities.

4. If participants are members of national organizations, such as antique automobile clubs, make contact with the group's headquarters about sixteen months in advance. (Smaller regional groups may be booked a year in advance.)

5. Find out what other activities are scheduled for the same date in your area. Publicize the date you have selected as soon as possible so that other organizations can plan their schedules accordingly. Take into account weather, previous attendance figures, and seasonal aspects of the event itself when you set a date.

6. Reach a clear understanding with participating groups or individuals regarding their fees, registration arrangements, special parking requirements, need for security, and insurance for items they may bring to the event. Define any limits on their participation regarding publicity stories, policies involving sale of their items during the event, and provisions to be made, for example, regarding meals and camping sites.

7. Because most participants help stage special events free of charge and frequently become volunteers and donors, they should be considered an important public. Nevertheless, the museum must insist that they maintain a high standard of interpretation. For example, modern clothing should not be allowed in a colonial military encampment. Also, the museum should require all participant organizations to make their exhibits and activities visible to the visitor at close range. For example, antique car clubs should agree to park their vehicles in such a way that visitors can readily view them. It should be understood by members of participating organizations that they are to be courteous and informative to visitors, but they should explain their own activity only and should not try to interpret the museum's overall programs and purposes.

8. Many special events held outdoors do not allow for a suitable substitute activity in the event of rain; however, the museum is responsible for helping participants protect their valuables when they are on display.

9. Plan publicity early, but do not forget people who might be attracted at the last minute. When the event is under way, be sure all visitors are made aware of it at the museum entrance.

10. The museum's appreciation for the participants' help should be

conveyed to them at the event. If possible, an evaluation session with key people from participant groups should be held soon afterward.

11. Determine what special services are to be accorded participants. Certainly they and their families should be admitted to the museum free of charge on the day of the event. Sometimes printed certificates and light refreshments can be provided. Depending on the type of organization, it might be appropriate for the museum to give a banquet.

12. If the event was well received but was attended by fewer visitors than were expected, bear in mind that one time may not be enough to test its pulling strength. Likewise be aware that it is not unusual for special events to produce a bell-shaped attendance curve over a three-to-five-year period. Assuming that bad weather or popular competing events do not depress attendance, major changes or a new event may be required as soon as the curve begins its downward path. If the event is to be canceled, show consideration for participant groups by notifying them at least a year in advance.

The Community

Just as most people strive to make their own homes and neighborhoods as pleasant and attractive as possible, most museums want to contribute to the betterment of their home communities and recognize that it is in their best interests to do so. Although they were sometimes isolated from their home towns in the past, many museums today are becoming community cultural centers where youngsters can throw clay pots on Saturday afternoons, teenagers can implement school projects, adults can take classes or engage in volunteer work, and senior citizens can participate in oral history interviews that will preserve their memories for future generations. For example, when the San Diego Historical Society assumed responsibility for an abandoned house in a neighborhood where the society had not operated previously, the neighbors were polled to determine what they would like Villa Montezuma to provide for them. Transportation to a swimming pool and karate lessons were among the services that the museum provided in response to needs expressed by the community. Today the neighbors are protective of a house museum that has become an important part of their community life.

Sound community relations involves striking a balance between what the museum receives from the community and what it gives. Among the benefits most museums receive are:

- police, fire, and health care services for employees and visitors;
- gas, electricity, water, and sewer lines;
- maintenance of streets leading to the museum, traffic and parking control, and directional signs;
- tax exemptions for museum-owned properties;
- educational, religious, and recreational services for museum employees and their families;
- zoning and other beneficial ordinances.

On the other side of the balance scale are the ways in which the museum gives to the community by:

- offering opportunities for full-time, part-time, volunteer, and temporary employment;
- attracting to the museum visitors who spend money locally during their stay;
- enriching the educational opportunities available to local schools resulting from class visits to the museum and from community involvement with the museum's educators;
- benefiting local organizations and enhancing the overall quality of life in the community—the museum's contribution to a better living environment.

Although a museum's situation will vary, depending on the nature of its local financial support and the size of its hometown, community relations objectives should probably include:

- making an effort to know the community's needs, problems, goals, and attitudes and to be sensitive to community feelings; for example, by deaccessioning artifacts closely associated with local pride, a museum might create resentment;
- involving local government officials in planning and participating in museum events and in serving on important committees;
- supporting special events in the community and refraining from scheduling museum programs that will compete with them for attendance;
- encouraging museum employees to participate in community affairs and to do their share in United Fund and other worthwhile communitywide causes, such as drives to register blood donors;

- developing special educational programs or exhibits on subjects of local interest, involving community representatives in the planning;
- offering use of museum facilities for meetings of local groups, making certain that charges and restrictions remain consistent for all groups;
- encouraging museum departments to use local businesses whenever possible.

4

Fund Raising:
Giving and Getting

Creating a climate in which prospective donors are aware of and have positive feelings toward the museum must precede fund raising. This task requires the publics audit, opinion surveys, and planned communication programs. "When a person is approached to give to an institution and does not know about the institution from previous, careful public relations and cultivation efforts, he or she will not respond unless there is strong peer pressure," according to John F. Schwartz, former president of the American Association of Fund Raising Counsel, Inc.[1] John Price Jones suggests that "fully 50 percent of all the time and effort in the average fund raising enterprise is in the field of public relations."[2]

The Fund-Raising Climate

In February 1981 President Reagan told Congress: "Historically the American people have supported by voluntary contributions more artistic and cultural activities than all the other countries in the world put together. I wholeheartedly support this approach and believe that Americans will continue their generosity." His words were uttered in the context of proposed major reductions in allocations to the national endowments, bad news for all museums dependent on federal support. Escalating inflation coupled with increased program and endowment needs have further cast museums into an unfavorable economic environment. The problem is not new; it dates to the establishment of the progressive federal income tax, which diminished the giving capability of the relatively few very wealthy individuals who supported many American museums. Many of the affected institutions sought to enlarge their support bases by establishing wealthy and sometimes elitist trustee groups who were expected to fund, personally, any annual deficits. When continuously rising operating costs surpassed the trustees' financial capabilities, new programs offered membership to anyone who paid a nominal fee. This step marked the end of elitism and the beginning of broad-based support for museums. But despite the larger support base, income often remained inadequate. Institutions next turned to the government for financial assistance. Now, with federal appropriations being reduced, many museums are focusing on corporate grants and are attempting to broaden their support base of individuals still further.

It is generally agreed that increases in the support base have been advantageous to museums. "The displacement of the individual donors of great wealth by a combination of small donors, businesses, foundations and others has created a shift in the material power balance within the institution. With the purse strings no longer so tightly gripped by a single fist, the manager is now freer than in the past to exert his own influence," says Alvin Toffler in *The Culture Consumers*.[3]

Diversified patronage also helps cushion institutions against fluctuations in the business cycle. Donors' tastes and interests are those not merely of individuals but of organizations representing broad publics and serving the needs of society, Toffler explains. Such links give cultural institutions social relevance, he adds. "[The museum] is exactly comparable to the self-employed professional who, because he works for many bosses, is his own boss in the end."[4] The new system has the additional benefit of encouraging support for projects of the greatest diversity and protects a museum from the disaster that would occur if it were to lose the single source of income upon which it depended.

An article in *U.S. News and World Report* predicted that individuals will again become the principal support of nonprofit organizations, that by 1984 their contributions will show an increase of 55 percent over 1979, and that total contributions received by arts and humanities groups will double by 1984.[5] Yet even though some museums are anticipating broader support, the public is receiving conflicting signals.

Many people believe that museums are profitable businesses. Perhaps this attitude stems from a confusion brought on by the publicity in recent years that has emphasized the dollar value of objects held by museums. The public also may have the mistaken impression that museums have profited significantly from "blockbuster" exhibits. Paradoxically, the belief that museums are on the brink of bankruptcy is also widespread—and counterproductive. Fund raisers are aware that people like to be associated with successful programs and institutions; if a donor thinks that an institution's failure is imminent, he or she is likely to direct an investment where it seems more certain to have lasting value.

Because museums generally have not communicated strong and consistent arguments for public support, the public relations person has a major task in building an awareness and understanding of needs and in stimulating a desire to contribute. PR staff need not be expert in fund-raising techniques, nor is it possible to deal with them in depth in this book. Still, a brief consideration of these techniques as they relate to public relations is appropriate.

Membership

Most museums have some type of membership that provides benefits such as free admission, merchandise discounts, and a magazine or newsletters. Memberships sometimes are priced at different levels in individual, family, and corporate categories. Because value is received, a membership is not tax deductible as a contribution.

Public relations has an important role in determining the target publics for a membership drive and in helping produce publicity and direct mail material that will motivate them. By writing the member magazine, newsletters, and renewal solicitations and helping plan member-only events, public relations can play a key role in keeping members interested and involved in the museum.

Because members are a prime target for fund-raising appeals, a conduit for word-of-mouth publicity, an audience for programs, and a market for on premises sales, you should consider them to be a high priority public when you are setting public relations program priorities.

Annual Giving

Annual giving programs seek funds to meet operating expenses. Because there is little donor recognition from an unrestricted gift, annual giving contributions can be difficult to develop and sustain. Yet they are the most important contribution to the many museums that are hard pressed to meet operating costs.

By continually placing consistent messages in media that reach members, corporations, foundations, and other annual giving targets, public relations can help develop and sustain the public perception that the ongoing operation of the museum is worthy of annual support.

Capital Giving

Capital giving involves campaigns to fund physical assets such as new buildings or major collection accessions. Such drives are conducted first among the museum's trustees. Commitments from board members should constitute a significant portion of the total funds needed and should be firm before a campaign is publicly announced.

Trustees should recruit campaign leadership and should be leaders in the drive.

According to the John Price Jones fund-raising company, the five essentials of a successful capital campaign are "a strong case, effective leadership, conscientious workers, prospects willing and able to give, and sufficient funds to finance the campaign during the preliminary period." [6]

Major capital campaigns usually begin with a feasibility study involving confidential interviews with 25 to 100 selected prospective major donors. Usually the interviewing is done by objective outside professionals employed by the fund-raising firm that the museum engages. Issues of concern include:

1. What is the general public relations and economic climate in which the museum will have to present its case for support?
2. How well is the museum serving its publics?
3. What do key supporters really think about the institution and its actual strengths and weaknesses?
4. Is the institution aware of its problems? [7]

The public relations person should be able to suggest candidates for interviews and to advise on the nature and relationships of groups within the museum's key publics.

Once it has been decided that there will be a campaign, the public relations person will usually assist in developing a "case statement"— the museum's statement of purpose expressed in terms of the need for funds to achieve high-priority goals and objectives. The case statement can take many forms and may be prepared by a development officer, a curator, or other staff member who is particularly knowledgeable about the subjects involved. Common sense should dictate ways in which the case statement will be published and distributed. An internal working document that includes detailed data on the need, costs, benefits, and strategies for implementing each aspect of the campaign can be refined into a variety of materials designed to motivate target publics such as members. These materials may be letters, inexpensive folders, or more elaborate brochures, depending on the size and nature of the campaign and the nature of the target public. One of the more unusual direct mail concepts is the gifts catalog approach developed by the Department of Interior and described in the U.S. Government Printing Office publication 1979-693-079.

Because direct mail is most productive when its message is focused on a specific audience and because it is expensive, public relations should help select high priority publics to receive these materials. In addition, you should learn as much as possible about what will motivate these publics to support the museum by using the research techniques discussed earlier in this book. A printed folder may be used to create interest and to make the case for support and could be mailed for arrival in advance of a personal contact. Backgrounders may be used by the media and by solicitors in connection with their calls. Special printed materials may also be produced to encourage previous donors to increase their gifts and to focus on publics with special interests.

Direct mail letters should be as personal and friendly as possible. If the number involved is small, or if the recipients are major prospects, the letter should be reproduced by automatic typewriter and personally signed by the sender. Such solicitations should be mailed first class, using a stamp rather than a postage meter. When larger numbers of letters are being mailed to a broad range of prospects, they may be duplicated on the letterhead of the executive director or the chairman of the board. "Dear Friend" is commonly used as a salutation; however, it may be more effective to begin with the opening sentence.

Crisp personal language should arouse the reader's interest, establish the importance of the campaign, create a sense of urgency, and suggest a specific course of action which can be taken by returning a check in the envelope provided. Studies indicate no significant difference in responses when the return envelopes are postage paid, but the return envelope should be of a size to accommodate a check and a return card. The card should make it easy for the contributor to indicate the category of gift that he or she wishes to make. It should be written in a personalized style, with provision for the donor to designate whether the gift should be credited to an individual or to more than one person. Typically the card might read: "Dear (executive director by name), I/we support the work of the museum and enclose a gift to help fund the important capital improvement)." Indicate in the letter that the way contributors sign their name or names on the card is the way it will be published in any donor listings.

Direct mail publications should be attractive, but do not use techniques that will make them appear excessively expensive. They should appeal to the emotion as well as to the intellect and whenever possible should have an illustration of what is being funded. The copy should be kept short and simple so the publication will be easy to read and understand.

In addition to assisting with the preparation of printed materials, the public relations person should be involved with special capital campaign activities. Major campaigns are often announced at a press conference with the chairman of the board of trustees and top campaign officials in attendance to answer questions. The architect, if a construction project is involved, or a senior curator, if the drive seeks to raise money for a major accession, should also be present. The kickoff dinner should have a speaker, and the program should be planned to excite workers into action. All major campaign officials including trustees should attend. Following the successful conclusion of a capital campaign, the public relations person may be involved in recommending and assisting with a variety of activities, such as a banquet in recognition of workers, dedication ceremonies, open houses, or exhibits of accessions acquired with the new funds.

Personal contact with large numbers of prospective donors is usually necessary to achieve broad-based support for a capital campaign. Museums can implement personal solicitation only by involving many people from all their publics as volunteer workers. The public relations department's success in linking the museum with its publics will be tested when efforts are made to convince perhaps hundreds of people to ask others for money.

Deferred Giving

Bequests, trust agreements, and life insurance programs are among gift possibilities that benefit the museum on a deferred basis. With a growing need for funds to increase operating endowments and a decrease in donors' gift reserves, museums will most likely intensify efforts to encourage this kind of support.

Prospects for deferred gifts, perhaps more than any other type of donor, must be personally committed to the purpose of the institution and must maintain their allegiance over a long period of time. Deferred giving is an area in which the public relations person's ability to communicate the museum's purpose, to maintain a congenial atmosphere, and to facilitate two-way communication is very important. Often there is no way of knowing which supporters have included a bequest to the museum in their wills, but PR staff members involved with deferred giving do know that donors can easily be prompted to cancel their bequests.

Opportunities for deferred giving may be described in the museum magazine or other publications or in descriptive literature provided upon request.

Special Gifts

Although most museum's special gifts will be donations of collection artifacts, gifts of sums of money large enough to erect buildings or to endow programs can also be classified as special gifts. As with all types of fund raising, the first task in stimulating special gifts is to identify prospects and to develop useful information about them. The public relations person's knowledge of the museum's publics is again helpful; other sources of names include attendance rosters from such activities as antiques lectures and seminars.

In identifying prospective donors of artifacts, a clearly defined collections policy is mandatory. Collection gifts are made in a very personal way, and the donor needs assurance that the museum is the right place for them. Adequate acknowledgment on artifact labels (unless donors ask to be anonymous), special exhibits of new gift accessions, and frequent publicity in appropriate journals will encourage contributions of collection gifts. Likewise, random and indefensible deaccessioning and a reputation for accepting collection gifts with the sole intention of selling them will discourage potential donors.

Grants and Grant Proposals

Most museums have the greatest need for funds that can be applied to operating costs. The Institute of Museum Services was established in 1976 as an independent agency within the executive branch of the federal government to assist museums in not only improving and increasing their services but also in maintaining them. In 1980, according to the IMS, "more than 425 general operating support applications that were turned down [due to limited funds] deserved to be funded." [8] In 1982 IMS reviewed 1,038 applications for funds totalling $10.2 million to be applied to salaries, utilities, maintenance, conservation of collections, education, and outreach programs at museums, aquariums, botanical gardens, planetariums, and zoos. In 1981 and 1982, the AAM and the AASLH, along with other associations, conducted lobbying efforts to prevent the rescission of IMS programs. Meanwhile IMS and other federal grants continued to be available but often were difficult to obtain and in late 1983 at this writing their future was uncertain.

Corporate grants are expanding and in 1979 for the first time surpassed the amounts given by foundations. Cultural institutions benefited most from the increase, with 19 percent of the funds being received by museums. If we consider that in 1980 corporations were allowed to give away a maximum of 5 percent of their income but on the national average gave away only 1 percent, we see that the potential is great.[9] Chairman of the Board C. Peter McColough of Xerox Corporation explained that one reason for his firm's support of cultural institutions is that "the types of people Xerox wants to hire are those who expect the company to support the arts." [10] Companies doubtless view their donations as serving their own interests in many ways.

Corporations usually require high public visibility for their support programs. Often they achieve it, as mentioned earlier, by retaining public relations counsel to work with gift recipients. The museum that is serious about developing corporate grants should view grant officers as a key public and should keep them informed about the ways in which the museum serves a corporation's interests. Foundations also often want their support to have public visibility. A museum can attract their interest only if its objectives are clearly in line with their aims and if this fact can be communicated to them persuasively.

Grant proposals should focus on the individual corporation or foundation involved and should address its needs and expectations as determined by research. The proposal should be clear, simple, direct, and as brief as possible. Common sense should dictate the proposal's format and length; proposals for major grants will usually need to be longer and more detailed than proposals for governmental funding. Many corporations and foundations will provide grant application guidelines. The following guidelines, developed by Raymond Pisney, director of the Missouri Historical Society, are useful in preparing longer and more detailed grant proposals.

1. Most applications require—and all should include—certain documents: a cover letter summarizing the background and purposes of the request for funds; a copy of the museum's 501 (c) 3 tax exemption letter from the Internal Revenue Service; a list of the members of the governing board of the requesting museum; and a copy of the museum's most recent financial statement.
2. Content is more important than format. It should cover:
    a. Purpose and objectives. What is the basic purpose of the proposal? Does the copy clearly define the problem to be addressed? Is this a request for general operating support or for funding for a new activity? If this is a continuation of an ongoing program, what are the past results, and how was the project evaluated? Is this a "pilot," "model," or "study" program?
    b. Plan of action. What activities will be undertaken? Who is involved in developing the proposal? What is the extent of the problem to be addressed, and how will the target population benefit? Is the applicant's staff adequate to attain objectives, or will additional staff be required?
    c. Evaluation. What is the process for evaluating the program? What will determine success or failure? Do evaluation plans include feedback and progress reports?
    d. Budget and financial information. Does the request include a detailed budget for the museum and for the specific project for which the funds are being requested?
    e. Background information:
        • The history of the museum. Does it indicate competence to carry out the proposed program?
        • What is the role played by the museum's governing board in forming policies, and how does the board relate to the program director? Has this relationship been adequately described?
        • Has the museum's governing board been involved in developing the project? Is board support indicated?
        • What are the relationships of this project to the overall goals and services of the museum?
        • Have requests for funds been submitted to other foundations or agencies?

- Has consideration been given to future sources of support?
- Has provision been made for appropriate financial accounting? [11]

Application forms for federal and state grants will vary among agencies, but the information sought will be similar. The National Endowment for the Humanities challenge grant form requests:

1. a description of the museum, the type of support requested, the proposed amount of NEH funding and funding from nonfederal matching sources, the project director, the institution's authorizing officer and payee and the type of institution;
2. the title of the project and a brief description of its use;
3. a detailed account of the project, including a statement of the problem, a description of any proposed solutions, the long-term capital campaign and matching fund development, the financial philosophy of the museum and conclusions;
4. a proposed budget including staff salaries for fund raising, a statement of the financial profits of the museum, previous national endowment support, and a timetable for matching funds development.

Fund-Raising Events

Fund-raising testimonial dinners and gala balls may help purchase an artifact or may help attract affluent people to the museum and increase its visibility to them. Such benefits usually have a ticket fee of at least $100 per person and are successful only if the museum is well connected socially, a factor dependent upon the museum's location and upon public relations efforts with prestige publics. Involvement of the members of the board of trustees and their peers in the planning and execution of such affairs is essential. Commercial sponsorship of food and other expenses incurred in staging the benefit should be sought so that all the money paid by participants may be turned to the museum's cause. Once the need and general direction of the affair is established, it is important for the museum to insist that volunteers execute the event. Because of the danger that the museum will give more than it receives at such events, they should be approached with specific objectives and should be carefully evaluated.

The Annual Report

Whether in the form of a speech, a letter with attachments, or a booklet, the annual report is the museum's public record of its performance and is an important development tool. It is usually produced in the form of a publication with an appearance of high quality that will interpret the museum's purpose, goals, and objectives in terms of the events of the past year. Museums are increasingly conserving costs by printing a limited quantity of annual reports and targeting their distribution. Summaries can be published in member newsletters and other museum publications. A story reviewing the year accompanied by a summary of the report may be sent to the media.

Annual reports may be organized in a number of ways, perhaps beginning with a statement from the chairman of the board of trustees. An illustrated narrative summarizing significant happenings during the past year sometimes appears next, under the signature of the executive director. The narrative can be divided into functional areas, such as interpretation, collections, exhibits, conservation, education, library, publications, personnel, membership, fund raising, maintenance, merchandising, and any auxiliary enterprises that the museum may have, such as lodging facilities. Statistics such as the number of memberships, collection and library accessions, and educational and general public attendance figures may also be included. The auditor's statement is sometimes next, followed by the statement of operating expense and revenue. Sometimes a pie graph sectioned to show budget percentages for salaries, wages, and fringe benefits and for maintenance, utilities, supplies, and administrative costs helps clarify the statement. A pie graph may also be used to show percentages of total operating income from each of the principal revenue sources, such as ticket sales and gift income. Donors are almost always listed by name and category of donation. It is critical that each name be spelled as it appeared on the return card or other communication that accompanied the gift and be located in the correct donor category. The museum's staff may also be listed.

The Museum Magazine

Although fund raising need not be a principal purpose of the museum magazine, it can lead to increased financial support by providing insight into the collections and programs and by developing an understanding of the museum's purpose. Although every issue should not dwell upon such subjects as needs for volunteers and for increased gift income, these and other topics of importance to the museum can be treated effectively in a magazine.

Governmental Relations

Because it is important that legislators in Washington be aware of museums' concerns and because few museums can afford their own representation, legislative efforts have been undertaken by AASLH, AAM, and other organizations. As these efforts expand and develop, they will draw increased attention to such issues as federal endowment appropriations and tax laws that affect individual and corporate contributors. The public relations person can assist in these efforts to influence favorable legislation by keeping federal, state, and local government officials informed and involved with the museum. A note of caution is necessary, however, because broad-based support will continue to be the foundation upon which most American museums are funded. Therefore, museums should not focus all their energy on attracting government grants. When seeking government grants, museums also should be certain that a proposed program serves the museum's purpose and is not being proposed only because there is funding available for it.

At the state level, the governor is almost always the most important single individual. A museum develops productive relationships with a governor and legislators by bringing them into contact with the executive director. "The degree of success you will achieve in the appropriations process, in obtaining special considerations when needed, and in bottling up legislation when necessary depends largely on the respect which legislators have for your president (or chief executive officer). The president symbolizes the institution," says Ray Hornback of the University of Kentucky.[12]

The museum's executive director should invite the governor or legislators to serve as speakers at ground-breaking ceremonies or on other major museum occasions. Likewise, members of Congress should be asked to participate in museum activities as nonpartisan speakers and to provide resolutions and citations of merit to mark milestones in the life of the museum and its collections.

It can be a responsibility of the public relations person to gather information on pending legislation, hearings, and other actions related to the museum's interests and to interpret this material for the executive director and for others involved. A file on legislators who are important to the museum is also useful. It should contain information on their interests and preferences that are relevant to the museum; dates of past visits; notes on what they have done for the museum; summaries of letters, telephone calls, and visits to them by museum representatives; and names of intermediaries who would be helpful in contacting them.

Local government is also important to the museum. Sidewalks, street lighting, traffic control, and various regulatory ordinances, and other facts of urban life all involve the museum with its home community. One should seize upon every opportunity to keep the mayor, city manager, council members, and others aware of and informed about the museum and its needs. The Indianapolis Museum of Art makes city council members honorary members of the museum. Local celebrations of national observances, such as Law Day or Museum Week, provide opportunities for involving local government authorities. All museums should consider placing key officials on the mailing list to receive, free of charge, selected publications, such as the museum's magazine.

Museums that maintain a continuous public awareness of the services they provide to society are in the best position to receive governmental support. The public relations person has a key role not only in publicizing the museum's good work, but also in influencing the museum to undertake programs that will benefit as many elements of society as possible.

5

The Publications Program

Unlike news releases, which are often rewritten by the media, and broadcast public service announcements, which may be aired to the wrong audience, publications can be carefully targeted. To maximize the publication's communication potential, it is important to understand the target audience and to develop and maintain the museum's mailing lists.

It is vital that every publication contribute to a better understanding of the museum's overall purpose, be consistent with the message base, and support themes that are developed in other communication efforts. When planning, writing, and designing a publication, you should keep in mind its objectives, its intended use, and the needs and interests of its target readers.

Distribution often does not receive adequate attention, yet it is one of the most critical concerns in addressing publications to a target audience. Relatively inexpensive computerized processing systems are available that hook into addressing machines and allow the user to combine several lists into one zipcode sequence, and eliminate duplicate names. There may be nearby institutions that would allow the museum to use such a system at a reasonable cost. By preventing duplicate mailing, the museum makes a better impression on recipients and avoids one form of waste.

Managing a Publications Program

Another form of waste results when many different publications are created to do a job requiring just a few. Only if existing museum publications, press kits, and other available materials cannot fulfill an important need should a new publication be undertaken. To prevent the duplication of effort and expense that occurs when each department produces its own printed material, and to achieve message and design consistency, publications should be coordinated through a central authority, which often is the public relations department.

Because each museum function best understands and is most capable of defending its own needs, each department often has its own publications budget. The PR staff or other coordinating office should estimate budget requirements for each department's publications needs, should obtain price quotations, and should produce an overall schedule for the year.

The schedule should have columns for each publication with deadlines for concept, copy, photos, art, editing, bid specifications, printing, and delivery. Planning well in advance is essential in scheduling publications, as is help from other members of the museum's management in establishing priorities. Each department will inevitably believe that its own projects are the most urgent and important.

The publications needs of most museums can be met by inexpensive folders to promote attendance, which can be distributed through literature racks and as enclosures with correspondence; by visitor orientation folders; by mailers describing the speakers' bureau and educational programs; by occasional fund-raising direct mail pieces; by an annual report; and perhaps by a quarterly magazine or newsletter. Employee and membership newsletters and exhibit backgrounders for visitors can often be produced by typewriter. Small shops can print typed fliers inexpensively. By exercising tight controls on minor projects and doing as much work as possible in house, one can concentrate budget allocations on publications that require professional art and production services, such as the promotional folder and the annual report.

Copy

The concept for a major publication, such as a visitor guidebook, begins with a clear grasp of the messages to be conveyed. The first draft may be written by the PR staff or by the department for which it is being produced. It is then the public relations person's responsibility to edit the copy, making sure that it expresses the desired message in an appropriate style that is grammatically correct. The client department should review final content, photos, and layout for accuracy. Writing style and graphics are the responsibility of the PR or other coordinating office working in conjunction with an in-house or outside designer.

Because people who are not accustomed to having their copy edited can be very sensitive to editor's changes, a great deal of diplomacy in working with the author may be required.

Design

By selecting the typeface, ink colors, and paper, and by laying out the pages and cover, the designer creates the visual impression that the publication will project. Unless an in-house staff member is skilled in design, this aspect of publication production is best left to a professional. An advertising agency may be willing to contribute design services occasionally. Design talent may also be obtained free of charge from a college or university design class. Free-lance designers are available in most cities, and all but the smallest printers will provide publication design and layout as part of a bid if they are instructed to do so. It is important for you to be familiar with the steps involved in designing a publication. With some practice, you may find you can design simple publications yourself.

Format

There are several important considerations in deciding on a format. What typeface, ink, and paper will be used? How will the design help communicate the message? Will there be one, two, or more columns per page? Will the publication be deeper than it is wide, square, or wider than it is deep? What photos or other art will be used? How can the cover be attractive, arresting, and thematically appropriate? How will this publication show a family resemblance to others produced by the museum? How can it be kept within budget constraints?

Start by making thumbnail sketches which establish the overall graphic concept. Experiment with different ways of arranging copy blocks and photos so that they appear balanced when the page is viewed alone and in conjunction with the facing page. Photos should direct the eye to the copy. To save costs, avoid graphics that create registration problems, such as two rules that run parallel to each other in different colors. See the sources at the end of this book for a list of books on producing publications.

When you have produced satisfactory thumbnail sketches of the cover and a few pages, try producing a layout of the actual size you plan to use. This can be done in two ways. For publications involving simple layouts, the copy and headlines may be typeset in lines of the correct column width, and photocopies of the corrected proofs may be cut apart for arrangement on dummy sheets that have column borders drawn to the actual size. Paper mats can be cut to the final size of photos for positioning on the dummy. Copy sections found to be too long may be trimmed to size with scissors. When all elements have been pasted into place, you can either return the dummy to the printer, who will do a final pasteup (called a keyline or mechanical), or you can save money by doing the mechanical in house. Because the keyline will be photographed to make a printing plate, the final pasteup must be done precisely and neatly, with all elements accurately aligned.

In the case of complicated layouts, you may translate thumbnail sketches into actual-size rough layouts by estimating the space required for copy and art before the type is set. In this way, several alternative layouts can be produced, each to correct copy and photo specifications.

Size

Consider selecting one of the following page sizes that take best advantage of standard paper cuts: 3½" x 6¼", 4" x 9", 4¼" x 5⅜", 4½" x 6", 5¼" x 7⅝", 5½" x 8½", 6" x 9", 7" x 5½", 8½" x 11", 8¾" x 11½", 9" x 12", 8½" x 14", or 11" x 17". Most common sizes are 4" x 9", 5½" x 8½", and 6" x 9". Publications with a large amount of copy and several illustrations generally benefit from the economy and the increased layout flexibility of a larger page size, such as 8½" x 11". If the publication is a flyer to be distributed in literature racks, 4" x 9" is usually acceptable. The 4" x 9" size is also most suitable for insertion with correspondence in a standard 9½" x 4⅛" business envelope.

Binding

You can save collating and binding costs by producing publications consisting of one sheet with several folds. However, publications intended for use by visitors while they walk around the museum can be awkward to handle if several panels must be spread open. If a publication folds to more than six panels, it should usually be saddle wire stitched (staples are punched through the edge of the fold into the center spread). Nearly all museum publications can be saddle wire stitched except when the number of pages is large or when the final product is to resemble a paperback book, with a flat spine on which copy is printed. In such cases the "perfect" binding technique, in which the pages are held by a flexible adhesive, is appropriate.

Reports can be bound in house using an inexpensive spiral binding kit, available at office supply stores. Often the cost of an envelope can be eliminated by meeting the postal requirements for a "self-mailer."

Typeface

Some museums own Varitypers, Justowriters, Selectric composers, or other machines which operate like a typewriter but will justify type (i.e., will set lines so that margins are straight on both sides). Each manufacturer offers a variety of typefaces that are interchangeable in that brand of machine. The machines can be operated with little training to compose copy that is ready for printing. You can also produce copy ready for printing (camera ready) using an ordinary typewriter, although the typescript will not have justified right margins.

In most cases when budget permits, you will want the readability and layout flexibility that come with type set professionally. Although most printers and typesetting houses have hundreds of typefaces, making a selection need not be bewildering. The face should be appropriate, readable, and readily available. A typesetter can tell you which faces are regarded as modern or traditional, casual or formal. Conservative readers usually prefer typefaces with strokes, called serifs, that project from the top or bottom of the main part of the letter. This is a serif E, this is a sans serif E.

Italic faces should be used sparingly because they are hard to read in large blocks. A large amount of reversed type (light on dark background) should also be avoided, because it strains the eyes. Boldface type should be used sparingly, or it will lose its ability to call attention to key words or phrases. There are condensed type faces (each letter is narrower than standard, so that more characters can be accommodated on a line) and extended faces (letters wider than usual, giving the page a feeling of openness). Lines of copy that are too short or too long or that do not have enough space between them are hard to read.

This copy is set without enough
space between lines.

This copy
has
adequate space
between lines but
the lines are too short.

Copy Fitting

By using the following procedure, one can estimate the space a given amount of copy will require.

1. Using a rule marked in picas (a "pica stick"), measure the width of the layout column.
2. Determine how many characters are in the typed manuscript, including punctuation marks and the spaces between words. (Multiply the number of characters in an average line by the total number of lines.)
3. Using a book of sample typefaces provided by a printer, pick a type face and look up the number of characters per pica in that face in the desired size (see figure 5.1). Multiply that number by the number of picas in the column width as determined in step 1.
4. Divide the total characters in the manuscript (step 2) by the answer to step 3. You will now have the total number of lines of typeset copy. For example: let us assume that you have a column 18 picas wide. There are 2,500 total characters in your typed manuscript, and you select 10-point Century Book type, which has 2.6 characters per pica. Then 18 x 2.6 = 46.8, or roughly 47 characters per typeset line. Divide 2,500 (the total number of characters) by 47 (number of characters per typeset line). You will have 53 lines of copy when it is set in 10-point Century Book.
5. Obtain a type gauge from a printer or a graphic supply store (see figure 5.2). When using 10-point type you will want one or two points of leading between lines. Read down the point column. If you use 10-point type with one point of leading, you will specify your choice as 10/11 (two points of leading would be designated as 10/12). Read down the 11-point column to 36 and read across to the pica column to find that the copy will, if set 10/11, be 33 picas deep.

Ink and Paper

Ink and paper (paper is termed "stock") affect readability as well as appearance. The ink must have a strong enough color value to be legible. Medium gray ink on a light gray paper might be unreadable. Imperfections in coverage can occur when you print large, solid masses of ink. Selecting one color or paper for the cover and another for the inside and using a colored ink that complements both papers will

CHARACTERS PER PICA BY POINT SIZE • NUMERAL WIDTH IN POINTS

Century Old Style Italic (077)	6	7	8	9	10	11	12	14	16	18	20	24
ABCDEFGHIJKLMNOPQRSTUVWXYZ	3.1	2.7	2.3	2.1	1.9	1.7	1.5	1.3	1.2	1.0	.93	.77
abcdefghijklmnopqrstuvwxyz	5.0	4.3	3.8	3.3	3.0	2.7	2.5	2.1	1.9	1.7	1.5	1.3
$1234567890	3	3½	4	4½	5	5½	6	7	8	9	10	12

Century Book (070)	6	7	8	9	10	11	12	14	16	18	20	24
ABCDEFGHIJKLMNOPQRSTUVWXYZ	3.2	2.8	2.4	2.2	2.0	1.8	1.6	1.4	1.2	1.1	.97	.81
abcdefghijklmnopqrstuvwxyz	4.4	3.8	3.3	2.9	2.6	2.4	2.2	1.9	1.7	1.5	1.3	1.1
$1234567890	3	3½	4	4½	5	5½	6	7	8	9	10	12

Century Book Italic (071)	6	7	8	9	10	11	12	14	16	18	20	24
ABCDEFGHIJKLMNOPQRSTUVWXYZ	3.2	2.7	2.4	2.1	1.9	1.7	1.6	1.4	1.2	1.1	.96	.80
abcdefghijklmnopqrstuvwxyz	4.3	3.7	3.2	2.9	2.6	2.4	2.2	1.9	1.6	1.4	1.3	1.1
$1234567890	3⅓	3⅞	4½	5	5½	6	6⅔	7¾	8⅞	10	11⅛	13⅓

Century Ultra (080)	6	7	8	9	10	11	12	14	16	18	20	24
ABCDEFGHIJKLMNOPQRSTUVWXYZ	2.7	2.3	2.0	1.8	1.6	1.5	1.3	1.1	1.0	.89	.80	.67
abcdefghijklmnopqrstuvwxyz	3.3	2.8	2.5	2.2	2.0	1.8	1.7	1.4	1.2	1.1	.99	.83
$1234567890	4	4⅔	5⅓	6	6⅔	7⅓	8	9⅓	10⅔	12	13⅓	16

Century Ultra Italic (081)	6	7	8	9	10	11	12	14	16	18	20	24
ABCDEFGHIJKLMNOPQRSTUVWXYZ	2.7	2.3	2.0	1.8	1.6	1.5	1.3	1.1	1.0	.89	.80	.67
abcdefghijklmnopqrstuvwxyz	3.3	2.8	2.5	2.2	2.0	1.8	1.7	1.4	1.2	1.1	.99	.83
$1234567890	4	4⅔	5⅓	6	6⅔	7⅓	8	9⅓	10⅔	12	13⅓	16

Century Schoolbook (084)	6	7	8	9	10	11	12	14	16	18	20	24
ABCDEFGHIJKLMNOPQRSTUVWXYZ	2.9	2.5	2.1	1.9	1.7	1.6	1.4	1.2	1.1	.95	.86	.72
abcdefghijklmnopqrstuvwxyz	4.2	3.6	3.2	2.8	2.5	2.3	2.1	1.8	1.6	1.4	1.3	1.1
$1234567890	3⅓	3⅞	4½	5	5½	6⅛	6⅔	7¾	8⅞	10	11⅛	13⅓

Century Schoolbook Italic (085)	6	7	8	9	10	11	12	14	16	18	20	24
ABCDEFGHIJKLMNOPQRSTUVWXYZ	2.8	2.4	2.1	1.9	1.7	1.6	1.4	1.2	1.1	.95	.85	.71
abcdefghijklmnopqrstuvwxyz	4.3	3.7	3.2	2.9	2.6	2.3	2.1	1.8	1.6	1.4	1.3	1.1
$1234567890	3⅓	3⅞	4½	5	5½	6⅛	6⅔	7¾	8⅞	10	11⅛	13⅓

Century Schoolbook Bold (086)	6	7	8	9	10	11	12	14	16	18	20	24
ABCDEFGHIJKLMNOPQRSTUVWXYZ	2.7	2.3	2.0	1.8	1.6	1.5	1.3	1.1	1.0	.89	.80	.67
abcdefghijklmnopqrstuvwxyz	3.7	3.2	2.8	2.5	2.2	2.0	1.9	1.6	1.4	1.3	1.1	.94
$1234567890	3⅓	3⅞	4½	5	5½	6⅛	6⅔	7¾	8⅞	10	11⅛	13⅓

Cheltenham (092)	6	7	8	9	10	11	12	14	16	18	20	24
ABCDEFGHIJKLMNOPQRSTUVWXYZ	2.9	2.5	2.2	1.9	1.7	1.6	1.4	1.2	1.1	.96	.86	.72
abcdefghijklmnopqrstuvwxyz	5.3	4.5	3.9	3.5	3.2	2.9	2.6	2.3	2.0	1.8	1.6	1.3
$1234567890	3	3½	4	4½	5	5½	6	7	8	9	10	12

Cheltenham Italic (093)	6	7	8	9	10	11	12	14	16	18	20	24
ABCDEFGHIJKLMNOPQRSTUVWXYZ	3.0	2.6	2.2	2.0	1.8	1.6	1.5	1.3	1.1	1.0	.90	.75
abcdefghijklmnopqrstuvwxyz	5.5	4.7	4.1	3.6	3.3	3.0	2.7	2.3	2.1	1.8	1.6	1.4
$1234567890	3	3½	4	4½	5	5½	6	7	8	9	10	12

Figure 5.1. *A sample of the Century typeface family.*

PICA	9 PT.	10 PT.	11 PT.	13 PT.	14 PT.	15 PT.	AGATE
	1	— 1	1	— 1	1	— 1	2
1	2	— 2	2		2		4
2	3	— 3	3	— 2		— 2	6
3	4	— 4		— 3	3		8
4	5	— 5	4	— 4	4	— 3	10
	6	— 6	5	— 5		— 4	12
5	7	— 7	6	— 6	5	— 5	14
6	8		7	— 7	6		16
7	9	— 8	8		7	— 6	18
8	10	— 9	9	— 8		— 7	20
9	11	—10	10	— 9	8		22
10	12	—11	11	—10	9	— 8	24
11	13	—12	12	—11	10	— 9	26
12	14	—13	13				28
13	15	—14	14	—12	11	—10	30
14	16	—15	15	—13	12	—11	32
15	17	—16	16	—14	13	—12	34
16	18	—17	17	—15	14	—13	36
17	19	—18	18	—16	15	—14	38
18	20	—19	19	—17	16	—15	40
19	21	—20	20	—18	17	—16	42
20	22	—21	21	—19	18	—17	44
21	23	—22	22	—20	19	—18	46
22	24	—23	23	—21	20	—19	48
23	25	—24	24	—22	21	—20	50
24	26	—25	25	—23	22	—21	52
25	27	—26	26	—24	23	—22	54
26	28	—27	27	—25	24	—23	56
27	29	—28	28	—26	25	—24	58
28	30	—29	29	—27	26	—25	60
29	31	—30	30	—28	27	—26	62
30	32	—31	31	—29	28	—27	64
31	33	—32	32	—30	29	—28	66
32	34	—33	33	—31	30	—29	68
33	35	—34	34	—32	31		70
34	36	—35	35	—33	32		72
35	37	—36	36	—34			74
36	38	—37	37				76
37	39	—38	38				78
	40	—39	39				80
	41	—40	40				82
	42	—41					84
	43	—42					86
	44	—43					
	45	—44					
	46						
	47						
	48						
	49						
	50						

Figure 5.2. A type gauge

create a good effect with only a one-color press run. Keep in mind that most ink is transparent and its color is affected by the paper.

Weight, opacity, brightness, grain, bulk, and finish are aspects of paper that you will need to consider in making a selection. You can save money by using a paper that the printer has already in stock or by making a large order that will last through several printing jobs. Paper weight is indicated in pounds ranging from 30 to 120. You will usually want at least 60-pound paper, which gives the page sufficient substance and prevents ink from showing through to the reverse side. Stiff cover papers are available in 65-, 80-, and 100-pound weights. In addition to weight, consider the bulk of the paper—its thickness. If you are producing a publication of only a few pages, a paper of high bulk will make it appear more substantial.

"Finish" refers to the surface of the paper. If the paper is uncoated, its finish will usually be rough and of a type not recommended for the printing of photographs. Some uncoated smooth finishes are available, however, for use when reproducing photos. Coated papers form the second major category of finishes. They are often more costly but give superior photo reproduction and impart a more elegant appearance to the publication. Coated finishes may be dull or glossy. Consult printers for paper samples and recommendations.

Art

Whether photos, charts, or other art are desirable depends on whether they will increase the reader's comprehension of the message. Course catalogs, for example, do not usually utilize art, while visitor promotion folders and annual reports almost always need illustrations to make the material comprehensible and attractive. Costs can be reduced by avoiding four-color printing unless it is important for the reader's comprehension, as it might be in a direct mail catalog illustrating several different museum reproductions of colored glassware. If photos or artwork are not of the highest quality, a printer can often suggest special treatments that will make them usable.

Photos are cropped for the same reasons that copy is edited—to take out unnecessary material, to emphasize that which is most important, and to make them fit the allocated space. You can construct a handy cropping guide by cutting two pieces of stiff 8½" x 11" paper in L shapes. Position them one over the other to create a window, then slide them around on the photograph until all unwanted parts of the image have been covered (figure 5.3). When you are satisfied that the photo

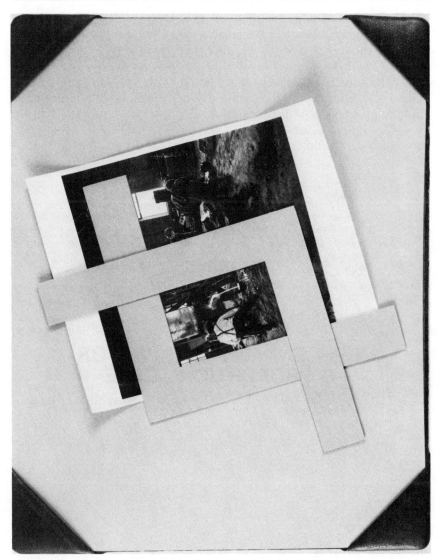

Figure 5.3. Cropping a photograph

has been cropped to appear exactly as it should when printed in the publication, draw lines on the photo's border with a grease pencil (available at art stores) to indicate the width and height of the cropped section. Do not extend these lines beyond the border into the picture. If a substantial portion of the picture is to be cropped out, draw an arrow in the border to indicate to the printer which portion is to be used.

The next step is to establish the height that the photo should have when it has been proportioned to fit the desired column width. You may determine this simply and accurately with a proportioning wheel (figure 5.4), which can be purchased at art stores. On the inner wheel find the present size of the portion of the photo that you want to use. If present width measures 4⅜″ and the publication has a column 3½″ wider, locate 4⅜″ on the inner wheel and rotate it until the figure lines

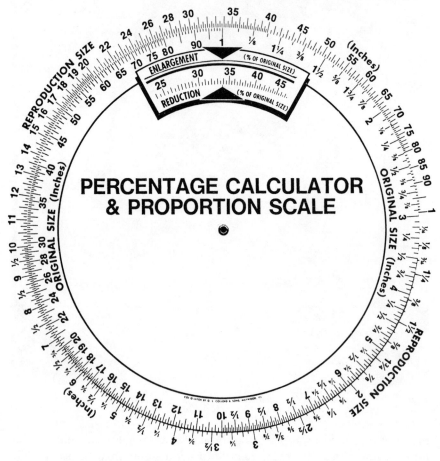

Figure 5.4. A proportioning wheel

up with 3½″ on the outer wheel. If the photo after cropping is 6″ in height, find 6″ on the inner wheel. The number closest to 6″ on the outer wheel (4¹³⁄₁₆″ in this case) will be the new height.

If you are baffled by the proportioning wheel, try a simple exercise in geometry. Measuring from the left edge of a clean sheet of paper, mark off the width of the cropped original with a vertical line. Then measure from the bottom of the sheet and mark the height of the cropped original. Draw a diagonal line from the lower left corner to the upper right corner. Finally draw a vertical broken line to the desired column width, in this case 3½″. The point at which the diagonal and column width lines intersect, shown in figure 5.5, is the final height of the photo (again, 4¹³⁄₁₆″). If the desired width is greater than the width of the original photo, the height of the needed enlargement can be plotted by the same method (figure 5.5).

Typesetters and Printers

There are several reasons for using more than one typesetter or printer. Few are equipped to handle all types of jobs well and economically. Also, the incentive to estimate jobs at the most economical price may be diminished in a noncompetitive situation. In addition, by spreading the printing work around you create a larger group of suppliers from whom you might occasionally request contributed services.

It is best to practice selective bidding, that is, to request bids only from firms that you know are capable of doing a particular job well. The museum should have a bid specification form with these headings:

job description	halftones (black-and-white photos)
quantity	color separations (for printing color photos)
size	binding
number of pages	typesetting/keylining
cover stock	delivery date
text stock	additional
color ink	

It is sometimes possible to effect greater economies by allowing a printer enough time to work the job into slack periods. Also, save money by ordering enough copies so that the job will not have to be rerun. The cost difference between 3,000 and 4,000 copies is very small compared with the difference between buying 3,000 copies now and

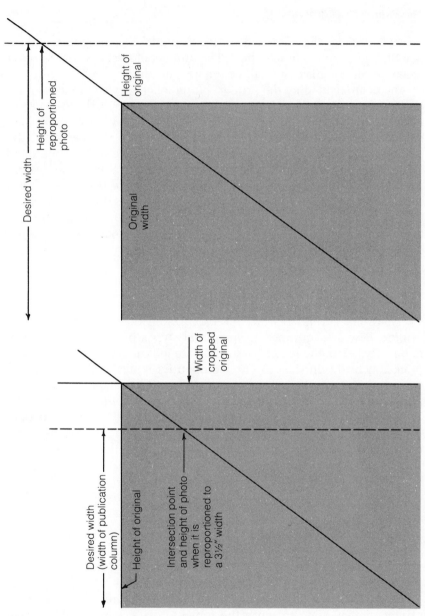

Figure 5.5. Scaling a photo reduction, left; scaling a photo enlargement, right.

ordering another 1,000 after the job has come off the press. Be aware that according to trade customs, unless a customer makes a special request, printers can deliver as much as 10 percent overrun or under-run and can adjust the bill accordingly.

You should always ask to see galley proofs (strips of copy for check-ing errors and for pasting up rough layouts) and page proofs (corrected copy including all art elements, with photos and captions in place). The typesetter can charge for alterations made by the museum after the manuscript is submitted. They are expensive and can delay the deliv-ery. Errors made during typesetting are corrected at no charge to you. When checking corrected proofs, look for new errors resulting from previous corrections. See the appendix for a table of proofreaders' marks.

Read your original typescript against the typeset copy. Check that no words are missing from sentences that continue from one page to the next; that headlines and photo captions are correct and properly posi-tioned; and that photos have been cropped as specified and have been screened adequately for good reproduction. The more lines in the screen, the sharper the photo image. A 133-line screen is standard.

In working with the printer you should specify where the publica-tion is to be delivered and how it is to be shipped.

Storage and Distribution

Publications should be stored in their cardboard shipping boxes off the floor in a dry room.

Check with the local postmaster for advice on the most economical mailing rate before the publication is printed. Second-class postage applies to magazines, newsletters, and catalogs that are mailed un-sealed at least four times a year. It requires a post office contract spec-ifying mailing frequency. Third-class bulk-rate matter includes such publications as form letters, flyers, and other direct mail that is not issued at fixed intervals. Bulk-rate mailings require a permit from the post office, must be sorted and bundled in accordance with postal regulations, and will not be accepted by the post office until a statement of mailing has been completed. Fourth-class material, which includes books, is charged at rates determined by weight and mailing zones.

6

Messages for the Media

A museum's message makes a strong impression when a person hears it on the car radio, sees it on the television evening news, reads it in the evening newspaper, and is told about it by a lunch companion the next day. Even with so much exposure, however, the message will probably be dismissed and forgotten if:

- the source is not credible;
- the message does not agree with the individual's preconceived notions;
- the person has no personal stake in the subject, has never visited the museum, and shares no common knowledge about it with the message sender;
- no specific and convenient action is indicated.

A publicity campaign will produce the best results when it is received so enthusiastically that people make an effort to share the information with their friends.

The written word is perhaps the publicist's most basic tool, and although public relations encompasses far more than publicity, the ability to write for the media is an indispensable skill. This chapter considers some common types of written communication. As earlier chapters have suggested, however, success will depend not merely upon the content of the message but also upon the extent to which its expression reflects the writer's awareness of the target audience and of the channels that will relay the words. The following guidelines therefore depend on those presented in later (as well as earlier) chapters of this book.

Describing the irrelevant puffery flowing into newspaper city rooms daily, Charles Honaker, a college communications director, exclaimed in the *Public Relations Journal* that few news releases are worth the paper they are printed on.[1] Explaining that many editors open only material coming from institutions and individuals that they regard as credible sources of pertinent information, he emphasized that most press releases are written to please an employer rather than to meet the media's needs.

Most museum messages inform consumers of available opportunities. It is critical that these opportunities be accurately described by the museum and the media so that no one is vulnerable to charges of misrepresentation. Visitors who feel that they have been misled or deceived will generate negative public opinion that will damage the museum.

The News Release

The release should be newsworthy, clearly written, arranged in the correct format, approved by appropriate museum staff members for accuracy, and issued with restraint. The copy should not be a thinly disguised advertisement. It will be published only when it is of local interest—within the city, state, or region—and is informative, useful, and timely. A story describing a forthcoming special event is useful information, and therefore news, to people living close enough to the museum to attend. It may not, however, be news to a reader 100 miles away. Usually only stories with universal appeal or linked with current issues hold interest beyond 100 miles unless a local person is involved.

Mindful of the message's objectives and of the informational needs and interests of the intended receiver, begin preparing the news release by isolating the most important, pertinent, and appealing elements of the story. For example, the essence of a special exhibit story might be that a scale model of the Massachusetts capitol will be shown for the first time.

Emphasizing this information, the writer prepares a simple and direct lead paragraph. The first two paragraphs should tell the who, what, where, when, why, and how of the story. For example, "A special exhibit, 'Boston's Bullfinch,' (what) opens at XYZ Museum (where) June 5. (when) It pays tribute (why) to architect Charles Bullfinch (who) by exhibiting models of his Boston buildings. (how)"

Depending upon the writer's intended focus, the lead paragraph can begin with any of the five W's, or the how, and can treat those remaining according to whatever sequence seems most appropriate, usually positioning the least important element last. Some subjects may not contain all six elements. The lead paragraph should be kept brief and should be interesting.

Although shallowness must always be avoided, it can occasionally be useful to write evocative descriptive prose to emphasize a point or to make the lead paragraph more arresting. An appealing lead sentence of this type might read: "The crackle of muzzle-loading rifles will pierce the quiet of XYZ Museum June 21 and 22. Participants from throughout the nation will recreate an early-20th-century turkey shoot."

Out-of-town newspapers are more likely to use a story that emphasizes local people in the opening paragraph. A lead sentence can be developed that will permit the release to be reproduced, leaving the name and hometown details to be typed on each copy. For example: "Three (name of city) area residents had winning entries in XYZ Museum's September 12 Old Car Festival judging. They are (leave two or three blank lines to type in their names and home towns)." In consideration of the participants' privacy, street addresses should not be used in hometown releases.

As you write, bear in mind that Americans have generally low reading skills and are spending less and less time with newspapers. They are too impatient to work at comprehending copy that is not readable. Communication expert Rudolph Flesch summed up readability guidelines in several numbers, three of which are seventy, seventeen, and ten.

Seventy is the percentage of words in any piece of copy that should be easily recognizable or of one syllable. In addition to being more comprehensible, trim words increase reading speed. Strive for no more than seventeen words in a sentence. When a long sentence is needed, offset it with a couple of short ones. Vary the sentence structure and keep paragraphs short. Flesch recommends ten personal references in each 100 words of copy. "He," "neighbor," and "husband" are all personal reference words. Titles of people, personal pronouns, and words denoting personal relationships humanize the copy and help readers identify with it.

Stocks are one thing on Wall Street and another at Colonial Williamsburg where they were a device for punishment. Such variations in word meanings are frequent sources of message noise. Jargon also introduces noncommunicative noise. For example, "gentrification," a word used by citizen groups protesting neighborhood changes wrought by preservationists, is meaningless to most people.

The most comprehensible written and spoken messages use common words in short sentences with human interest anecdotes that amplify clearly written statements of fact. Personal references and active verbs sweep the reader from one sentence to the next. Polysyllabic words are barriers to readability and should be avoided whenever possible. By using quotations the writer personalizes copy and also establishes its credibility. Parenthetical expressions are also enlivening, as are questions, examples, and human interest anecdotes. Always use a woman's name—Mary Jane Brown, not Mrs. James Brown. Triple check to be sure that all names are spelled correctly.

As writer Philip Lesly has noted, "The biggest occasion for sins of discommunication is thinking about oneself instead of the audience. Ego is singular, and likely to be massaged in solitude. Communications, being plural, involves interaction with others, and makes it possible to move multitudes. Ego is the enemy of good communication." [2] Clarity, readability, and appeal require finding the elements of the story in which the museum and the readers share a common experience. An article about an antique automobile collection, for example, can be made meaningful by discussing the gasoline mileage that the cars attained. Restatement is another device for establishing clarity. You may wish to repeat a tightly written version of the museum's message base at the end of each release for the purpose of reinforcing in the editors' minds the museum's purpose and uniqueness.

By arranging the required information in the proper format you will greatly assist editors in evaluating the material and will improve its chances of being read and published. Format considerations begin with the mailing envelope. The name and address of the museum and the office from which the release is being mailed should be printed in the upper left corner. If the museum has a corporate color, use it. A colorful postage stamp helps personalize the envelope's appearance.

The release should be on 8½" x 11" paper suitable for clear copy reproduction. Never type a release on erasable bond paper. Ideally, the letterhead should consume a depth of no more than two inches and should be printed in the museum's corporate color and typeface, if any. The word "News," the name and address of the museum, and the name and office telephone number of the public relations person or designated media contact person should be prominent. If the museum switchboard is closed evenings, holidays, or weekends, the contact person's home telephone number should also be listed. Otherwise the switchboard operator should be prepared to answer questions or advise media callers of appropriate home telephone numbers.

A consistently used graphic symbol and/or typeface quickly establishes that a news release or any other material is from the museum. The symbol should be professionally designed, and should be bold enough to reproduce in reverse (light color with dark background) or when it is screened (a lighter value of any color). It should also reproduce well when stamped on museum reproduction items or on business cards. It should not require two-color printing, should not duplicate or strongly resemble anyone else's symbol, and should be appropriate for the museum.

The museum's name as it is printed in conjunction with the symbol should always appear in the same typeface. The typeface chosen should be attractive, distinctive, and readable even when reversed. Refrain from using incongruous typefaces, (art deco styles would seem out of place for an eighteenth-century museum); consult a printer for advice. The Tennessee State Museum symbol (figure 6.1) illustrates how a typeface and a design can be integrated in a symbol.

Use a dark ribbon when typing releases and avoid typefaces that are hard to read. With elite type one can fit more copy on the page than with pica. Leaving six spaces below the letterhead, type "For Immediate Release" flush left and underline it. These words advise the editor that the story can be published any time. If the story is being offered only to one outlet, add "Exclusive to the ABC Newspaper." It is wise to call a newspaper before you offer it an exclusive story to gauge its

Figure 6.1. The logo of the Tennessee State Museum, designed by Phil Kreger of the museum staff

interest. You should follow up your call if the story is not used within a few days because it can be placed elsewhere if the first newspaper does not use it. Exclusive releases are usually done only to make your material attractive to a large metropolitan newspaper and are used infrequently because they limit media use of your materials. If it is being widely distributed, but only to one newspaper in multiple-newspaper cities, add "Exclusive in Your City." If the newspaper is published in several regional editions, the release can be offered on an exclusive or an "exclusive in your city" basis to only one of them.

A story given to one newspaper a short time before it is provided others is a "break." Breaks should be made only when there is a specific reason for doing so, for example, a release about a local person winning a museum award could go to the local weekly first. When a release is being issued as a break, that fact should be indicated. Distribution to several people at one newspaper is to be avoided. When it is done, the names of all recipients at the newspaper should be noted on the release. To specify the date and time when a story can be used, simply substitute "For Release June 17" for the usual "For Immediate Release." Imposing such release requirements on the media should be avoided if possible. Although many media will honor release dates, some may not.

Next, in parentheses four spaces down and to the right of "For Immediate Release," type a suggested headline. It should be capitalized to distinguish it from the body copy and should be short and to the point. Because all newspapers write their own headlines, the one you provide merely helps the editor establish the gist of the story at a glance.

Leaving at least six spaces in which the editor can write his or her own headline and can rewrite the lead sentence (which newspapers almost always do), type the dateline flush left. It includes the city (in all capital letters) and the state (upper and lower case), and the date of mailing, in parentheses followed by two hyphens. Then begin the lead sentence.

Always double space unless single spacing the last one or two paragraphs will keep you from having to use another page. Never print releases on both sides of a page. Do not split words at the ends of lines, and try to avoid splitting paragraphs between pages. If the release is more than one page, type "-MORE-" at the end of each page and "page X of X pages release, XYZ Museum" at the top of each following page. The number "-30-", the typographer's symbol for end, should be

XYZ Museum

XYZ MUSEUM NEWS

252 West Street, Monroe, Vermont 45206
Tel.: Jean Smith (212) 568-1473

For Immediate Release

(XYZ MUSEUM VOLUNTEER PROGRAM
TO BE DISCUSSED SUNDAY EVENING)

MONROE, Vt. (June 10)--The XYZ Museum volunteer program will be discussed June 21, 7 to 10 p.m. in the Museum auditorium. All interested adults and children over twelve are invited.

Director of Education Emily Stroede and Director of Special Events Ave Barr will speak briefly on their programs. A film on the many opportunities that await volunteers also will be shown.

During 1982 more than 10,000 hours of work was contributed by 50 volunteers who were involved in the Museum's public school programs, summer festival and Victorian Christmas. "Without their much appreciated effort, we could not have conducted these programs," according to Museum President Jane Adams. "At least ten more volunteers could be put to work immediately on interesting and worthwhile projects of great benefit to the Museum and this community in 1983" she said.

Now in its fifth year of operation, the XYZ Museum volunteer program has produced 35,000 hours of contributed work valued at more than $175,000.

−30−

XYZ MUSEUM IS A NON-PROFIT EDUCATIONAL INSTITUTION SPECIALIZING IN 19th CENTURY VERMONT HISTORY.

(GDA, 1, 4, 75)

Figure 6.2. A sample news release

centered four or more spaces below the last sentence. Do not use staples or paper clips on releases.

If you need to add a clarification statement, type it in capitals at the bottom of the last page. Below it, type coded information that will be useful in the future, such as the initials of the person who wrote the story, the code letters of the mailing lists used, and the total number of copies mailed. Figure 6.2 shows a sample release.

The Broadcast Media Release

Releases prepared for newspapers are usually used by broadcast media only for background. Radio and television news departments stress immediacy and want to receive news information by telephone. However, if there is adequate advance time and the story has strong local or state interest, a printed broadcast news release can be sent to news directors. A radio announcer may read it over the air, or it may prompt a television news department to assign coverage.

The broadcast media generally determine whether a story is news by measuring it against the following criteria, according to writer Gabe Thurston.

1. Does it affect a large number of people?
2. Will it make a perceptible difference in the safety, life-style, or well-being of these people?
3. Is it surprising (or at least novel) to many of those in the audience?
4. Does it convey or involve information that is of importance or value (or at least of interest) to a large segment of the audience?
5. Will it interest, appeal to, excite, or entertain the audience?[3]

In summary he says, "A good broadcast news story has universality, impact, immediacy, informational content and emotional appeal."

Radio and television share the same writing style and format requirements. Because most broadcast stories are aired in fifteen to forty-five seconds, they should be no more than 100 words long, (25 words equals ten seconds), triple spaced, and typed in all capital letters. Radio and television stations want to be told when the story should be used. Sentences should be short, should flow, and should use informal conversational language. You should write for the ear, rather than for the eye. Contractions and simple words will help meet this requirement. As much as possible, the passive voice should be avoided.

Jamming the who, what, where, when, why, and how into the first paragraphs is usually impractical in a broadcast release, but you should come to the most important and interesting part of the story quickly. The lead sentence should emphasize the story's immediacy and should include the source of information, but do not place key details at the beginning of the opening sentence; they will probably be missed by listeners. Lead up to a name or other important subject with a descriptive phrase that will cue the listener or viewer to the information that will come next. For example, to say in a broadcast release that "the coveted historian of the year award offered annually by XYZ Museum will go today to Jim Brown of Boston," is better than to say, "Jim Brown of Boston receives XYZ Museum's historian of the year award today."

Insert hyphens between letters that are to be read as letters, and use abbreviations only when they are to be read as such. Titles are easier to read when they appear before the names unless they are very long. The phonetic spelling of any difficult name or unfamiliar word should follow the word in brackets. It can be any combination of letters that is easy to understand. Never use museum jargon or words not commonly spoken or understood. Use punctuation marks with restraint and only to tell the announcer where to pause. Keep quotations short, and introduce them with a statement such as "in her words" rather than "quote."

Read the release aloud before printing it, change any words that cause you to stumble and make sure the release communicates the intended message clearly. At the end of the release, suggest interview possibilities for radio stations and visual possibilities for television. Circle these suggestions and type them below the end mark so that announcers will know they are not to be read on the air. It is appropriate to include with television releases closeup horizontal 35mm slides of high quality illustrating the subject.

The positioning of release instructions, suggested headlines, name and number to call for further information, dateline, end symbol, clarification statement, and coded information is the same as for the print media release.

Calendars

Reproduced on 8½" x 11" mimeograph paper, the museum activities calendar can be mailed biweekly, monthly, or quarterly to all media outlets except magazines. It should have the same color, design, and letterhead that appear on the news release, with the word "Calendar" substituted for "News." The calendar should be mailed first class and should be timed to arrive two weeks prior to the month covered. The envelope should be imprinted "Dated Calendar Material." Special exhibits and performances, film presentations, and weekend special events should be listed with dates, one- or two-sentence descriptions, fees, and notations of any special visual or interview possibilities. The material can be divided into first-time and repeat listings. A sample appears in the appendix.

Editors of monthly magazines need a long lead calendar that provides information about activities six months before they occur. Released each January for the period July through December and each July for January through June, this version can use the same format as the monthly or biweekly calendar. It should include only those activities that would be of widespread regional or national interest.

The Writer's Guide

A writer's guide that includes costs, hours, and other basic information may be released annually in the first quarter of the year to all media lists. Extra copies should be printed for inclusion with press kits and query letters (described below) and for reference use by the museum's volunteer speakers and by staff members doing media interviews. For filing convenience an 8½" x 11" size is recommended. Copy can be typed and printed on both sides of the sheet to keep cost and the number of pages minimal. A typical writer's guide might be organized as follows:

- a printed letterhead reading "1983 Writer's Guide for your convenience in using the staff and resources of XYZ Museum. For additional information call the public relations office at (telephone number) or write (address)";
- a selection of two or three photographs that give an impression of the museum's size and appearance;
- the museum's message base statement;
- the names of museum public relations personnel to contact for information;
- the names of the chairman of the board of trustees and the museum's executive director;
- the year's special exhibits and activities listed by date;
- crafts demonstrations listed by operating season;

- education department services;
- special departments such as archives, research, library, traveling exhibits, reproductions, and sales, briefly described;
- major collections, organized by subject headings with a descriptive sentence and a brief description of selected highlights for each. For example:

  Agriculture Collection. Excellent examples of early twentieth-century sources of farm power and dairy and grain harvesting equipment. Highlights are: comprehensive exhibits of traction steam engines; the first Fordson tractor; a 1938 Massey Harris combine, one of the first to be self-propelled.

- on the back cover, a fact sheet, separate copies of which could be printed as single-sheet handouts. Information should include hours, admission, group programs, rides or other special attractions for which there are special fees, eating places, sales shops, and directions to the museum from freeways, airports, train stations, and bus terminals.

Print Media Fillers

Newspapers, especially small weeklies and special interest tabloids that do not use computerized typesetting, take filler copy to plug holes in page layouts. A number of filler paragraphs, each four to six sentences in length, can be reproduced on a letterhead titled "Fillers" and can be sent to appropriate media at least three weeks prior to any date that is mentioned in the copy. Birthdays of famous people associated with the collections and historical antecedents of objects that are making news are useful filler subjects because they are timely or connected with the day's events. See the appendix for a sample of a filler release.

Securing Approval of Publicity Copy

Information provided to the media must be reviewed by appropriate museum personnel to assure that facts are correct. When the staff is small, approval by the executive director and the appropriate curator is usually sufficient. At larger museums the curator most involved with the subject, his or her supervisor, the public relations director's supervisor and the executive director may okay the copy.

When circulating the release to various museum offices, you can attach a form printed on colored stock so that it will stand out in the day's mail. The form should note the date the story is scheduled for mailing and should explain that any factual errors should immediately be brought to the attention of the public relations office; otherwise the copy will be assumed to have been approved.

The Feature Story versus the News Story

The news story emphasizes the facts, is written for a general audience, and is reproduced in a press release for simultaneous distribution to many media outlets. In contrast, the feature amplifies the facts through research, interviews, instructions, anecdotes, and vivid descriptions. It seldom opens with the who, what, where, when, why, and how in the first two paragraphs, as does the news story. Rather it may begin with an interesting fact, a question, or some other attention-getting device. It is longer than the news story and usually develops a specific angle or aspect of the subject.

Most museum news releases are a news-feature blend. While they are based on hard information, they use feature techniques to give the story interest and appeal.

Instead of writing the feature, the museum public relations person usually calls an editor or sends a query letter with an exclusive feature story idea. The newspaper, magazine, or station either writes the story or advises that it is not interested, in which case the idea can be offered elsewhere. A feature idea is most acceptable to an editor when it is on his or her specialty and is of particular interest to his or her readers. For example, a feature idea on color trends as illustrated by a costume exhibit would be of interest to a newspaper fashion editor, while a general story on the opening of the exhibit should be directed to the news editor, with an information copy to the fashion department. (See the appendix for a sample feature story.)

Most magazines are published for target audiences and will provide a description of the characteristics of their readers. Reference books such as *Writers Market* (see the sources section of this book) also provide this information. Knowing these facts, one can select the magazine most likely to be interested in a feature idea.

You can increase your chances of placing a feature by providing totally different story angles to two or more noncompetitive media. For example, if you were publicizing a tobacco festival and a tobacco company's employees were prospective visitors, a feature idea on a participant who was scheduled to demonstrate the processing of snuff could be sent to the editor of the company magazine. Meanwhile, the editor of a newspaper Sunday supplement magazine could be offered another angle with an idea on the methods of tobacco harvesting to be demonstrated at the festival. You might also query a free-lance writer who is known to have published in magazines that are of interest to the museum. Free-lancers can accept paid assignments from a museum, but it should be established at the outset who pays for what.

Because editors will consider ideas only if they meet current needs, you can improve the chances of placement by consulting periodicals that publish information on stories being developed at various magazines. (See the sources at the end of this book.) Museums most frequently fail to secure feature magazine coverage because they do not query far enough in advance or do not query the right magazine. National magazines commit their editorial pages from four to six months in advance of publication.

To determine where best to place a feature idea, study several issues of magazines to determine their editorial interests. The samples you consult will reveal differences in emphasis. From these possibilities, select the magazine that seems most appropriate and that reaches the largest portion of the target audience. Check a reader's guide to periodicals to determine whether the magazine has published a story on the subject recently. If not, and if the idea seems consistent with the type of story the magazine publishes, mail a query letter to the editor with a self-addressed stamped envelope for his or her reply.

The query letter should emphasize why the idea would be of interest to the magazine's readers. It should state that an exclusive story idea is being offered and should give a clear, concise summary of it. It should not request any favors or suggest that the story must be treated in a specific way. Always be sure that the museum can follow through on promises that are made. Following is a sample magazine query letter:

Dear Mr. Smith:

We have just finished one of the largest exhibit reinstallations ever attempted by a museum. More than a quarter million objects were moved and reexhibited.

Knowing of your readers' interest in museums and your emphasis on the people connected with museum programs, we are suggesting a story on our director of interpretation, who supervised this project.

As an articulate interpreter of modern museum exhibit concepts, he would make an excellent subject for an interesting story on how this reinstallation was accomplished.

I have enclosed his vita. Please advise if you would like additional information.

We are offering this story idea to you on an exclusive basis and will look forward to your response.

Sincerely yours,

The term "exclusive" applies only to those elements of a story that the publication decides to use. For example, if a magazine is queried with regard to a Christmas feature at XYZ Museum and decides to cover only a special exhibit on holiday crafts, other aspects of the Christmas program could be suggested to other magazines. To prevent complications, a letter should be sent to the editor confirming the details of the story idea that he or she has accepted and has been granted exclusively.

Interested editors will usually respond to a query by making a survey visit to the museum to see if the story offers what was promised. If a recipient does not respond, one should wait a suitable length of time (fifteen days, according to the Code of Ethics and Good Practice of the American Society of Journalists and Authors) before contacting the magazine to establish if it has an interest. If the idea is rejected, one is then free to offer it to another magazine. Small magazines might ask the museum to write the story. If it is written by the museum public relations person it should be done as part of their job and neither the writer nor the museum should accept payment from the magazine. Curators and other professional staff who write a story on their own time should be allowed to accept payment when a magazine offers it.

The following types of magazines and their interests are appropriate targets for most museums:

- general history and art—stories on the museum generally and its collections, new accessions, exhibits, antique forums, and other special events;
- specialized collection—definitive features on single artifacts or classes of artifacts, photo features on collections that are in the periodical's interest area;
- shelter and womens' interest—ideas that decorators could adapt from museum room settings, special Christmas decorating ideas, uses for museum-licensed reproductions, instructional stories on how to perform simple crafts;
- travel—consumer features on seasonal activities at the museum and on other attractions in the museum's area;
- Sunday newspaper magazines—weekend get-away trips involving

a visit to the museum, regional historical facts revealed by the museum's exhibits and programs.

One can never be certain that a story will be used until it appears in the magazine. Even if a magazine completes the copy and photography, the article may still be canceled in favor of another that the editor thinks will be of greater interest to readers.

Photography

An up-to-date file of interesting pictures is one of the public relations person's most important resources in filling media requests. Most newspapers and magazines have a greater need for good photographs than for copy. If one can provide pictures on demand, the museum can be featured time and again in stories involving a wide range of subjects. Because artifacts must be visualized to be understood and appreciated, photos are especially important in stories about the museum.

Not only is there great media need for good pictures, but photographs are the most looked-at element on any magazine or newspaper page. Captions are often the most frequently read copy. Because photos will be seen by nearly all readers, it is important that they picture the museum in ways that make it immediately identifiable and show it busy with satisfied visitors rather than as an empty hall.

Wire Service Criteria

An effective way to secure media use of museum photos is to call shooting possibilities to the attention of wire services (on an exclusive basis) whenever possible. To do so you will need to be constantly on the lookout for photo opportunities in all events in the course of a day at the museum. The wire services demand photos that tell an interesting story. Although they usually take their own pictures, they will occasionally use those provided by the museum on an exclusive basis. Knowing what the wires require will provide insight into newspaper photo needs in general.

The subject should be interesting or uncommon or timely. For example, the registrar might unexpectedly find a 200-year-old love letter in a collection desk. Or maybe the collections contain an artifact like a cooling fan, which is propelled by a kerosene burner that actually heats rather than cools a room. A photo of it with an appropriate model is

Plate 1. Despite recent headlines, the drive to create lighter, more fuel-efficient cars is not new. This experimental 1925 Pierce Arrow at Michigan's Greenfield Village is about 85 percent aluminum, including the engine, body, wheels, front axle housing, braking, and steering systems. Although the car was never put into production because of the scarcity of aluminum at that time, the metal is now plentiful enough for use in disposable beverage containers, as guide Dennis Carnevalle points out. Credit: Mark Gordon, Chacma, Inc.

almost certain to appeal to a wire service for use during the hottest days of August. The photo of an aluminum automobile was used by the Associated Press when lightweight automotive components and returnable aluminum cans were in the news. Sometimes successful wire photos simply have a human appeal, like the one of the father responding to his daughter's curiosity about the contents of a huge ceramic pot. This photo was used nationally by UPI.

The wire service photo should be a well lighted 8″ x 10″ glossy with crisp blacks, a full range of mid-tones, and bright clear whites. There should be no dust specks, scratches, or other imperfections. Excessive

Plate 2. Getting inside of things at Dearborn, Michigan. With a little help from her father, Tracy Hill of Warren, Michigan, checks out the "inside" story on one of the largest ceramic pots ever manufactured in this country. Now on display at Greenfield Village in Dearborn, the pot was acquired from the General Ceramics Company of New York in 1920 by the museum's founder, Henry Ford. The giant jug's function, if it ever had one, is not recorded. In addition to the jumbo crocks, the unique historic complex includes a fourteen-acre museum and eighty-five buildings spanning 300 years of American history. Credit: Mark Gordon, Chacma, Inc.

grain should be avoided. Wire photos often are shot in 35mm format using available light. They should generally include no more than two or three people, doing something museum visitors are allowed to do. Children are appealing subjects. Composition is important. The subject must fill the frame, as it does in the picture of the Greenfield Village Bakery. The services will not use compositions that have a band of grass across the base of the photo, then a band of subject under an

Plate 3. The subject fills the frame in this bakery photo. Credit: Mark Gordon, Chacma, Inc.

empty sky. The bakery and ice cream parlor photos illustrate that models can direct the viewer's attention to the principal subject. Closeup and action photos are well received by the wire services; see the picture of Benjamin Franklin showing a Susan B. Anthony dollar to a young

Plate 4. Models can direct the viewer's attention to the principal subject, as illustrated by this photo. Credit: Mark Gordon, Chacma, Inc.

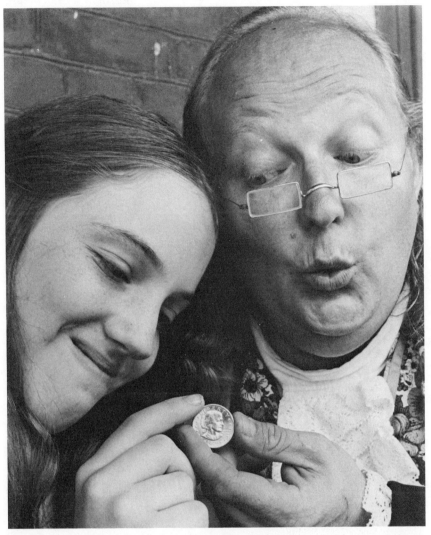

Plate 5. "An Anthony Saved . . ." Benjamin Franklin, who was born 278 years ago this January 17, would probably be pleased to know that his memory is being kept alive by look-alike Ralph Archbold at historic Greenfield Village in Dearborn, Michigan. Archbold recently received a birthday gift of a new Susan B. Anthony dollar from Lori Kentschaft of Upper Montclair, New Jersey. Credit: Mark Gordon, Carl Byoir Associates.

Plate 6. Action pictures are attention getting and in demand by the wire services. Credit: Mark Gordon, Carl Byoir Associates.

admirer or that of the two Greenfield Village visitors in front of the Wright Cycle Shop. Whenever possible, pictures for the wire services should be composed so that they can be cropped either horizontally or vertically, as illustrated by the photo of the pewterer.

Plate 7. An example of a photo that can be cropped vertically or horizontally. Credit: Mark Gordon, Carl Byoir Associates.

One should not publish pictures of artifacts that are not on public view in the museum. In addition, if the subject of the photo is not owned by the museum or if it is a reproduction, the caption should so indicate.

Newspaper Criteria

Newspapers exercise the same standards as wire services but will accept photos that have local, if not universal, appeal. For example, if a museum in Ohio is sponsoring a muzzle loaders festival that will attract participants from Houlton, Maine, the Houlton newspaper will not be interested in a general photo of last year's festival but might publish one that shows a Houlton resident who will be participating again this year.

Duplicate prints of photos can be sent to several newspapers, but

Date _____ 19 ___

I hereby consent to and grant XYZ Museum permission to use for publication, advertising, and exhibition, either using or not using my name, the photographs of me
taken at _____ .

_____   _____
(witness)   (signature)

Figure 6.3. A photo release form

avoid providing the same photo to two that share the same circulation
area or to morning and evening editions of the same newspaper. If a
photo is being released on an exclusive basis, it must go only to one
newspaper in a given circulation area. The practice of slightly shifting
the camera angle or repositioning subject elements so as to provide two
"exclusive" pictures of the same subject is not acceptable from the
standpoint of newspapers or wire services.

Whenever a photo is being taken by the museum for its own use, a
photo release form must be signed by everyone who is recognizable in
the picture. A person in the photo could be on a weekend holiday with
a neighbor's spouse! Although the release form shown in figure 6.3
would be adequate for most museum's needs, you should check with
the museum's legal counsel to learn of any special requirements.

Stock Photos

Many of the magazines that are most interested in developing
museum-related stories have a small circulation and will need photos
provided by the museum. Free-lance writers who produce articles for
these magazines are not paid enough to contract for photography and
will also need to have photos provided. Unlike story copy, which a
magazine can edit to meet its standards and style requirements, photos
cannot be altered except by cropping and must meet a publication's
criteria. It is not unusual for magazines to kill a feature story because
adequate photos are not available from the museum. To meet the
media's needs, public relations office files should contain three types of
photos—general, studio, and human interest. Each type requires different photographic skills.

General pictures showing such subjects as panoramic views are used by newspapers and magazines when unspecific illustrations are required. Such shots are a basic ingredient of any museum press kit. These are often "pretty pictures" involving handsome building interiors or sunsets and colorful foliage. To produce them the photographer needs an understanding of composition and natural lighting. They should portray scenes that are consistent with the image that the museum wishes to project. For example, an open air museum that emphasizes industrial history should not be portrayed as a farm. Although people in the photo are useful to establish scale and to add human interest, they are not usually the focal point in such pictures. The picture of Greenfield Village's covered bridge is an example of a general photo that has been used extensively by the media and has been found to generate a large response when used in coupon advertising.

Plate 8. This general purpose photo has a scenic quality that people find appealing. Credit: Mark Gordon, Chacma, Inc.

Horizontal and vertical views of each of the museum's annual special events, its major properties, its most interesting exterior views in each season of the year, and its most attractive exhibit galleries should be adequate to fill most requests for general photos. They should be 8" x 10" black-and-white glossy prints and 35mm color slides. The most attractive views could also be photographed in 2" x 2" or 4" x 5" color transparencies for use by magazines on their covers and could be enlarged for publicity use on display boards. It must be possible to crop them to a vertical format, and they should have open space in the upper right section where a magazine can print its name. Because magazines will usually demand original rather than duplicate slides that may or may not be returned, take the same photo many times, thereby creating several identical originals for the file.

To illustrate stories about museum collection artifacts, magazines and newspapers will request studio photos, usually in black and white but occasionally in color. Slides will also be used by curators in their lectures. Studio photos should be sharply focused against a neutral background to bring out details. It is best to create a studio setting within the museum building so that artifacts vulnerable to damage will not have to be crated for moving. When it is important for the viewer to know the size of an object, you may wish to include a posed model or a bar scale in the picture.

Studio photos in black and white and 35mm color slides that show front and three-quarter left and right views of the most important, best-known, and most interesting objects in the museum's collections should be kept on file. The studio setting can also be used to take photographs of someone illustrating a process. Published in a series, such photos, for example, showing how to make a clothespin doll, are well received by small newspapers and by tabloid collectors' periodicals as space fillers. To conserve expense when offering such a series, one may print as many as four views on one 8" x 10" sheet.

Human interest pictures that show people actively enjoying the museum are difficult to produce but are very useful. In addition to emphasizing people, good human interest photos capture the subjects acting spontaneously and appearing unselfconscious. Although some of the photos of people reproduced here have this candid quality, it was achieved by posing the subjects in natural situations. Such posed candid photos can be effective only if the photographer is skilled at directing the subjects.

Excellent candid human interest pictures can be produced using an

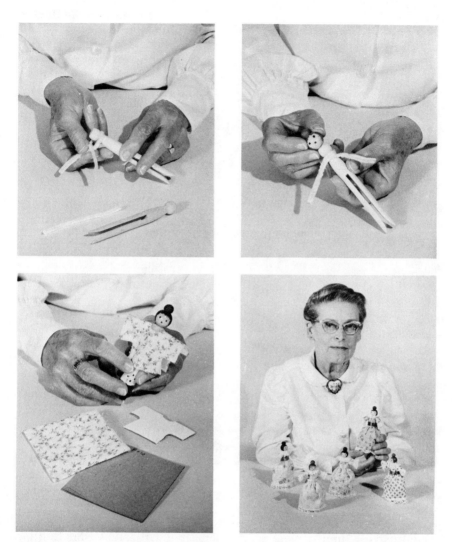

Plate 9. Greenfield Village craftsperson Norma Samuels shows how to make clothespin dolls. First she wraps pipe cleaner arms around the head of the clothespin (top left). Next (top right) she attaches a special wooden head (that of the clothespin may also be used). She clothes the dolls (bottom left) using the simple patterns shown and displays several examples of her handiwork (bottom right). Credit: Rudolph Ruzicska.

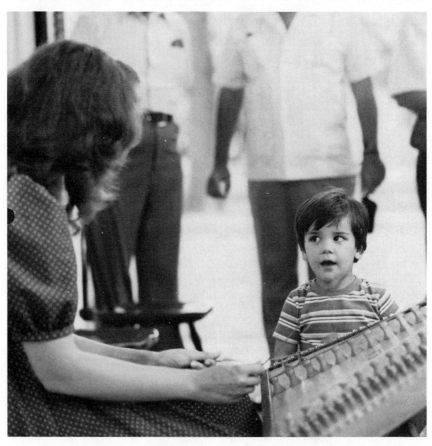

Plate 10. A museum's impact on its visitors can best be captured through candid photography. Credit: Tim Hunter.

unobtrusive 35mm camera with a lens that will allow shooting far enough away from subjects so that they will not know they are being photographed, as illustrated in the picture of the boy who is captivated by the dulcimer player. Immediately after shooting, seek permission from all subjects to use photos in which they appear. The photographer must have a quick eye and must be skilled at working with available light. Great care must be exercised in enlarging 35mm negatives to 8″ × 10″ prints to avoid scratches and dust spots. Newspapers, wire services, magazines, and designers of the museum's publications all prefer candid photos with human interest; they are believable, interesting, and lively.

You will occasionally want to arrange for publication of special events pictures prior to the event so that they help generate attendance. There are two ways of securing pictures for this purpose: stage a portion of the activity early, or photograph this year for release in advance of the event next year. Using advance photos will be especially successful in the hometown newspapers of those appearing in the photos. You should always obtain the permission of the people in the photos and should not reveal their street addresses.

Captions

All media require captions. Each person in the photo should be identified from left to right. The caption should be short and should focus on the most interesting and appealing aspects of the photo while emphasizing the name of the museum enough so that it will not be edited out. Caption letterhead paper should be printed following the guidelines suggested for release paper, but the word "Caption" should replace "News."

One of the most successful producers of wire feature photos explained that he plans the caption before he takes the picture. Captions appearing in this section, with the exception of the series photo and those that explain a photographic concept, are examples of those published by the wire services. Each caption should be attached to prints with a small amount of rubber cement, as illustrated in figure 6.4.

Caring For and Mailing Photos

It is best to store prints in a steel file, making certain that they will not be bent, creased, or torn. File drawers equipped with folders suspended from rods offer the most protection. Print life will be prolonged if photos are not constantly exposed to light, heat, or extreme humidity.

Because magazine editors may ask when and where a photo has been published before, it is helpful to keep a record. One should also record with each print any restrictions on its use that have been imposed by the photographer or by the people in the picture. To help prevent unauthorized use of the photo in advertisements and to discourage one publication from selling a print to another, consider stamping on the back "Not to be sold or used in advertisements without

DEARBORN, Mich. -- Center foreground in this overall view of the
automobile collection in Henry Ford Museum is a 1909 Ford Model T which
is painted in its original red color. It was on later models that only
black was available.

Figure 6.4. Photo with caption attached

written permission from XYZ Museum.'' The back of every print
should also show the name of the museum as it should appear in the
credit line. It is recommended that the location of the museum be part
of the credit line. Write lightly on the back of prints with a soft lead
pencil. Felt markers are particularly likely to show through on the face
of the print. Use a grease pencil for crop marks and keep them within
the border of the print.

File prints with their captions. File numbered negatives in glassine
sleeves. Write the negative number on the back of each print so that

editors can identify the picture when calling for additional information. Old photo prints or tintypes that are part of the museum's collections should never be provided to the media. Instead, supply new prints made from a copy negative.

Prints should always be mailed between two pieces of stiff cardboard cut to fit tightly into the envelope, which should be imprinted "Photos—Do Not Bend." In addition to helping protect the prints, this notation will encourage the busy editor to open the envelope. The image side should face the back of the envelope so that postal machines will not damage it. Never use staples or paper clips on photos. If the photo must be returned, enclose a stamped self-addressed envelope. Usually it is best to let the photo stay in the media's files so they can use it again. Do not be surprised if the print comes back in poor condition, with crop marks and bent corners.

Slides should be mailed in the plastic pockets of 8½" x 11" protectors designed for three-ring binders and available at photo supply shops. Rather than using separate caption sheets, number each slide and key it to captions typed on a single sheet.

Stretching the Photo Budget

Getting the right picture requires a photographer who is equipped with two cameras to produce color and black-and-white photos. Very few professional photographers are equally skilled at taking general, studio, and candid human interest photos. Volunteer photo hobbyists are usually most skilled at taking general photos. You might contact hobbyists through photo clubs. Or the museum might consider organizing a photo contest, providing prizes, and keeping the prints. College and university adult education photography classes and workshops sponsored by camera and film companies and photo retailers are other sources of volunteer talent. If possible, the museum should secure unrestricted rights to the use of contributed pictures.

It is difficult to locate volunteers who can produce convincing human interest candid photos that will be enticing to newspapers and wire services, but with a little searching it may be possible to find a nearby source. Begin by checking the nearest wire service bureaus to determine if there are any staff photographers who moonlight. They might suggest area free-lancers they have used successfully. Notes on photographers credited with good candid photos in local publications might also help you find a capable free-lancer. Local photo studios can sometimes produce human interest candids, but their photographers are usually most skilled with studio setups.

When wire service, newspaper, or magazine staff photographers shoot at the museum, ask if their employer would permit them to make prints available. Often prints can be obtained free if one does not intend to provide them to the newspaper's or wire service's competitors.

Media Lists and Their Selection

By sending too many releases to too many media outlets, museum public relations people make a serious error in judgment and waste much of their publicity material. Overmailing is costly, and editors may learn to discard mail received from the museum unopened if they have been sent useless material in the past. An economical and effective publicity program operates from lists that include only those media that are likely to use the material. Such lists are kept current and are annotated with the information needed to make sound decisions regarding media distribution.

To generate attendance and to maintain general public awareness, most museums will need four media lists.

- List A (local area): newspapers, magazines, and radio and television stations in the museum's hometown area. A metropolitan area or a one-hour drive-time radius could be considered local, depending upon the geographic dispersion of the museum's audience.
- List B (local region): newspapers, magazines, and radio and television stations within one to two hours' distance from the museum by car. Excluded are media on List A.
- List C (general interest): wire service bureaus, statewide newspapers and those in the nearest regions of bordering states, and magazines published in these areas. The greater the distance from the museum, the more difficult it is for out-of-town broadcast media to localize material, so they are not usually listed if they lie beyond a one-hour drive-time radius.
- List D (special interest): newspaper editors and columnists, syndicated columnists, magazine editors, and free-lance writers throughout the nation whose interests relate to the museum's collections and objectives. Likely to be on this list are newspaper travel, antique, or art editors and columnists as well as antique and art magazine editors.

Media Personnel

Although titles vary, those listed below are common.

Newspapers
- Publishers are the owners or the owner's representatives who set and supervise policies.
- Managing editors determine and implement such overall news coverage policies as how much of a reporter's time and how much column space should be devoted to a subject.
- News editors supervise reporters, editors, and writers, determining the emphasis that a particular story should receive and when it should be used.
- City editors serve as filters for most releases received from public relations people and supervise local reporters.
- Editorial page editors express the opinions of the newspaper through editorial columns. They also select editorial page materials and therefore can support or attack an institution or a point of view. Sometimes they edit the "op ed" sections, where opinions not written by the newspaper's staff are published.
- Sunday editors coordinate and supervise the production of this large edition.
- Special editors concentrate on one or two subjects, such as travel, entertainment, food, business, education, or society.
- Columnists are the "personalities" of the newspaper. They usually have a following among their readers, who believe what these writers say. Columns are bylined and thematic and use ideas from public relations people.
- Wire editors select from the offerings of the wire services to which their newspaper subscribes those stories that are to be considered for publication. The Associated Press and United Press International are the two principal wire services. Both serve newspapers and broadcast media. Each employs "stringers," who report from outlying suburbs and rural areas and are paid for each story they submit. The wire services operate through regional and city bureaus from headquarters in New York (see the sources section of this book) and have "A" wires, which carry the bulk of the news, and "B" wires, which carry overload and regional news and features. In some cities public relations staff may transmit a publicity story over the independent PR Newswire. For access the museum pays the service an annual membership fee and a fee for each transmis-

sion. Check with your local newspaper wire editor for information on the closest PR Newswire office.

- Reporters gather facts either working on their own or on assignment for an editor. Their copy is usually channeled to their editor through a rewrite person. A reporter may or may not have certain subject specialties.

Broadcast media

- Station managers represent owners, set policies, and provide overall supervision.
- Program managers supervise the selection and scheduling of material to be aired, which may or may not include news. If there is no public service director, the program manager may determine the extent to which the station will use public service announcements (PSAs).
- News directors supervise camera crews, reporters, and all others associated with producing news shows. Ideas for stories that do not have to be covered that day are usually called in or mailed to the news director. Because many small radio stations do not have a news department, news is often prepared by commentators or other available personnel.
- Assignment editors, who usually report to news directors, dispatch reporters to cover stories. Consequently they determine in large part what will be covered locally by that day's news programs and are a key contact for the public relations person who wants a crew to visit the museum to cover a story that day.
- Public service directors determine what public service material the station will produce and which of the public service announcements received from public relations people will be used.
- Producers originate and implement show ideas by being in charge of content, talent, and technical production. They also write material, appear on camera, and are important contacts for placing guests on shows.
- Show hosts select guests and material directly or through their producer and are on the air in any of several types of programs, such as talk shows.
- Announcers, together with show hosts, are on-air or on-camera personalities. They may or may not write their own material. Contact with them is usually made through their producers.
- Reporters are often on general assignment and are not briefed on the stories they are covering. They will be too busy to spend time

on a story unless it is scheduled for that day's news. Some reporters specialize in certain subjects, such as consumer affairs, or lifestyles, and have a hand in choosing their own material. They usually report to the news director. One may contact specialized reporters directly with appropriate story ideas.

Annotating Media Lists

The local area and one-hour drive-time lists are especially important because they will be used on almost every occasion when there is a message to be transmitted. Persons on this list should be addressed by name. Because newspaper editors prefer that only one person at the newspaper receive a story, remember to list on the release all recipients if it was sent to more than one. Broadcast media do not usually mind having more than one person at a station receive a story.

Annotate local and one-hour drive-time lists with the following basic information, which should be kept current.

- Local daily newspapers: names of city, Sunday, and or weekend editors; feature, entertainment, antiques, calendar, art, and education editors; columnists; reporters who are assigned to the museum (if any); preferred general news-feature contact persons; subjects of major interest for each editorial department, deadlines for copy and black-and-white or color photos for each department, apparent familiarity with the museum.
- Out-of-town daily newspapers: geographical coverage area and names of regional editors covering the city in which the museum is located; bureau chiefs (if any) located in the museum's home town; reporters assigned to the area; the Sunday and/or weekend editor; feature, art, entertainment, or calendar editors; columnists; preferred general news-feature contact persons; copy and photo deadlines; apparent familiarity with museum.
- Local and out-of-town weekly newspapers: names of managing, feature, entertainment, or calendar editors; the community editor, if the paper is part of a chain; the preferred contact person; localities covered by the newspaper; photo and copy deadlines; apparent familiarity with the museum.
- Magazines: names of editor or local bureau chief if the magazine is national; subject interests (entertainment, travel, and so forth); advance time required for story queries, calendar announcements;

photo requirements; policy on using material from nonstaff writers; exclusive requirements; apparent familiarity with the museum.

- Radio stations: name of the station manager and of news and public service directors, talk show producers; principal on-air personalities; reporters (if any) assigned to museum; preferred news-feature contact person; format preferences (telephone interviews or releases, etc.); station format (all talk, middle of the road, all classical, etc.); requirements for public service material.
- Television stations: names of news director, assignment editor, on-camera reporters, public service director, talk show producers; preferred news-feature contact persons; format preferences (telephoned advisories or mailed releases, slides with script or film clips, etc.); deadlines; requirements for public service material.

List Maintenance

Update Lists A and B at every opportunity, keeping them current with the continuous changes in media staff positions. New staff at the local media will have to be familiarized with the museum. Long-term media employees who move into positions where they will start to cover museum stories will also need to learn about the museum. Because of their numbers and distance it is difficult to keep as well acquainted with List C, general interest media. Usually it is necessary to address mail to people on this list by title only, sending general news releases to news editors and other materials to the most appropriate departments. An updated media directory should be purchased each year. See the sources at the end of this book for recommendations.

The public relations office or the curatorial departments should subscribe to most magazines on special interest List D, thus making it simple to keep names current and to keep abreast of format changes. Names of travel editors and travel free-lance writers (List D) can be obtained from the Society of American Travel Writers or Midwest Travel Writers directories (see the section on sources). Columnists are usually identified by name in column mastheads.

Selecting the Most Appropriate Media

Newspapers are most appropriate when the message:

- is local, involving a subject of special interest to readers in the publication's circulation area;

- has news value—is interesting and useful to readers and answers their questions;
- fits the interests of a particular writer at a newspaper;
- establishes a local connection with a national story.

Wire services are most appropriate when:

- the story or photo has broad state, regional, or national appeal even for readers who are located too far away from the museum to visit;
- is newsworthy because it is already in the news;
- a photo has a striking, universal appeal.

Magazines are most appropriate when the message:

- relates to specific interests of a particular audience;
- lends itself to feature treatment by involving information and photo possibilities that can best be explored in depth and can be developed as much as a year in advance of publication date.

Radio is most appropriate when:

- there is a need for immediacy in transmitting the message (when a special event must be canceled, for example);
- the visual element is not necessary to convey the message;
- the story can be told adequately in thirty to sixty seconds;
- museum personnel can be used to convey a message in a spoken format;
- the story has a local appeal and the station involved covers local news (some only use network feeds for news shows or do not broadcast news at all);
- one wishes to reach people outside their homes, for example, when they drive to and from work;
- the story has a dramatic appeal that can be developed by the listener's imagination. A radio feature can transport listeners back into history without the stage sets and special art required by television;
- the treatment of a subject in a studio interview can be enhanced with music and sound effects.

Television is most appropriate when:

- the message is entertaining and has a strong visual appeal—people engaged in active, interesting pursuits;
- the story has local appeal and involves people—rather than discuss the exhibit with a curator, a television news producer might prefer to interview a group of schoolchildren for their reactions;

- the activity can be covered as it takes place;
- the story requires physically demonstrating how something is done;
- the treatment of a subject in a studio interview can be enhanced by showing films and visual props such as artifacts.

The following media deadlines are only guidelines. Deadlines vary with each newspaper, station, and magazine.

MEDIA DEADLINES

Newspapers

A.M. dailies	General news	10:00 A.M. to noon of the preceding day to make all editions
	Features	Several weeks before desired publication date
P.M. dailies	General news	No later than mid-afternoon of the preceding day
	Features	Same as A.M. features
Sunday	General news	Preceding Thursday noon if intended for regional editions, preceding Friday noon for local editions
	Features	Same as A.M. features
Weeklies	General news	One week prior to publication date
	Features	Same as A.M. dailies features
Wire Services	All material	Anytime, but weekday business hours are preferable

Magazines

Weekly	Features	If color photos involved, three months in advance, otherwise two months in advance
	Calendars	Two weeks in advance
Monthly or quarterly	Features	If for annual event, one year in advance, otherwise six to eight months ahead
	Calendars	Six months in advance

Radio

	General news	Mailed material should arrive one day in advance, telephoned material one hour in advance of newscast. Breaking news should be called in when it is happening.
	Public service scripts and tapes	Two weeks in advance of intended use
	Talk show queries	Two to four weeks in advance of intended date

Television

	General news	Coverage suggestions are best called in the morning of the day preceding the event. Later news should be called in three hours prior to

	air time. Breaking news should be called in while it is happening
News clips	Should arrive two days before an event and not over a weekend
Talk show queries	Six weeks in advance
Public service spots	If about a specific event, at least two weeks before desired air date, if generic filler, whenever it is most timely

(Note: Use a PR newswire or telephone to reach newspapers and broadcast media quickly, twenty-four hours a day, when there is an urgent breaking story such as a fire.)

WHEN A STORY IS MOST LIKELY TO BE USED

Daily newspapers

	Light features	Sundays or the day after a holiday
	General news	Mondays, weekends, Wednesdays, or Fridays
	Calendars	Thursdays or Fridays

Weekly newspapers

	All material	Most publish on Thursdays

Radio

	Light features	Weekends, holidays
	General news	Weekends, holidays
	Calendars	Usually aired Fridays and weekends

Television

	Light features	Weekends, holidays
	General news	Any day, but stations have the greatest need for material on weekends, holidays, the day after holidays
	News clips	Day before or day of event
	Calendar announcements	Usually aired on Fridays

Wire services

	News	Any day
	Features	Any day

(Note: Use will vary with individual media outlets.)

7

Meeting the Media

Most museums experience an occasional media story that is inaccurate and unfair. The story can develop as a result of many factors:

- the reporter did not understand the story. Perhaps the museum did not brief the reporter or perhaps the museum and the reporter did not share any common experience;
- the story was covered by the wrong reporter; for example, an investigative reporter was sent out to cover a feature story;
- a personality conflict developed between the museum representative and the reporter, or some action during the visit, such as a comment by a surly museum employee, affected the reporter's frame of mind;
- the timing of the story was wrong; the museum fell victim to controversial issues over which it had no control such as criminal behavior by an artist whose works were on exhibit;
- the museum representative tried to control who the reporter talked with diverting the reporter's attention from the story and focusing it on the possibility of an attempted cover up.

This chapter will discuss policies, methods, and materials that can help reduce confusion and unfair media treatment and will explore ways to increase the museum's visibility through public service material.

Media Conferences

Media conferences for anything other than visits from major newsmakers or in response to crises usually are an unnecessary imposition on reporters' time and should be avoided. Possible exceptions might include the opening of a new wing or the announcement of a major new accession. If you stage a media conference, the media should be notified a day in advance whenever possible. A room with an adequate number of electrical outlets and sufficient space to accommodate the expected number of reporters should be arranged. The conference should start at the announced time, with brief remarks followed by a time for questions. Adequate time should be allowed at the end for the conference principal to fill reporters' requests for interviews. Media conferences favor the broadcast media, which can cover them live or within a few minutes, thus giving them a considerable advantage over newspapers.

Media Kits

A media kit is simply a compilation of materials that will assist print and broadcast media in becoming acquainted with a museum or in covering an activity. Usually these materials are gathered in a folder that has pockets to hold unfolded press releases and 8″ x 10″ black-and-white glossy photos. A folder with a simple cover design imprinted with the museum logo and an attractive photo of the property can be used for years whenever a media kit is needed.

Media kits usually contain the following information:

- the writers' guide or a general fact sheet;
- the print media news release on the activity;
- a fact sheet on the specific activity briefly describing the who, what, where, why, when, and how, with recommendations for interview subjects and filming opportunities;
- appropriate black-and-white photographs with captions and a note on the availability of slides or motion footage for television and tapes for radio;
- a general background story on the museum, including its history and its collection and program strengths and offerings;
- appropriate museum publications such as a promotional folder and an annual calendar.

Depending on the situation, several other materials might be included in a media kit: vitas and photographs of lecturers, artists, or museum employees who are central to the activity; a list of participants and their hometowns; instructions with photos depicting craft activities, such as how to make simple tree ornaments for a Christmas exhibit opening. If materials are not redundant and will help the media cover the story and if they are consistent with the museum's message base, include them in the media kit.

The Media Reception

Normally, public relations staff members host media representatives simply by inviting them to the museum individually to cover stories. Occasionally, if budget permits or if funding is available from such sources as members of a trustee public relations committee, you may wish to hold a media reception. There are two types of receptions: luncheons, which reporters and other working press attend in the course of their business day, and evening cocktail parties with hors d'oeuvres, which are often social and are attended by invited representatives of media management and their spouses or guests.

The luncheon reception is for working reporters who are collecting material for a story. It can be built around such subjects as an exhibit preview, a new special event, or the launching of the summer season. Invitations should require an RSVP. Names and affiliations should be printed on tags in advance for distribution at a registration table as guests arrive. Reserved parking should be arranged, and museum staff members who are to be present should be briefed with information about individual guests, such as the names of reporters who should be commended for recently published museum stories. Depending on the community, the media may be accustomed to having a full-service bar at such occasions; good food, however, is always appropriate. Remarks should be limited to an explanation of the activity involved. The museum staff person who knows the most about the activity should be available to talk with reporters individually and to answer their questions.

Backgrounders and a supply of four to six different 8" x 10" black-and-white photos with captions should be distributed. The backgrounders should describe a story's most important facts and should answer the questions that are most likely to be asked by reporters. They are also useful as enclosures with newspaper and broadcast releases, with magazine query letters, and with followups to telephone tips and are helpful references for museum staff members and volunteers who are participating in media interviews or in a speakers' bureau. They should be tightly written, with material arranged in descending order of importance, and should be confined to one page if possible. See the appendix for a sample.

Evening receptions, usually held from 6:00 to 9:00 P.M., are social occasions involving publishers, editors, bureau chiefs, station managers, columnists, and other media executive and management personnel. Reporters and other working media may also be invited. Evening receptions often have a full-service bar, a variety of hot hors d'oeuvres, and a chamber group, classical piano, or other appropriate background music. In most cases no formal remarks are made. Press materials are not distributed, but backgrounders should be available for people who request them. Although one cannot expect stories to result immediately, acquainting media management with the museum's staff and programs is always worthwhile.

The Print Media

Newspaper Interviews

Interviews may be conducted in person, or over the telephone. The public relations person should advise people who are to be interviewed of what to expect and how to prepare.

The person being interviewed must be thoroughly briefed on the museum in general. Even when the interview is on a specific topic, the interviewer is apt to ask questions about admission prices, the attendance to date, and activities of special interest. The writer's guide, fact sheet, and backgrounders are helpful.

Be sure that the person being interviewed understands the questions and answers them in a straightforward manner. Answers should be complete but concise. Also be sure the interviewer has understood the answer. If you are being interviewed, do not waste time and redirect the conversation by introducing unrelated information. By practicing in advance with a tape recorder, you can evaluate the clarity of your answers. Respond truthfully to every question that is asked, and anticipate sensitive ones. If you are uncertain of the correct answer, explain that you will have to contact the reporter later. Do not speculate or become defensive or argumentative. If you are under fire, calmly answer with a statement of the facts. If a reporter tries to draw false conclusions, listen carefully, question any of the interviewer's assumptions, restate the question, making it pertinent, and answer it. Avoid off-the-record remarks and comments about other institutions.

Media Admission Policies

Museu s should waive any admission fee for all print and broadcast media personnel who contribute directly to the production of stories and to their immediate families, whether they are at the museum on assignment or for pleasure. Normally this policy does not extend to press operators, secretaries, and other support personnel employed by the media.

Ticket sellers should be instructed to allow free passage to all persons who can produce a credential confirming appropriate employment in the media. When free-lance writers, who will not have such credentials, or media personnel without this identification seek free admission as media representatives, it is usually best to trust their claims.

Some media representatives and independent writers may not accept free admission at museums because they are prohibited from doing so by their employers or by professional or personal ethics. Special annual admission passes may be issued to all the media representatives on your lists but this procedure is not recommended because of the difficulty in making sure that they are received by all who are qualified.

Hosting the Media

Most often you will simply call a reporter or editor with an invitation to come to the museum for lunch, perhaps to view a new accession or special exhibit or to discuss a forthcoming event. Such invitations can be especially important when a new media person moves to the area. Also make it a practice occasionally to write or telephone media personnel within an hour's drive-time radius, suggesting that they tour the museum next time they are in the area. The public relations person should be contacted to greet media and to offer assistance when reporters arrive unexpectedly and are on assignment. In the public relations person's absence, the reporter should be asked to register his or her name and affiliation at the ticket desk. This information should be forwarded to the public relations office for any appropriate followup or assistance.

Media representatives should receive an information sheet explaining admission prices, hours, and special attractions. Though customary at many museums, it is always a wise policy to prevent media representatives from going beyond the visitor barriers unless accompanied by a museum representative—usually the curator responsible for the collection involved. For everyone's protection, most museums also have a policy stating that collection objects may not be touched or handled in any way by anyone other than the curator. Such a policy should be explained to reporters to prevent embarrassment and to facilitate their work. Although not always necessary, many museums prefer that reporters on assignment be accompanied by a museum public relations person. At no time should reporters be prevented from photographing anything that is on public exhibit unless conservation considerations prohibit it. Likewise, they should not be prohibited from talking with anyone on the museum staff or discouraged by museum employees from doing their jobs unless they are endangering the collections or upsetting visitors.

Because sessions involving media representatives who need to go inside the normal visitor barriers to move objects for photographs or for other purposes can be lengthy, it is important to let curators know well in advance when they will be needed. Demands upon curators' time should be kept as minimal as possible. Media visitors arriving without advance arrangements cannot expect the kind of access to the collections that requires a curator.

Visiting the Media

Practiced judiciously, visits to the media can be an excellent way to communicate story ideas to writers. Overused, they can be counterproductive.

It is cost effective for the executive director and other management personnel traveling on museum business to make visits to introduce the museum to editors and writers. Advance appointments should be arranged by the museum public relations person. Make the visit cordial but brief, and do not be critical of other institutions or other media. Do not expect a story to result. Because most media visits are for the purpose of getting acquainted, it is appropriate to leave a general media kit. The visit also provides a good opportunity to present exclusive story ideas to an editor.

If a museum's position on matters such as its use of public funds or its contributions to the local economy need to be explained, arrangements can sometimes be made for the executive director and public relations person to meet with a newspaper or magazine's editorial board at their offices.

Hosting Travel Writers

Even the smallest museums have the opportunity to generate major publicity by hosting out-of-town travel writers. Nearly always state and regional travel bureaus include all the museums in the area when they host travel writer's conferences and familiarization trips. The following recommendations will help assure that visiting writers' needs will be met.

If you wish to bring travel writers to the museum, purchase the membership directories of the Society of American Travel Writers (SATW) and Midwest Travel Writers Association (MTWA) (see the sources section of this book). Next determine who the most productive members are by consulting media acquaintances and by reviewing the credentials that are described in the directories.

Most museums will invite the most productive writers one at a time or in small groups of four to eight people. This approach involves less planning and less cost than hosting a travel writers' conference. Also, by bringing writers in one at a time or in small groups, the visit can be planned around activities certain to be of special interest, thus improving the possibility that stories will result. Another advantage of visits by lone writers or small groups is that several writers will not all be trying to develop a story around the same subject at the same time, a duplication of effort which can limit results.

Although newspaper policies increasingly prohibit reporters from accepting gratuities, whenever you invite a writer to visit, you should offer to pay all expenses including travel. Ask public relations departments of airlines that fly into your area to consider free passage for travel writers who are making familiarization trips from cities that are on their schedule. If a newspaper or magazine staff writer indicates an interest in visiting but is not allowed to accept gratuities and has an insufficient budget, you may arrange for food and lodging discounts to keep expenses minimal. Free-lancers not on a specific assignment almost always will need to have all their expenses met.

When the museum has become experienced at successfully hosting small groups of travel writers, you may consider making a bid to host an MTWA conference or the meeting of a SATW chapter. Attendance will range from 50 to 125, with the SATW group larger in number. In addition to practicing travel writers (active members), associate members who are public relations personnel employed by travel attractions will attend with their spouses. The exception is the Free Lance Council of the Society of American Travel Writers, in which only active writers attend conferences. SATW meets in Canadian, central states, middle Atlantic, Northeast, Southeast, Caribbean, and western chapters. MTWA meets as one association, with members from Ohio, Kentucky, Indiana, Iowa, Wisconsin, Mississippi, Minnesota, Michigan, Illinois, Nebraska, South Dakota, North Dakota, and Kansas.

Several considerations are involved in determining whether to make a bid to host a travel writers' conference. Writers attend these conferences in order to develop the largest possible number of stories in the shortest period of time. Even the largest museum, if it is the sole attraction in the area, is not enough to warrant a bid. Several sites of high quality must form part of the program. Museums usually become involved with travel writer conferences by being included on the itinerary of a conference sponsored by someone else in the area rather than sponsoring it themselves.

Active member participants usually pay only expenses involved in reaching the site and returning home. Almost invariably in the past, hosts have paid all other expenses, with the exception of a small registration fee which may be levied at the discretion of the host. Writers whose employers make it a policy to pay their expenses will need to be billed. As costs continue to rise, however, hosts sometimes discuss with the group's program chairperson the possibility of charging associate members and all spouses for their accommodations, requiring everyone to pay a conference fee, reducing the length of the conference, or in other ways balancing the group's needs with the host's budget. Do not make a bid for the conference until you are satisfied that there are firm commitments from an adequate number of host-sponsors to make the visit interesting and worthwhile for the writers and to keep it within each host's budget. A bid is usually made one or two years in advance of the conference date. Host commitments should therefore not be subject to change.

Conference bids are presented at regular meetings of the associations. If you attend the meeting to make the bid, observe how the gathering is organized, and note which arrangements seem to work well and which do not. Use the opportunity to meet some of the participants. The bid presentation and direct mail publicity that follows should emphasize the number of story possibilities that will be available during the conference.

Assuming that your bid is successful, there will be the costs of printing and mailing advance publicity (samples appear in the appendix) and registration materials; chartering buses; producing name tags and media kits; and contracting for entertainment, lodging, meals, meeting, and banquet rooms and for setups and hospitality rooms.

Planning Guidelines for the Principal Host

1. Check with the chairpersons from the last two conferences for advice on costs and on the number of participants to expect.
2. Ask state and regional travel bureaus to sponsor part of the cost, such as bus transportation. A travel writers' conference benefits the entire state.
3. Involve at least four hosts in addition to the museum. Each should pay all expenses incurred at its site and should share local bus costs in proportion to the time required to transport the group to that site.
4. If possible select a hotel that will provide rooms free or at a substantial discount. If more than one hotel is involved, busing charges can be expensive. Lodging charges that are not complemented will have to be divided among the hosts.
5. Involve the local convention bureau, chamber of commerce, travel bureaus, and businesses in sponsoring breakfasts and other meals. Airlines and national hotel chains will usually sponsor hospitality suites and an occasional meal. Printed material and an inexpensive souvenir could be provided by (or paid for by) local merchants.
6. Consult airlines regarding the possibility of free passage for active members attending the conference, with discount fares for associates and spouses of actives and associates.

By observing the following guidelines you will be better able to deliver what travel writers need.

- Do not begin advance publicity for the membership prior to the conclusion of the organization's preceding conference.
- Inquire in the advance registration material about special interests that writers would like to pursue during the conference, and make arrangements to meet these requests. For example, a food writer might wish to sample a particular restaurant and interview the owner or chef. A writer working on a book on state parks might like to visit one that is nearby.
- Do not overload writers with material. The conference's main host should assemble literature on all the conference sites in a press kit

that participants find in their hotel rooms when they arrive. A participant roster and a conference itinerary should also be in the room.

- An association conference typically involves touring sites on Thursdays and Fridays, a business meeting on Saturday mornings, more tours in the afternoon, and a return home Sunday. Time is limited, and travel writers do not take long to evaluate a site. A fact sheet containing prices, directions, days and hours of operation, seasonal attractions, and special events should be given to each writer upon arrival. A display of available black-and-white prints and color slides with an order form is also helpful.
- Provide comfortable buses with good sound systems, and tip the driver to keep the interior of the bus clean at all times.
- In organizing the conference, remember that the writers' mission is to inform his or her readers about what they can expect to see and do if they visit the site. Including activities that are not available to regular visitors only wastes travel writers' time and leads to confusion. See the appendix for a sample program schedule for a SATW conference.

The Broadcast Media

Spot News Coverage

When an event is taking place at the museum that might be of interest to radio or television news, the public relations person should call the news or assignment desk. If a television news department is interested, it will assign a crew if the day's schedule permits. If it is a slow news day, one's chance of coverage is improved. If the museum is part of a breaking story, the broadcast news departments should be called immediately. The public relations person should arrange for the museum people who are most involved with the story to be available for interviews.

On occasion, reporters may call to ask whether the museum has artifacts that establish a local connection with a national story. The public relations person should be familiar enough with the collections to be able to expedite such requests by determining quickly which holdings might be relevant. Because there may be little advance notice when a station initiates such coverage, you must be prepared to obtain curatorial assistance promptly when crews need to go beyond visitor barriers. You may also need to make arrangements at the museum so that television vehicles are able to park near the activity being covered.

A crew may or may not include an on-camera reporter. If it does, the reporter will voice the piece on the premises. If not, the crew will shoot "B Roll," which will be used as the visual for a story read by an announcer on the newscast. A piece done by a reporter usually has a better chance of being used.

A reporter may instruct the crew to shoot a "standup" and "cutaways." The standup is a short segment introducing or wrapping up the story. Usually the reporter will be facing the camera with the site of the activity in the background. Cutaways are action closeups or scenic segments that are shown while a reporter or interviewer is talking. Be prepared to suggest locations that will meet the station's needs and will picture the museum at its best. Do not be surprised if in the midst of shooting the crew receives a call from the station newsroom and leaves immediately to cover a breaking story.

When there is a major activity of broad interest or a short feature possibility that relates to the day's news, you may generate radio or television network interest by calling an appropriate producer (see appendix for information). If the network is not interested in assigning coverage, you might ask if they would use a local affiliate's coverage. If the producer expresses interest in the story, you should follow up with the same type of query letter that is sent to magazines and then call the producer to establish the network's intentions.

Documentaries and Minidocumentaries

Documentaries are television and radio versions of the newspaper or magazine feature story, usually in a half-hour format. Documentaries not only present the facts but also interpret them. They may express a point of view or may develop a historical perspective on a subject. They may also be instructional. Both television and radio documentaries often emphasize narration and interviews rather than dramatic acting. They are usually produced from written scripts, which the museum should if possible check for accuracy. Minidocumentaries, often presented in a series of three-and-one-half-minute segments, are increasingly being used by radio and television news departments. Radio news departments may spread them throughout the broadcast day; television may air them at 6:00 P.M. and 11:00 P.M. or may run them as a series during a period of a few days.

To assure that the museum will not be overlooked in these important features, which are broadcast to large, prime-time audiences, you should keep stations informed on ways in which the museum's programs and collections relate to subjects of current local interest. Museums with the proper resources may be able to produce their own documentaries. A commercial television station in Cincinnati, Ohio, broadcasts Cincinnati Historical Society programs in its evening prime-time hours and in the mornings for use in schools.[1]

News-Feature Interviews

Whenever a news release has been sent out, keep pertinent information at hand in case a radio station reporter calls to ask for a telephone interview. Most news interviews are edited to thirty seconds, so expect only a fraction of the conversation to be used. With this fact in mind, have one major point to communicate. If the interviewer's question does not address that point, bridge to it as quickly as possible.

Listen very carefully to questions. In many cases it will be obvious that the reporter has not been briefed on the story, and clarification will be necessary. It is helpful to watch or listen to different shows to become familiar with interviewers' styles and program formats. Address your responses directly to the interviewer as if you were having a normal conversation instead of talking to the microphone or camera; this trick will make you feel more relaxed and confident. Avoid fidgeting with papers. Allow a couple minutes to catch your breath if you have just walked to the interview site. If a television interview is conducted on the museum premises, you can increase the visual impact and enhance the museum's visibility by using a collection or outdoor scenic area as a backdrop.

Talk Show Interviews

Become acquainted with talk shows by watching or listening to them before queries are made to place museum guests. Queries are made to the appropriate producer by telephone or by letter. Slides, photographic prints, films, or videotapes of the activity will help the producer evaluate the query. Some hosts inject controversy into interviews whenever possible. Others feature calls from listeners. Some are consumer oriented and would be interested in learning how visitors can most greatly profit from the museum visit. Many shows are taped for later broadcast. Museum staff should always be notified in advance of air dates for broadcasts in which they will appear.

On the day of the interview, plan to arrive at the studio at least fifteen minutes early. If you know who the other guests will be that day, you may be able to guess on what the topics of discussion will be and how you can best relate them to the museum. Do not wear bright white clothing or a loud print pattern for a television interview, and avoid big pieces of jewelry which will reflect the studio lights. If you perspire easily, take a handkerchief. Have a glass of water handy.

Be well prepared on the subject, but answer questions conversationally and not from notes. Do not give long answers or leap from one idea to another, even if you are worried about covering a certain amount of information. Be aware that the fast pace required to hold a radio or television audience's attention requires frequent exchanges between host and guest. Be responsive to the host, use his or her first name, and do not be defensive.

You can enliven a television interview by bringing visuals such as small artifacts related to the topic or horizontal slides. You should not describe in detail what the viewer is already seeing in the slide. Instead, use the slide in a general way to make a subject more understandable and appealing or as a mechanism to introduce a new subject. Rest objects against a surface when they are being shot close up. If the museum has 16mm film on the subject or videotape footage of good quality, suggest that it be shown while you provide a voice-over description. Discuss visuals with the producer of the show in advance of the interview day. It is worthwhile for the museum to provide printed material for the station to mail free of charge to listeners who request it. For example, if the interview is about a gristmill that grinds corn, recipes using cornmeal would make appropriate giveaways. If the museum cannot provide quantities of such material, sometimes the station will print it. This approach gives the museum a second and more lasting exposure to the audience and indicates to the station the size of the show's audience. A large response will encourage the station to make more frequent use of museum guests. Television stations will need advance notice of plans to offer listeners printed material so that they can prepare address slides. If you take a tape of general sound effects and music from the museum to radio interviews, it can sometimes be used to enliven talk show appearances.

Remote Television Coverage

When an important museum event takes place during the news hour, nearby stations may cover it live, transmitting the signal by microwave, which requires only a small antenna. Stations sometimes produce videotape on site, using portable equipment, for delayed broadcast. When several stations wanted to shoot an event taking place in a small building in Greenfield Village, on-site videotape production made it possible for one crew to shoot a tape that was duplicated in a few minutes and was given to all who wanted it. Using satellite technology, television images can be transmitted live across the country. During the 1982 Superbowl, a television station transmitted live voice and picture from the floor of Henry Ford Museum in Dearborn, Michigan, to a news show in San Francisco.

When a television station plans to produce footage from the museum for live or delayed transmission, you should make the following arrangements.

1. Plan to be with the crew at all times.
2. Encourage the producer to make an advance visit to the site.
3. Obtain any required approvals from museum staff.
4. Inform the museum's security department of any need to control crowds around the shooting area.
5. If the crew does not use battery-powered lights, check to determine whether the museum electrician will need to provide an electric cable that has at least two 120-volt circuits. When museum power is being used, a museum electrician should be on call. A wheelchair or hand truck will help the crew make pan shots.
6. Arrange in advance for any curatorial or custodial assistance and for meeting any special requirements such as providing a shooting platform or a "green room" where guests who will be interviewed can wait.
7. Give the crew some printed material on the activity that is being covered before they leave. The station may use the material to introduce or embellish the story so it should emphasize the message that you want conveyed.

Remote Radio Coverage

Radio can undertake remote broadcasting more easily than television. Take advantage of this capability by inviting producers of appropriate talk and entertainment shows to originate them periodically at the museum. On such occasions you will need to:

- arrange for the show's guests to reach the broadcast location without having to pay museum admission fees;
- provide adequate space for folding chairs to accommodate show guests and museum visitors who will want to be in the audience (most hosts prefer to broadcast from busy areas of the museum);
- furnish a special broadcast telephone line as specified by the station;
- Take into account environmental noises that might interfere with broadcasting.

Radio Actualities

The actuality "feed" permits a radio station to achieve the effect of live coverage without traveling to the site and enables the museum to place material on news shows economically.

An actuality is an on-the-scene interview recorded by the museum with audible background sound. It gives the listener the sense of being present at the museum and usually consists of a twenty-second introduction, a thirty-second actuality interview, and a ten-second tag (conclusion). The introduction and tag are voiced by the museum public relations person and are usually revoiced by the radio news announcer, who will broadcast only the interview segment of the tape. Below is an example of a hypothetical actuality taped at a carousel while it was operating.

This is (museum public relations person) from (name of museum) with a ten-second actuality interview for use May 18, 1983.

Museum public relations person's voice:

XYZ Museum's new carousel went into operation today.

Actually, it's a 1914 carousel that was brought to the Museum last year from Montpelier, Vermont, and restored.

Six-year-old Steve Halleran of Plainfield was one of the first riders.

Actuality (the actual voice of the person being interviewed with the sound of the carousel in the background):

I rode the green frog. It's really neat. The carousel man told me next time it stops I can go again.

Museum public relations person:
The beautifully painted carousel will be operating all summer. From XYZ Museum, this is Jane Smith.

You can ask visitors or staff people to participate spontaneously in actuality interviews, but be prepared to record a considerable amount of material to secure thirty seconds of usable tape. It will be easier to edit the tape to the correct length if it is transferred from the cassette to a reel-to-reel recorder.

Actuality tapes can be fed to radio stations over the office telephone. Simply call a station, and if it is interested it will tape the actuality as it plays into the telephone receiver. To improve the sound quality, a voice transmitter can be screwed onto the telephone to replace the mouthpiece. You will still be able to talk over the telephone, but the tape recorder can be plugged into it as well. The best transmission can be achieved by having the telephone company install a line coupled directly to a cassette-type telephone answering device of high quality. The cost of this system makes it impractical, however, unless actualities are being produced continuously.

Actualities do not have to be only on time-specific subjects for distribution to news departments. They can also be produced as short public service features on your permanent exhibits and ongoing programs. Several such features of varying lengths can be produced on a single tape and distributed periodically to station public service departments.

Television News Clips

News clips are produced on 16mm film or videotape. Because they are read by the station newscaster, they are produced silent or with background sounds only. The museum produces and distributes them to television news departments with a printed script. Although they are designed to be used on the news, they frequently stimulate the television news director to assign a crew to cover the event instead.

News clips should provide useful information on specific activities that relate to local audiences. They should be less than a minute in length and should be presented in a straightforward news style.

The script should be typed on 8½" x 11" paper, in all caps, double spaced, on the right half of the page. Video instructions should be indicated on the left, as shown in figure 7.1. The sample shows that background sound has been added in the form of music ("SOF" means

THE EDISON INSTITUTE
Henry Ford Museum
& Greenfield Village

Subject: "Victorian Holiday"
TN 82-12-01
Film: 16MM, COLOR, SOF

Length: :44

TV Newsfilm

Release: 12/25/82 at 6 p.m.
through 12/30/82

Office of Public Relations, P.O. Box 1970, Dearborn, Michigan 48121, (313) 271-1620

VIDEO		AUDIO
LEAD-IN, ON CAMERA		HERE'S A WAY TO EXTEND YOUR CHRISTMAS CELEBRATING...AND TO KEEP THE KIDS ENTERTAINED DURING THE SCHOOL VACATION WEEK.
		PACK UP THE WHOLE FAMILY AND TAKE THEM OUT TO GREENFIELD VILLAGE IN DEARBORN, MICHIGAN.

- -

MUSIC UP

1. LOOKING IN KITCHEN WINDOW	:04	THE FOLKS THERE HAVE A PROGRAM GOING ON NOW CALLED "VICTORIAN HOLIDAY."
2. CANDIES	:06	YOU CAN SEE COOKING DEMONSTRATIONS... INCLUDING SOME GREAT CANDIES AND OTHER TREATS.
3. FLAGS	:04	ALSO, HOW PEOPLE MADE THEIR OWN ORNAMENTS AT HOME,
4. GILDED NUTS	:02	USING MATERIALS THEY HAD AROUND THE HOUSE.

- MORE -

Figure 7.1. Script for a television news clip. Source: The Edison Institute.

5. Tree trimming	:02	It's designed to show how our modern, commercial Christmas
Ornaments & guitarist	:09	season developed during the 19th century.
6. Pie baking	:06	And you can really see the difference between the activities in the earlier buildings,
7. Popcorn stringing	:06	and in the ones built later in the century.
8. Guitarist	:05	The Victorian Holiday program is going on right through New Year's weekend, except for New Year's day, in the historic setting of Greenfield Village.

Music up to end

- 30 -

HENRY FORD MUSEUM AND GREENFIELD VILLAGE ARE PART OF THE
EDISON INSTITUTE, A NONPROFIT EDUCATIONAL INSTITUTION.

121682   JS

"sound on film"), and that each shot lasts from two (:02) to nine (:09) seconds. A 35mm closeup slide can be included to be used as a visual during the announcer's lead-in to the clip. The film clip, manuscript, and slide should be distributed to stations the Monday preceding the weekend of a special event or about five days preceding a mid-week activity.

Public Service Material

Public service time is available on radio and television free of charge, provided it is used for the public welfare.[2] Materials provided to stations to be used in public service time are called public service announcements (PSAs). PSAs may relate to specific activities or may be general (generic) in nature so that they can be used any time. The PSA may be printed on letterhead release paper indicating "Public Service Material," for a station announcer to read, or it may be produced on audiotape, videotape, or film. Occasionally a radio or television station will produce a PSA for a museum and will allow dubs to be made for distribution to other stations.

Radio PSAs. Radio PSAs are issued in three formats: printed script, audiotape, and audio disc (record). They are timed to run approximately ten, twenty, thirty, or sixty seconds. Ten-second public service spots are popular with stations because they fit into breaks for station identification. The scripted radio PSA should be written in a conversational style and should be typed in all capital letters, double spaced on an 8½" x 11" sheet imprinted with a letterhead indicating that it is public service material and listing the sender, the date or dates when it should be used, and the sender's address and telephone number. The length should be indicated in the upper right corner. The number "30" should mark the end of the PSA. Figure 7.2 shows examples of ten-second and thirty-second scripted radio PSAs.

Audiotapes and records are more time consuming and costly to produce than scripted PSAs but can be effective if budget allows. They should be voiced by professionals and recorded so that they meet broadcast standards. Before producing PSA tapes, verify that the stations in your market will use them.

Records can be cost effective if they are produced in quantities larger than fifty, but there are seldom enough radio stations in a given market area to make them cost effective. The amount of recording and production time required prevents them from having immediacy, on

PUBLIC SERVICE ANNOUNCEMENT   LENGTH: :30

SUBJECT: ANTIQUE FIRE APPARATUS   FOR USE: JULY 19 - 25, 1982
           MUSTER
           JULY 24 & 25, 1982

ANNCR: A GREAT EVENT FOR FIRE ENGINE CHASERS THIS WEEKEND AT GREENFIELD

VILLAGE -- THE ANTIQUE FIRE APPARATUS MUSTER.

     THAT'S WHERE YOU CAN SEE ALL KINDS OF FIREFIGHTING EQUIPMENT IN

ACTION, FROM HOSE CARTS AND HAND PUMPERS TO BIG, SHINY, 20TH CENTURY

ENGINES.

     THEY ALL FUNCTION, SHOWING OFF THEIR CAPABILITIES IN CONTESTS AND

DEMONSTRATIONS.

     THAT'S THE ANTIQUE FIRE APPARATUS MUSTER, THIS SATURDAY AND SUNDAY,

9 TO 5, AT GREENFIELD VILLAGE IN DEARBORN, MICHIGAN.

                              - 30 -

           HENRY FORD MUSEUM AND GREENFIELD VILLAGE ARE PART OF THE
           EDISON INSTITUTE, A NONPROFIT EDUCATIONAL INSTITUTION.

062582   JS

*Figure 7.2. Script for a thirty-second radio public service announcement.
Source: The Edison Institute.*

PUBLIC SERVICE ANNOUNCEMENT   LENGTH: :10

SUBJECT: COLONIAL MUSIC AND   FOR USE: JULY 5 - 11, 1982
           MILITARY MUSTER
           JULY 10 & 11, 1982

ANNCR: THE SPIRIT OF '76 IS ALIVE AT GREENFIELD VILLAGE THIS WEEKEND,

AT THE COLONIAL MUSIC AND MILITARY MUSTER.   THAT'S SATURDAY AND SUNDAY,

9 TO 5, AT GREENFIELD VILLAGE IN DEARBORN, MICHIGAN.

- 30 -

HENRY FORD MUSEUM AND GREENFIELD VILLAGE ARE PART OF THE
EDISON INSTITUTE, A NONPROFIT EDUCATIONAL INSTITUTION.

062582   JS

Figure 7.2. Script for a ten-second radio public service announcement. Source:
The Edison Institute.

which the broadcast media place a premium. The quality of records is not as good as that of one-quarter-inch tapes, and they are difficult to store.

In 1983 the equipment necessary to produce radio PSAs on tape cost approximately $8,000—a figure that would be within the reach of some museums. This price includes two reel-to-reel tape recorders of broadcast quality; a mixing board, which permits mixing live voice and prerecorded music; a microphone of broadcast quality; a monitor; and a timer. The studio should be a room with good acoustics. The walls and ceiling of a small room in a quiet area can be fitted with acoustical tiles and foam baffles to deaden unwanted noise. Alternatively, you might book time at a local recording studio or radio station. Ways of reducing costs by enlisting the help of broadcast stations, students, and freelance professionals are discussed below, in connection with television PSAs.

Television PSAs. Television PSAs may be issued as scripts with 35mm slides or as films or videotapes with or without synchronized sound. They are used by commercial and cable stations and sometimes by closed-circuit systems in such locations as hospitals, nursing homes, and hotels.

The most basic television PSA is a station identification slide. The museum should be immediately recognizable in the slide, which should include some open space on which stations can superimpose their call letters. You need only identify the subject of the slide in a note to public service directors, suggesting that it may be useful for a station identification PSA. The script, prepared by the station, might say "You are watching WCAX TV, Channel 2, Buffalo, home of the XYZ Museum."

You may also submit a slide with a script to be read by a station announcer. The script should be ten to twenty seconds. A script sent with a slide of a museum's distinctive facade or logo might read, "Step back into Ohio's history by visiting the XYZ Museum, open every day, in Cincinnati."

Multiple-slide PSAs should usually be timed for approximately thirty seconds, with no less than five seconds allowed per slide. The slide script should be arranged in three columns and should be printed on the public-service letterhead. The left column describes the slides by number; the right column contains the copy to be read by the announcer; and the center column lists the amount of time required to read that copy. The script for a typical twenty-second television slide PSA might be the following.

TELEVISION SLIDE PSA

Slide		
1. Youngster at potter's wheel	:07	THEY'RE PASSING OUT WORK APRONS AT XYZ MUSEUM THIS MONTH, BUT YOU HAVE TO PROVIDE THE KICK POWER. THAT'S AT THE MUSEUM'S "EVERYBODY IS A POTTER" EXHIBIT, WHERE THEY LET YOU SIT AT A POTTER'S WHEEL AND SHAPE SOME CLAY.
2. Closeup, youngster getting help shaping pot.	:03	IT'S NOT HARD WHEN A PROFESSIONAL POTTER SHOWS YOU HOW TO DO IT.
3. Closeup, youngster's feet on treadle	:05	KEEP THE WHEEL GOING WITH YOUR FEET AND PULL THE CLAY INTO SHAPE. IT'S CALLED THROWING A POT.
4. Youngster with finished pot	:05	YOU CAN DO IT ANY DAY THROUGH MARCH 1 AT XYZ MUSEUM IN CEDAR RAPIDS.

The slides should be horizontal, with contrast that is not too high, and protected for mailing by special envelopes or plastic sleeves, available at photo supply shops. In addition to the slides, you may also submit background sounds on tape for possible use with the script.

Television public service films are produced with synchronized sound in either thirty- or sixty-second spots or as four- to five-minute short features. Occasionally a public service short feature will run if a sporting event concludes earlier than scheduled or if a movie does not fill a time slot. A 1980 study of 419 stations by Planned Communication Services, Inc., revealed that television PSAs were used in the following broadcast hours.

Daytime	62.6%
Early fringe	11.5%
Prime time	10.9%
Late fringe	3.4%
Late night	11.6%[3]

The same study cited the PSA length preferences shown in table 7.1.

The public service film or videotape should be placed in a suitable container with the title, length, and name of the museum typed on a label attached to the edge of the flap, where it will be visible on a storage shelf. The contact person's name and telephone number should also appear on the box, which should be mailed to the station's public

Table 7.1. Lengths of public service announcements preferred by television stations

	Length (seconds)			
	60	30	20	10
Prefer (%)	42	67	30	25
Accept (%)	53	33	58	57
Will not use (%)	5	0	12	18

Source: *TV Public Service Announcements: What Do Stations Want?* (New York: Planned Communication Services, 1980).

service director in a padded bag. Because stations randomly pull public service films off the shelves whenever they are needed to fill open time slots, your films should be generic in character so they can be used any time. Time-specific activities, such as weekend special events, are better handled by a television news clip and a news actuality tape. If you use PSA material to promote a time-specific event, it is safest to personally retrieve it from the station after it has been used so it will not be accidentally used again after the event is over.

The PSA should be entertaining and colorful and must have an informational rather than promotional tone. It should show action and should move smoothly from one segment to the next. In producing thirty- or sixty-second public service spots, the challenge is to attract attention and to tell a story in a fleeting moment. In a four- or five-minute public service short-feature film, the task is to hold attention.

To minimize the costs of a fully produced PSA you might ask a station's public service director to have the station produce it or to assist with its production. If a station will contribute voice or on-camera talent, camera and sound crews, and a film editor, the museum's costs will be limited to film processing, printing, and distribution. Alternatively, check with local colleges and universities to determine whether they have radio or television production classes that would be capable of producing museum PSAs. Also, you can sometimes contract with station writers and technicians for work on a free-lance basis. A local cable system may also produce a PSA or may provide production assistance. In some communities it may be possible to interest advertising agencies or corporate electronic media departments in producing PSAs as contributions to the museum.

It is generally less expensive to produce PSAs on film than on videotape. Film is also less costly to distribute and mail because commercial stations require that videotape materials be packaged in three-quarter-inch U-Matic video cassettes. Another advantage of 16mm film is that at present it can be used by all television stations, including those that broadcast only in videotape. Planned Communication in 1980 conducted a study of 419 television stations' PSA preferences. The results indicated that some stations need two-inch videotape, whereas others require three-quarter-inch tape.[4] It is therefore impossible for a museum to have a videotape system that will meet all stations' needs, as table 7.2 shows. As videotape technology develops, recommendations regarding film versus videotape will probably change.

Production equipment for 16mm film is significantly less costly than comparable videotape equipment. The 1983 cost of basic equipment needed to produce a 16mm synchronous-sound film is $35,000 to $45,000. This price includes a quiet-running synchronous camera; a one-quarter-inch synchronous tape recorder; a six-plate flatbed editor and editing bench with editing tools; a projector; microphones; lighting; and a grip kit. If you plan to use this equipment only occasionally, consider renting it from motion picture and video agencies.

A museum that plans to produce many television PSAs should consider employing a staff member who can produce them with help from free-lance writers and on-camera talent. At 1983 prices, to contract with a recognized local producer for a thirty-second color 16mm spot to be shot in one day costs $5,000 to $15,000 plus the cost of making prints for distribution. In 1983 the same spot could be produced in house for $1,500 plus the cost of prints.

You might begin production of a short public service feature film by organizing a small ad hoc museum staff committee to outline a story that the museum wishes to tell. The next step is to contact a qualified producer, who could be a student intern with film or video production background or a professional who is capable of taking full advantage of

Table 7.2.   Television stations' format preferences for public service announcements

	Format			
	16mm film	2" tape	¾" tape	Slide/script
Prefer (%)	63	49	15	16
Accept (%)	34	41	38	50
Cannot use (%)	3	10	47	34

Source: TV Public Service Announcements: What Do Stations Want? (New York: Planned Communication Services, 1980).

television's special capabilities. The producer's responsibility would be to assimilate the committee's ideas into a script with a scenario that indicates the sequence of visual action, sound, music, and other special effects. Because such a person exercises overall responsibility for producing the film or videotape, he or she must be allowed to decide how the material should be written and presented—providing, of course, that it is accurate and consistent with the museum's professional standards and message base.

The PSA shot on 16mm film will be sent to a processing laboratory, where a work print will be made and sound recordings will be transferred to magnetic film to allow them to be mechanically synchronized with the work print. Next, by cutting and splicing the sound and film to lengths that correspond to the script and scenario, an edited work print with synchronized sound tracks will be made. The film then goes to a mixing studio, where the various sound components are rerecorded onto a single sound track. The original film is pulled from storage and matched frame for frame with the work print and magnetic sound track. Finally the laboratory makes the first composite print for the producer's approval before multiple prints are prepared for distribution.

Museum staff who must approve the film may recommend changes at two stages. The first review is at the rough cut, when the footage is edited the first time. Final changes should be at the next stage, which is the fine cut, when the footage is edited with sound to the correct lengths. To make changes at the next stage, when the fine-cut work print has been interlocked with the mixed sound track, is expensive. The answer print, which is the first to include titles, optical effects, color corrections, and mixed sound track, is the last stage before the creation of multiple prints. As the film progresses through each stage, the cost and labor involved in making changes increase.

You should not expect television stations to return prints, and you should be aware that print costs are a major part of the production budget. At 1983 prices each 16mm 30-second print costs $5 to $8. Five-minute prints cost $15 to $20 each.

Sponsored Films

"A sponsored film is a moving picture, in any form, paid for by anyone controlling its content and showing it for public entertainment or information," according to writer Walter J. Klein.[5] Sponsored films are produced for free distribution to motion picture theaters, colleges, schools and libraries, cable television outlets, and commercial and educational television. They may also be shown at civic clubs, churches, fraternal meetings, women's and garden clubs, hospitals and other health care institutions, homes for the aged, hobby groups, and cultural educational, professional, historical, and fine arts organizations.

Although the film should have promotional value for the museum, its emphasis must be informational and entertaining. It may be produced in 35mm for theaters and in 16mm or videotape for television. Sponsored films are most adaptable to both theater and television use if they are either ten or twenty-five to twenty-eight minutes in length. Travel relates to museums more than any other of the most popular subjects for sponsored films. Other popular subjects for sponsored films that are pertinent to museums but less in demand include history, art, science, conservation, crafts, ceramics and sculpture, festivals, and special events.

Before making the commitment to produce a sponsored film, the museum should be aware of the research and other time-intensive assistance required of the professional staff. In addition, compromises may be required to accommodate not only the museum's objectives but also the goals of any funding agencies that are paying the bill.

Funding. At 1983 prices a ten-minute film for television contracted out for professional production would cost a minimum of $20,000. The only way such an expense could be met by most museums would be through outside funding. The public relations department with the help of others in the museum would prepare a funding proposal presenting the story line and explaining why the film should be produced, why it should involve the museum, and how and to whom it would be distributed. The proposal can be sent to private, corporate, and governmental funding agencies as well as industrial and business associations.

Should funding be granted, select a producer carefully. The museum public relations person should work closely with him or her to be certain that the museum's objectives are being met as much as possible and that the film is presenting correct information.

Distribution. Any film's distribution strategy and cost should be determined at the outset, and figures should be incorporated into the budget. Usually when a film is produced with grant funds, the funding organization will want it to be distributed to a large audience. Whoever is paying for the distribution should contract with a professional distributor to promote, schedule, and ship the film and the accompanying printed materials. The distributor also handles replacement of damaged prints and maintains the film and collateral materials inventory. See the sources section of this book for a list of distributors.

Cable Television

Cable television had its beginnings in rural areas, where it was an antenna service amplifying signals for subscribers who could not otherwise receive a good picture.

Today cable programmers such as Home Box Office, a subsidiary of Time, Inc., occasionally produce documentaries that can involve museums. Cable system owners such as Teleprompter and Cox Cable are also competing for business by offering museums time on special local channels specializing in cultural and educational programming.

Cable's immense need for material makes it a major outlet for public service films. Some cable companies may also be interested in producing or allowing you to produce with their equipment documentary features on a museum which you could use for additional purposes, such as visitor orientation. In most cable communities citizens have free use of equipment to produce their own shows for transmission on a public access channel. When such programs involve the museum, the public relations department should monitor them, making sure they are consistent with the museum's objectives and of a quality that reflects well on the museum.

If you work with cable, do not overlook the Cable News Network (the address appears in the sources at the end of this book) as an outlet for museum material.

Satellite Cable

When RCA launched Satcom 1 in 1975, a satellite era began. Now any broadcaster who has reserved space on a satellite can send signals to it that will shower down to receivers located across the country or around the world. As the number of satellites and earth receivers grows, many national satellite cable networks are expected to develop, each with its own earth receiver and a specific program focus. The concept is called "narrowcasting," which simply means producing programming that is targeted to the specific interests of a single segment of the audience. Narrowcasting could lead to cultural networks that would emphasize the kind of programming to which museums relate best. Modern Talking Pictures Services, Inc., provides a satellite transmission service. The National Geographic Society is working on plans to form an alliance of nonprofit organizations to produce programs for cable or satellite transmission.

Video Discs

Video disc players connect to standard televisions and permit the viewer to watch programs reproduced on discs which resemble phonograph records. If the cost of these units decreases and they become more popular for home use, production companies may wish to reproduce a museum's existing films and videotapes on discs for retail sale. Meanwhile the machines promise to be important for such uses as the storing of artifact slides on discs that can easily be accessed and viewed and for the storage and presentation of general educational and archival images. They are also practical in exhibits if a video presentation is repeated continuously.

Home Videotapes

Currently home video half-inch VHS, or beta, tape recorders are not of sufficient quality to have significant television broadcast application. They can, however, be used to produce training and interpretive films to be shown in conjunction with exhibits. A few independent videotape producers are now approaching museums for approval to shoot videotapes for retail sale. Evaluate such proposals with caution to be certain that the producer expresses the museum's point of view, that the publicity value is worth the museum's effort and that the museum will receive sales royalties or other financial benefits.

In November, 1982, the Whitney Museum of American Art became the first major museum to produce home videotapes of its collections for retail sale.

Media Do's and Don'ts

In working with the media, a museum and its public relations staff will find it helpful to observe (or at least to be aware of) certain customs pertaining to fees and regulations. Your institution will also want to formulate some operating policies with respect to the media to assure that the relationship is smooth and mutually advantageous.

Photography of Museum Properties

You should establish a policy that provides for a consistent response to requests to use museum properties as photography locations. The policy should provide for good media relations and can allow for income from appropriate fees if such charges are allowed in your museum's operating policy.

Although some museums do not charge any fees for providing materials or services to the media, others charge photographic print and location fees and direct costs. Photographic print fees could be charged for providing photos requested by the media that will not have any publicity value for the museum. Location fees may be charged to a photographer or filmmaker for using museum property as a set. The amount charged depends upon the publicity value. Direct costs involve regular and overtime wages paid to museum employees who must be on duty to assist with a project.

When the museum is the subject of a story, the publicity value is obvious. In such cases a fee for using the museum as a location for shooting still or motion pictures or a fee for providing photographic prints should not be charged unless the cost of the prints cannot be absorbed by the public relations budget. Also, it is inappropriate to charge a location or print fee when the museum initiated the story idea. In determining whether to charge a fee, do not overlook the long-term value of cooperating with the media as much as possible.

Magazines. A collectors' magazine might request a photo of one of the museum's Chippendale chests to illustrate a story on a cabinet-maker. The subject of the story is the cabinetmaker, not the museum. In such a case one must determine whether collectors who read this magazine are one of the museum's high-priority publics and whether the magazine's use of the photo will produce enough publicity value to offset the fee that could be charged for the print. A photo credit alone has little publicity value. The museum must at least be mentioned in the caption and preferably in the body copy as well. This requirement should be communicated to the magazine that has made the request. In most cases, if a magazine assigns a photographer to shoot at the museum, the resulting story will have enough publicity value to make a location fee unnecessary. However, you should still discuss the museum's publicity requirements with the magazine's editor.

Newspapers. You will be expected not to charge a location fee or direct costs to any reporter shooting news material on the museum property. Therefore, a newspaper producing a news story or feature should not be charged a fee. Although newspapers could be charged for using the museum to shoot photos for such nonnews material as a fashion supplement, charging local newspapers a location fee might threaten your relations with the press. Newspapers could, however, be expected to pay for photographic prints used to illustrate stories that do not mention the museum.

Television. As with newspapers, you should not charge a location fee or direct costs for spot news or for news feature shooting by a television news department. Likewise, because of the publicity value, you should not charge location or direct fees to stations developing documentaries that significantly involve the museum or to stations producing talk or entertainment shows that will be broadcast from the museum.

In most cases it is important to recognize that by assisting local television producers, the museum will benefit in the future when there is a need for coverage that does have important publicity value. If the museum is only incidental to a documentary, however, or if there is only an occasional script reference to it and a crawl credit at the end, you might consider charging a location fee and direct costs.

Photo and Film Regulations. Copyright requirements must be met in the use of museum photos, and a prescribed credit line should appear with the photo when it is published. You should stamp "Not to be sold or used in advertisements without written permission from XYZ Museum" on the back of each print. It is impractical to require that all photos be returned unless they are 4" x 5" transparencies, which are usually lent.

Be sure to caption all photos. Because visitors often travel to a museum to see an object that has been pictured in an article, do not release photos of artifacts that are not on public view. If an object is not owned by the museum or is a reproduction, mention the fact in the caption. Models should not be shown breaking museum rules, and photographers should not be allowed to use inappropriate props.

If the photo or film subject is a new accession that a member of the museum's curatorial staff is using to illustrate an article he or she is in the process of writing, its use could be delayed until the article is published, depending on museum policy. Such a restriction should not, however, extend for more than six months. An immediate need to recognize a donor could supersede this policy.

A photo or film shot at the museum should not be used to endorse any cause or any promotional or quasi-promotional activity, such as an auto show or fashion tabloid, unless such use is approved by the museum. Photos or films involving museum properties should not be used for raising funds for any institution other than the museum.

Films by Independent Producers. Independently produced films are made under contract with television networks, corporations, and private or governmental agencies for distribution to such outlets as television (commercial, public, educational, or cable), schools, theaters, and libraries. Corporations sometimes contract to have them produced for internal training purposes.

When responding to requests from independent producers first try to obtain the following information:

- the names of all organizations and their representatives involved in financing, producing, and distributing the proposed project;
- what the project is, its intended purpose, to whom it will be shown, and the means of conveyance;
- how and why the producer wishes to use museum properties or personnel;
- proposed shooting dates and times;
- the promotional, educational, or other benefits of the project;
- evidence of liability insurance in the event of injuries to personnel and/or property damage.

Assuming that the answers to these questions are satisfactory, recommend that the producer visit the museum to see what is available and to provide a very specific list of items to be filmed. Because plans for curatorial assistance and other arrangements will be based on this list, the producer must understand that other subjects and locations cannot be added on the day of shooting. Depending on the nature of its collections, a museum may need to approve the film's treatment or script to make sure portions involving the museum and its collections are accurate and consistent with its educational objectives.

The museum public relations person should schedule the shooting and should oversee all arrangements, providing electricity at the site, places to park vehicles, any required rearrangement of objects, and other services. Direct costs could be charged. Often an independently produced film does not have enough publicity value to warrant waiving a location fee; however, the public relations department and the producer could possibly negotiate a partial waiver if a significant portion of the film involves the museum.

Advertisements and Commercials. Museum assets should generally not be utilized for the purpose of selling products unless a location fee and direct costs are charged. Exceptions could be made for state, regional, or city travel and convention bureaus, air and bus lines, and hotel chains with advertising that encourages people to come to the area and visit the museum. For such types of advertisers, one should consider waiving or reducing the location fee.

If your institution wishes to accommodate other product advertising, consider doing so for its revenue-producing rather than publicity value. The policy of charging a location fee for commercial product advertising and the possible implications of product endorsements should be evaluated by the museum's legal counsel, however. All regulations pertaining to any photographic use of the museum should apply. The product and the theme of the advertisement or commercial should not conflict with the museum's message base.

Books, Films, and Photos for Commercial Sale. Whether to charge photo print fees to book authors depends upon the publication's publicity value for the museum. If it is a travel book that will encourage people to visit the museum, no fee should be charged. Otherwise, unless a significant portion is about the museum, charge a print fee.

A letter of permission should be signed by the book author before the photo is provided. In it the author should agree to:

- specify the intended use of the photo;
- use it only once and for the purpose specified, without permitting others to reproduce it;
- credit the museum, preferably in the caption or on the facing page;
- give the museum one complimentary copy of the published work.

A sample letter of permission is in the appendix.

Producers of films, reels, videotapes, or video discs that are to be sold commercially to schools or through public retail outlets should be charged a location fee and direct costs. If the museum is the subject, the content should be approved by the museum public relations department before the film's release. In such cases, the museum might negotiate royalties with the producer.

Photographers who wish to take photos of museum properties to sell for a profit should be charged the museum's direct costs plus the location fee, which could be reduced or waived, again depending on the publicity value.

A Sample Fee Structure (1983). Fees should be set individually by each museum, depending upon the nature of its collections, publicity needs, and institutional policy.

Still prints
(direct costs could be added)

8″ x 10″ print from existing negative	$10.00
8″ x 10″ print, new photography	25.00
35mm duplicate of existing slide	8.00
35mm original of new photography	25.00
4″ x 5″ color transparency, existing,	10.00
sixty-day loan	
4″ x 5″ color transparency, new photography,	25.00
sixty-day loan	

Location fees
(still and motion)

Nonadvertising $100.00 per hour plus direct costs
Advertising $200.00 per hour plus direct costs, minimum $1,000.00

Where direct costs are concerned, you may charge the regular and/or overtime wages of employees who are involved in the project. These could include security guards, grounds, electrical, carpentry, maintenance, public relations, interpretation, curatorial, and library staff members as well as any work museum employees would do that is not part of their regular job, such as modeling for photos.

Media Relations Summary

DO:

- Know and understand the museum and its collections.
- Know and understand the media, be mindful of its needs and deadlines, and keep lists edited and current.
- Send a news release only when the information has news value and then only to the most appropriate media.
- Develop peer relationships that encourage the media and the museum to share in building public understanding of the institution and its programs.
- Be certain that materials fit the needs of the media to which they are being offered—that they have local appeal or that they are directed to the interests of the media's target audience or are of universal interest and are timely, relevant, and useful.
- Be helpful and available to the media both in good times and in periods of adversity. Make quick and courteous responses to inquiries, and send thank you notes when appropriate.

- Be sure news release information is accurate and complete, including event dates, location, admission fees, mailing date, and the telephone number of a museum contact person. News material should answer every reasonable question that a reporter or editor might ask.
- Time releases to arrive early enough to meet media deadlines. Do not overlook the telephone as a means of keeping media aware of special opportunities.
- Anticipate requests with a file of readily available backgrounders and photos.
- Use local angles to link the museum and its collections with regional or national news.

DON'T:

- bluff, exaggerate, lie, or pad a story or hinder reporters in their coverage;
- hold press conferences except when major newsmakers or news events are involved or in a time of crisis;
- apply pressure to the media to cover stories;
- ask that a story be killed or expect it to be killed because the museum does not provide information; complain about a story treatment unless it was seriously inaccurate (then talk first with the reporter); ask to check reporter's copy; call to find out why a story was not used; or request that the reporter send the museum tear sheets of the published article;
- use advertising purchases as levers to place stories, consistently favor one media outlet over another; or expect every interview to produce a story.

8

The Promotional Campaign

Promotional campaigns help motivate the public to attend a museum's special programs, and also can focus public attention on ongoing exhibits, membership benefits, and other offerings. They can portray a museum as an enjoyable and worthwhile place to spend leisure hours and can even make a museum a regional or national travel destination.

A campaign's success depends upon utilizing all the media, exploiting advertising possibilities even when there is little or no advertising budget, and, if necessary, evaluating and correcting the messages that are being conveyed. Promotional campaign planning requires determining how to communicate and distribute messages so they will be accepted by various media channels, controlling timing so the publicity can be sustained, and developing creative ideas to make the museum interesting and appealing to the media and the public.

Publicity

Messages transmitted periodically through media visits, news releases, media coverage, and speakers' bureau activities can help maintain awareness of the museum at a low level.

To persuade people to buy an admission ticket or to tell their friends about the museum, however, requires well-planned publicity that uses each medium's special strengths.

A study made by the U.S. Department of Agriculture suggests that publicity must effect a five-step process if it is to motivate people to act. As stated by authors Cutlip and Center, these steps are:

Awareness. The person learns of the existence of the idea or practice, but has little knowledge of it.

Interest. The person develops interest in the idea. He seeks more information and considers its general merits.

Evaluat n. The person makes mental application of the idea and weighs its merits for his own situation. He obtains more information and decides to try it.

Trial. The person actually applies the idea or practice—usually on a small scale. He is interested in the practice, techniques and conditions for application.

Adoption. If the idea proves acceptable, it is adopted.[1]

The Department of Agriculture found that although the media played an important part in creating an awareness and interest, contacts with people were most important when a farmer wanted to learn more about a subject and to evaluate it.

Messages placed with the print and broadcast media can never take the place of word-of-mouth publicity. Your chances of benefiting from this most desirable form of promotion are greatest when you use all the media in a coordinated campaign. The following guidelines may help you develop a promotional campaign for a special program.

1. Urge that publicity planning begin as far in advance as possible, at least seven months to a year ahead.
2. Be involved in the initial planning of the activity that the campaign is promoting, recommending approaches that could increase story possibilities, could align the event with the interests of prospective audiences, and could take into account problems to be resolved and factors in the museum's environment to be considered.
3. Develop objectives that serve the needs and resolve the problems (attract a new audience, call attention to new program offerings, etc.). Always strive to improve the public's understanding of the museum as a whole and its purpose.
4. Establish a strategy. Rather than telling the whole story in the first release, employ the technique of releasing one angle at a time, building up to the event but also following up on it as much as possible when the event is over.

In implementing the plan, tailor each element of the story to the most appropriate medium: give strong visuals to television, colorful interview possibilities to radio, in-depth feature subjects to magazines, news and feature angles to newspapers, human interest photo opportunities to wire services.

Often a snowball effect develops as the campaign proceeds. If a wire service features an element of the story, a radio show producer may read it and may call to arrange an interview. A newspaper feature can stimulate television's interest. You thereby achieve an integrated publicity campaign, with different media responding to the story in ways that best use their own strengths.

The Publicity Schedule

A publicity campaign schedule with weekly deadlines is a must to keep one's efforts directed toward objectives. It should list the events, the stories, and the target media. For purposes of the schedule, the stories can be listed by merely tentative titles and with details only briefly sketched. The schedule should be flexible to accommodate unexpected opportunities.

A hypothetical publicity campaign for the relocation, restoration, and activation of an outdoor museum's 100-year-old steam-operated gristmill is outlined below. List A includes local newspapers, magazines, radio and television stations; list B includes one- to two-hour drive-time newspapers, magazines, and radio and television stations; list C includes statewide and border states' regional newspapers and wire services (no broadcast media); and list D includes national newspapers, magazines, and syndicates that have special interests related to the subject.

September

Weeks 1 and 2
- Media lists A,B,C, and D newspapers— "XYZ Museum Plans to Rescue Historic Grist Mill."
- Lists A and B television—thirty-second film or slide news clip about mill on its present site.
- Lists A and B radio—telephone actuality of curator discussing mill on its present site.
- List D—query letters to long-lead monthly magazines, each with a different angle such as: "How a Museum Rescued a Historic Gristmill"; "Early American Industry to be Interpreted at XYZ Museum's Gristmill"; "XYZ Museum Gets All Steamed Up about Grinding Cornmeal"; "It Is Not Your Everyday Stones That Will Grind Corn at XYZ Museum's Gristmill."

October

Throughout the month
- Follow up on magazine queries; mail new queries with self-addressed, stamped envelopes when subjects are rejected.

November

Week 2
- Lists A,B, and C newspapers—"Moving Day for a 100-Year-Old Gristmill"; fact sheets on how the move is to be accomplished.
- Actuality interview tapes for radio, slides or film for television.

January

Week 2
- List A print and broadcast releases—"Local Steam Enthusiasts Will Restore XYZ Museum Gristmill."

March

Week 2
- Lists A and B print and broadcast releases— "XYZ Museum Awarded Steam License to Operate 1880 Gristmill."
- Invite media to demonstration firing.

April

Week 1
- List A, newspapers—"Stone-Ground Cornmeal to Be Produced at XYZ Museum Gristmill, Search is on for a Miller."

May

Whenever appropriate
- List A, newspapers only—"XYZ Museum Employs John Doe as Miller." Offer Doe to List A and B talk show hosts.

June

Week 2
- Lists A and B, release—"XYZ Museum to Dedicate Gristmill July 20." Invite those interested from Lists A,B,C, and D to cover the dedication.

July

Week 2
• Lists A,B, and C—"Governor Smith to Speak at XYZ Museum Gristmill Dedication July 20, Souvenir Recipes for Using Cornmeal to Be Given Away."
• Offer discussion of cornmeal for baking to List A and B radio and television talk shows.

Week 3
• Lists A,B,C, and D print media followup story—"Governor Emphasizes XYZ Museum's Cultural and Economic Contributions to the Area and the State at July 20 Dedication of 1880 Gristmill." Send backgrounders and photos to those not covering the dedication.

Evaluating Publicity

Publicity evaluation begins with retrieving material on the museum that has been published or aired. Clippings can be obtained by contracting with a clipping service that will search for museum mentions in newspapers or magazines. The museum may choose to contract for clipping on a national, regional, or statewide basis. Larger clipping services will also provide broadcast transcripts or tapes. Expect to retrieve about 60 percent of the material published. The cost per clip will be high. See the sources at the end of this book for the addresses of clipping services.

To save money, you might post a notice in the museum's magazine or newsletter asking readers to send clips of newspaper and magazine articles to the public relations department, noting the date and the name of the publication. Readers could also be asked to advise the department of television or radio mentions on a given subject and to indicate the station's call letters and date. A postage-paid envelope should be provided for readers' convenience in responding, and a fresh envelope should be supplied to anyone who sends in a clip. You should read and clip local newspapers and special interest magazines daily and should make every effort to hear all broadcast interviews and reports that involve the museum so that dates, times, admission fees, and other vital information can be checked for accuracy.

When it is known that a radio or television show will involve the museum, you may record it on audiotape using an inexpensive cassette recorder. A transcript may later be typed from the recording. Most television stations will, for a fee, produce a videotape of talk show segments in which museum guests have appeared, or you may supply a blank videotape, to which the station will usually transfer the museum segment at no charge. To be able to view these videotapes and to dub them onto a single storage tape, you will need a three-quarter-inch U-Matic video recorder, a video player, and monitor (for a total cost in 1983 of about $4,000). The recorder and monitor may be rented from an audiovisual supplier or video production house for about $100 a day. Broadcast tapes should be played for museum staff people who were involved as a means of showing appreciation for their help and as a way for them to evaluate their performance.

Although clippings and typed broadcast transcripts are often glued into a clipping book, they can be organized effectively by storing them in acid-free file folders labeled by month or by subject category. Most public relations departments circulate the clips and broadcast transcripts to the executive director, the trustee public relations committee, and departments whose activities were publicized. Summaries of the total number of placements are helpful in comparing amounts of material published in different years. Such reports can also help motivate public relations staff members by setting placement goals. The number of media requests for information or for assistance that you receive each year can be a measure of the extent to which reporters view the museum as an interesting and reliable information source.

More important than these quantitative summaries are qualitative evaluations which focus upon what the media are actually saying about the museum. Because newspapers almost invariably rewrite release headlines and lead paragraphs, be alert to the possibilities that the media may misrepresent or misinform even in publishing articles based on information received from the museum. To help determine whether the museum is saying what it means to say, perform a content analysis. One technique involves picking words that denote aspects of the museum's program objectives, such as "entertaining," "educational," "fun," "inspiring," "quiet," "worthwhile," or "informative." Then skim a random selection of clippings and broadcast transcripts, checking off each occurrence of these words or of words with similar meanings. Although releases may stress the educational aspects of the museum, "entertaining" and "fun" may be the words most often used by the media.

Another type of content analysis involves listing the museum's publicity objectives and totaling the number of clippings and broadcast transcripts that address them. Your publicity objectives might include communicating the museum's role as a positive influence upon the quality of life in the area, or as an economic stabilizer, a generator of tourism, or an educational asset for area youth and adults. Do not be surprised if you learn that none of your objectives is being communicated by the media. This may be because you are not treating these objectives as integral parts of the story but are simply tacking phrases that speak to them onto your releases and the media are editing them out. Also it may be that the museum's programs are not supporting your publicity objectives and that you need to have greater input in program planning or change your publicity objectives.

Advertising

Use advertising to complement publicity, and vice versa. Neither form of promotion should be expected to replace the other. Instead, plan your campaign to use the strengths of each. Advertising offers several advantages.

- By having control over when and where the message appears, you can position it for maximum exposure to a target audience. For example, if suburban commuters are the principal audience for the museum's weekend adult education courses, you can purchase the radio drive-time advertising that they hear. You can also control the emphasis. If a discounted price is the principal appeal, you can feature it in the ad.
- Researchers believe that the advertising message motivates action better than the publicity story, especially when the advertisement is repeated many times.
- Advertisements can incorporate a greater variety of feedback mechanisms than publicity stories. Clip-out coupons, telephone numbers and addresses encourage the audience to make contact with the museum.

For its part, publicity offers other advantages.

- Because publicity stories make the museum a part of the day's news, most readers view them as more believable and legitimate than advertisements.
- The media do not charge a fee for running stories.
- Stories are more effective than advertisements in acknowledging

people who have helped the museum, in reporting on its successes and interpreting its failures, and in providing a multifaceted view of the institution that will lead to public understanding and support. (Museum advertising for the most part should aim simply to generate attendance and is not usually an appropriate means of raising money or explaining policies.)

Be alert to imaginative uses of direct mail. Although list development and maintenance and production of collateral materials and postage are expensive, direct mail has advantages:

- contact can be confined to target markets;
- messages can be focused to motivate recipients to take a desired action;
- format and message variations can be tested by sending out different versions to specific segments of the market and then comparing results;
- repetitive exposures can be achieved for such purposes as motivating membership renewals.

Often the most productive direct mail lists come from recent visitor names. You can provide a guest book at the entrance to generate names and then send events calendars and membership solicitations to them. People who buy museum merchandise can be invited to fill out a card if they wish to receive announcements. A guest book at eating areas will produce lists to mail menu announcements and invitations to holiday meals. Coupon returns from your advertising can be converted into lists to mail discount package announcements and other attendance generators.

To expand your direct mail program, you can exchange your lists with other museums. Also, magazines whose markets are similar to yours sometimes will exchange regional subscription lists. Perhaps a nearby symphony orchestra would exchange its membership list with yours so both could solicit members in new markets. If you exchange lists, your list must be in a format that the other party can use. This may mean putting the list on computer tape. Lists of teachers and group leaders probably will have to be purchased from list brokers either on mailing labels or computer tape. These lists are expensive; order only those geographical segments that are most pertinent to your needs.

High direct mail costs can be controlled somewhat by testing lists and using only those that produce good results, by designing collateral materials for production and mailing cost efficiencies, and by seeking contributed funding and services wherever possible for production and distribution. Occasionally you might recover some list development costs by selling your most productive lists to commercial merchandisers.[2]

The Greatest Value for Your Dollar

Use your imagination to think of ways to achieve maximum value at least cost. Every situation offers different opportunities, and the following guidelines are intended simply to stimulate your own creativity.

- Approach media, particularly radio stations, about providing air time free or at a discounted price in exchange for museum admission tickets or cost-saving coupons for food or other museum sales items. The museum not only saves advertising money, it gains exposure when the media publicizes the ticket giveaway.
- Keep broadcast media weathercasters informed about the museum's special exhibits and events. Suggest that they might note on a Friday that "It will be a good weekend to attend X,Y,Z Museum's Folk Festival," for example.
- Explore joint promotional projects with area museums. Such programs can provide shared funding for projects that a single museum could not afford such as advertising or hosting travel writers. Museums might also apply as a group for outside funding. Increasingly, formalized museum consortia are undertaking programs at many levels of museum operation.
- Produce joint advertisements with other area attractions, splitting the cost. Travel destinations with multiple offerings are particularly attractive to tour bus operators and agents, planners of auto club package tours, and tours commissioned by special interest groups. Be aware that packages usually involve the museum in offering some admission price discounts.
- Develop visitor packages built around a special museum feature such as an exhibit or event and include the price of overnight accommodations and meals as an option. All participants should share in the advertising costs.
- Ask area retailers and other advertisers to sponsor the museum's ad or, when appropriate, to include its message in their own ad. A free ride in someone else's ad can be especially successful with airlines

and hotel chains that are eager to attract visitors to the area for their own business interests. One should also ask to have the museum mentioned in the promotional folders and customer magazines of such businesses and illustrated in their advertising posters.

- Ask for mentions of the museum on the outdoor signs of hotels and shopping malls.
- Ask sign companies to contribute space on vacant billboards and bus cards. By giving the empty space to the museum, the company supports a local institution and advertises its own good citizenship. If the sign company cannot pay for art preparation, see whether an advertising agency will contribute it.
- Enlargements of museum promotional photos can be offered to retail stores, hotels, banks, utilities, schools, and libraries for display in windows and public areas. They can also be used to advertise the museum at antique shows, art galleries, and other locations frequented by prospective visitors.
- Sales brochures, employee orientation films, or other promotional materials produced by local companies should mention the museum as one of the strengths of their home community and as one of the recipients of their support.
- Print inexpensive stuffers for utilities, financial institutions, and retailers to distribute free of charge with their monthly billing statements. The printing cost might be assumed by anonymous contributors. Be sure that the piece is light enough not to increase the mailer's postage.
- Build and maintain good working relationships with state travel bureaus and with local and regional convention bureaus, chambers of commerce, and tour bus operators. The museum should always be included in their promotional efforts and the public relations staff should work closely with them. You should urge the state and the city to picture the museum and identify it in its travel advertising and literature.
- State highway signs indicating the exits that are most convenient to the museum should be produced, erected, and maintained by the state free of charge to the museum. Municipal signs welcoming travelers to the community, and directional signs to the museum, should be provided by the municipality or local service clubs at no cost. State, city, and auto club maps should identify the museum free of charge and should include a photo of it when possible.
- Print inexpensive promotional folders for stuffing in packets dis-

tributed at conventions meeting in the area. If necessary, sell advertising space to cover the printing cost.
- Emphasize any ways in which your museum presents a region's unique qualities. Travelers usually want to experience whatever is distinctive to the area and tour planners often have difficulty providing such opportunities.
- Contracting with professional distribution services is the best way to be sure your marketing material will be in literature racks. But you can distribute museum information free of charge by personally requesting that state and local travel bureaus, state highway information centers, hotels and motels, restaurants, and banks make your materials available. You will need to replenish supplies. You can make your material more visible by providing inexpensive plastic counter-top racks to which you have affixed a museum promotional sticker.
- Ask local hotels and other businesses exhibiting at travel shows to display promotional photos of the museum and to distribute its literature.
- Do not overlook the promotional value of merchandise sold in museum stores. The museum can receive free publicity by printing its name on appropriate items.[3] On a different level, ask licensees who manufacture your museum's reproductions to promote the museum in their literature and their advertising. By doing so they will enhance the product's prestige while publicizing the museum.
- If the museum's collections policy allows the loan of artifacts for exhibit at other museums, ask that borrowers mention the museum in their publicity.
- Consider asking a corporation to sponsor a month-long museum special event or other attendance generating activity. Corporate marketers are increasingly undertaking such programs not only to gain exposure to an institution's visitors, but also to enhance their product's image. Ticket giveaways and other promotional partnerships can be developed that will benefit the museum and the sponsor. Any sponsorship program should be carefully evaluated for its appropriateness and for the positive and negative impressions and results it might produce.
- Allow plenty of advance time to meet deadlines. Be sure media are quoting the nonprofit rate, which is 10 to 20 percent below retail, and are advising on best ad locations and sizes. Newspaper activities pages, published on Sundays one and two weeks before a spe-

cial event, daily entertainment pages, and spaces near calendars are usually productive for museums. In large newspapers an ad three columns by ten inches is recommended as the minimum size likely to be noted or read. Be cautious of deals offering editorial use of the museum's publicity stories in return for the purchase of ads.

- Study audience demographics reports, available free from the media, before deciding which are the most appropriate media buys.
- Whenever possible, incorporate a feedback mechanism into advertisements. Generate attendance by including coded clip-out coupons with space for the reader's name and address to get further information or to be redeemed at the museum entrance for an admission discount. Such coupons can provide feedback indicating which media pull the best and which geographical areas are being reached.

Despite how well conceived and executed the promotional campaign may be, the public relations objective of having supportive publics will not be achieved unless visitors actually experience what is promised. This involves collections, facilities, and interpretive programs that are of high quality and are accurately presented in the museum's promotion.

As was emphasized earlier in this book, there is a message cycle at work that helps shape the museum's image. Previsit publicity and advertising messages promise benefits; on-site experiences convey messages that either do or do not deliver on those promises; postvisit messages, conveyed by the word-of-mouth of visitors to their friends, create new previsit messages and new promises. This word-of-mouth communication network strongly influences people's relationships to the museum.

9

Daily Operations and Troubleshooting

When evaluating public relations successes and failures, it is all too easy to overlook some of the basic reasons why things happened as they did. For example, something important in the life of the museum may have gone by unnoticed because no one on the staff saw in it the potential for publicity or felt capable of working with the media. Sometimes, too, museums mistakenly conclude that the media are not interested if they do not check with the museum regularly. Administrators may not realize that busy reporters and editors expect the museum to take the initiative in telling its story. There is no magic in gaining the media's acceptance of a message. Rather, publicity is achieved through simple techniques that can be practiced by qualified part-time employees or by volunteers who have only minimal time and budget.

Successful institutions issue news releases with restraint, carefully selecting from the available media those that will use their material. They give the media adequate lead time to develop stories. Their messages are presented in formats that meet media requirements. There is substance to everything that successful institutions publicize. They do not issue "fluff," misinterpret facts, or exaggerate minor activities. They have a plan to help assure that their interests and the media's will be served in times of emergency or crisis. They maintain awareness of their institutions by addressing their audiences time and again and from all sides, using personal contact, speeches, publications, exhibits, and media stories.

The successful institution's staff and the media's reporters and editors work together as peers sharing the responsibility for keeping the public informed. Editors and reporters view these institutions and their public relations person as dependable, credible, and professional peers. Successful public relations requires more than plans, schedules, budgets, and staff, however. Your ability to meet the needs of the museum and the public will depend in large measure upon smooth, coordinated daily operation.

Organizing Daily Operations

Daily operation of the public relations office involves keeping yourself informed, providing input in overall museum planning, organizing work in progress, using the telephone and telephone special systems to best advantage, organizing files, writing memoranda, responding to requests for information and to complaints, hosting VIP visitors, and arranging meetings.

When your department is working on a special event, it is best to make one person responsible overall. That individual should attend the event's planning meetings, draft the publicity proposal, oversee the preparation of the event's publicity, and be at the event to assist with media coverage. If possible, the following year the assignment should be given to someone else who may bring a fresh approach.

Because much of the work in small and large public relations departments will be generated by incoming telephone calls and letters, it is very important for each person to know what the others are doing. Such awareness is particularly critical when exclusive stories are being offered. Two individuals could unknowingly promise the same story as an exclusive to two separate newspapers. By reviewing the flow of activity daily, however, the department director could catch the problem in time to develop a new story angle that satisfies both editors.

Evaluating the Staff

Staff administration and motivation are subjects that lie beyond the scope of this book. In public relations, however, where results are often intangible, it is important to develop ways by which everyone can measure his or her individual performance in contributing to the museum's fulfillment of its purpose and goals. The director of the department should meet privately with each staff member at least annually to answer questions of personal concern and to discuss performance. In offices where there are more than three or four staff members, scheduled weekly meetings may also be advisable.

Using the Telephone

Because the telephone is a major vehicle in the museum's two-way communication with its publics, it is important to observe a few guidelines.

- Be certain that during business hours someone is always on hand to answer the telephone for the public relations department.
- Include on news releases a telephone number where the public relations person can be reached in the evenings and on weekends if the museum switchboard is closed.
- When initiating calls to the media, get to the point immediately. If you are telephoning a radio station, be prepared to do a live or taped telephone interview at the time of the call. When calling a media outlet with story background information, avoid off-the-record comments and long, detailed accounts and descriptions. Never joke about a story; there is no way of knowing whether or not the reporter will view the humorous aside as a comment to be used.
- Practice good telephone manners.
- Always confirm in writing any agreements reached over the telephone.

Museums that offer numerous activities may wish to install a recorded telephone message system for the public's convenience. The caller dials a well-publicized number and hears a message as long as two minutes which can be rerecorded at any time and is accessible twenty-four hours a day. Most systems have a counter which totals calls received, thereby indicating the number of people who expressed interest during specific time periods.

Organizing Files

With the exception of a good secretary and good working relationships with curators and other information sources, nothing is more important for prompt service to the media than well-organized files. They should include the following materials:

1. Folders of media lists, well-organized and up to date, are a first priority.

2. Next in importance to media contact names and lists are files of photographs and captions.
3. A "brains" folder contains information that must be available quickly—prices, hours, directions from the nearest airport, and so forth.
4. A tickler folder listing future commitments that must not be forgotten is of critical importance.
5. A telephone conversation folder recording the name, telephone number, title, and affiliation of the person calling and the subject and date of the call can be very helpful many times during the year.
6. A contacts folder can save embarrassment and can help you use personal contacts. As you answer the telephone, call on media, and attend meetings and conferences away from the museum, you should record the names and affiliations of the people you meet. At the end of each year these names should be alphabetized and should be added to a permanent record.
7. Lists of names, telephone numbers, and addresses with pertinent background information on key travel associations and on governmental, educational, and community departments and agencies should be kept up to date.
8. A biographical folder with concise information and multiple copies of 8″ x 10″ glossy portraits of the museum's trustees, officers, and professional staff members should be kept current.
9. A collections file will help when media call to ask whether the museum has a particular artifact. Such a file may be organized by indexing artifact label copies in ring binders. Copies of the interpreters' manuals, accession committee meeting minutes, and collection backgrounders should also be filed.
10. The museum's publications, news releases, public service materials, advertisements, and speeches are important information sources that one needs to be able to retrieve easily.
11. Survey findings produced by the museum and by other agencies with which the museum shares an interest should be filed. File reports on pending governmental legislation can also be useful.

Memoranda

Used with discretion, memoranda serve the important purpose of confirming assignments and keeping key people informed. Brief, clearly written memos can:

- confirm agreements made by telephone;
- establish the specifics of requests for assistance from curators and others in the museum;
- explain or summarize performance reports, survey results, and other materials that otherwise might be misinterpreted;
- provide the deadline for the return of copy that has been sent to other departments for approvals, as well as any background information that those approving it may need;
- notify the museum's security department, guides, and other appropriate personnel in advance of visits by reporters.

Letters

Requests for Information

Letters received from people making specific requests for information can suggest the extent to which publicity has generated interest in a subject and can provide another opportunity to gauge public feedback.

Although there may be hundreds of letters in response to a well-publicized offer of free information, each inquiry should be answered within one week. If prompt reply seems impossible with existing staff and equipment, consider contracting with a fulfillment company. For a small charge per piece, such agencies will pick up letters daily, will open and sort them, and will type labels, stuff and bundle the materials, and mail them.

Complaints

It is realistic to assume that if one complaint letter is received on a subject, there may be many other people who also feel the same way but did not write. The complaint letter is important because it is one of the most direct forms of feedback. It should be read carefully, perhaps by more than one person, to be sure that the message has been correctly understood. Its contents should be checked with museum staff members to determine whether the complaint is legitimate. If it is not, a letter explaining the misunderstanding should be mailed promptly.

Because a vocal complainer can quickly dominate the word-of-mouth communication network that leads most people to visit the museum, legitimate complaints should be answered immediately with an explanation of steps being taken to prevent a recurrence of the problem. You might wish to enclose a complimentary admission ticket.

All complaint letters should be filed; subjects should be summarized and reported to the executive director weekly or immediately if a critical issue is involved. PR staff should insist that the museum take all reasonable steps consistent with its capabilities and professional standards to eliminate the situation that prompted the complaint.

VIP Visitors

One way to attract attention to the museum as an important institution is to encourage visits by notable people. This can be done by contacting area colleges and universities, chambers of commerce, theaters, and nightclubs to request that they incorporate visits to the museum into the itineraries of visiting VIPs. Another way is to send invitations to notables who have announced that they plan a trip to the area.

When a major government official intends to visit, you will need to consider many details.

1. Date, time, and method of arrival. If arrival is by motorcade, a local police escort and special parking space may be required. If arrival is by helicopter, special landing clearances and a site blocked off from the public may be needed.
2. Security. Do sections of the museum and the grounds have to be sealed off from the public? Are security clearances required for museum employees who will be working?
3. Press. Who is the museum's contact with the official's press aide? Will a press corps be accompanying the VIP, and if so, is a press room required? What are press room requirements, especially for telephones? How will local media that are not a part of the official press corps be accommodated while the VIP is at the museum? Will there be a press conference, and if so, how and by whom will it be managed? Unless you are authorized to do so, you should not arrange media interviews with the VIP. Never during a visit by a government official should you offer to arrange exclusive interviews. Rather, if there is no press conference, the media should be left on their own to secure interviews. Most reporters actually prefer to go their own way in such situations. If the museum wants photos of the visit for its own use, it should arrange for its own photographer.

4. Protocol. It is always appropriate to have the VIP greeted by the museum's executive director. A simple souvenir gift from the museum presented with a minimum of ceremony is usually appropriate.
5. The museum tour. Any advance information on the VIP's special interests is helpful. A foreign language guide may be required. Wherever possible, museum staff members and volunteers who are especially interested should be given assignments that will enable them at least to see the guest. Regular visitors should not be shunted off into a corner of the museum when the VIP arrives. If the visit is during regular hours and if the secret service requires that portions of the museum be closed, these facts should be made known to visitors that day before they purchase tickets.

The accommodation of a celebrity who may visit the museum while in the area to give a lecture or performance will not require all the special planning necessary for the major government official. It is critical, however, that one check with the celebrity's agent and be able to meet any special requirements before agreeing to act as the host.

Arranging Meetings

A public relations person may be asked to make arrangements for a meeting at the museum, perhaps an antiques forum or a travel writers' conference. One person, who may or may not be the museum public relations director, should be authorized to make major decisions and to coordinate plans.

When arranging for meetings, you should:

1. estimate attendance based on the number of people invited, and tentatively reserve hotel conference rooms and food services eight months to one year in advance;
2. check calendars to be sure other activities that will compete for attendance are not scheduled for the meeting days. Check with a few prospective participants to find out if the dates selected pose problems. Try to plan meetings for Mondays through Thursdays starting no earlier than 9:00 A.M. and concluding no later than 6:00 P.M.;
3. personally check the hotel. Will there be signs available to direct participants to the meetings and to welcome them at the entrance? Is the meeting room large enough for a suitable seating plan? Is

there space for coffee breaks? Are restrooms and telephones nearby? Is the room insulated against noise from adjoining rooms, properly lighted, equipped for audiovisual aids, and available early enough in the day to allow for adequate setup of equipment? Is hotel staff available if it will be required? What is the name of the person in charge of the room, and how may that person be contacted? Do not forget to arrange for the hotel bell captain to help you meet your participants' needs;

4. review lunch and dinner arrangements. Are spouses or guests to be invited? It is usually customary to include them if the activity is being described as social in nature. Is seating adequate, and can suitable tables be arranged? Are there enough servers? Who will be the person in charge? What is the location of the private bar, if one is required? Does the museum pay by the drink or by the bottle? Is the bar to have selected liquors or to be fully stocked? Will it include a nonalcoholic beverage? Where will the bar be located? Will hors d'oeuvres be served? How will gratuities for the bartender and parking lot attendants, as well as bills for food and other hotel services, be handled?

Six months before the meeting, registration forms with a return deadline and specifics on all costs should be sent to prospective participants. If the number of people who can be accommodated is limited, state in the form that registrations will be on a first come, first served basis and mention the maximum number who will be accommodated. Four months in advance, a followup registration form should be sent to all individuals who have not replied to the initial mailing. Three months before the conference, the lodging and food commitments should be made firm. Most hotels require 90 percent of monies forty-five days in advance unless credit has been established.

In addition to managing or assisting with advance registration, the public relations person may help oversee the smooth functioning of the meeting itself. This work could involve:

- providing press kits and arranging for a media room where reporters can talk with key meeting participants;
- helping make sure the needs of VIP speakers are met;
- arranging for the transportation, payment of honoraria, and general accommodation of VIP participants;
- preparing name tags. They should be printed in large letters so that they can be read easily and should include the person's affiliation.

All the members of the staff registering participants should be thoroughly briefed so that they can answer questions or can locate someone who is able to do so;

- preparing a printed program and perhaps a daily agenda to be available at each table along with glasses, water, pencils, and note pads;
- making food arrangements, not overlooking coffee breaks, cocktail receptions, and snacks in a hospitality room. Lunches and evening banquets may require that you designate head tables and supply table markers, place cards, and centerpieces.

Troubleshooting

Because museums depend upon their publics in many ways, there is the potential for problems in almost every aspect of day-to-day operations. You will be better prepared to cope with problems if you develop procedures for:

- diagnosing whether the problem is real or imagined, major or minor, urgent or long range;
- communicating urgent and serious problems to the executive director immediately and to other involved museum personnel and appropriate outside authorities as soon as possible;
- involving experienced and clear-thinking colleagues in making sure the problem is understood and in developing possible solutions;
- objectively examining solutions from public as well as museum perspectives and for consulting respected colleagues for their reactions.

Although one cannot inventory all the problems that are likely to develop in a year or even in a day, the following areas of operation are among those that should be monitored for their problem-causing potential.

Advocacy

That large museums particularly may be called upon to be advocates can create public relations problems. Bruce H. Evans of the Dayton, Ohio, Art Institute, observed:

The tours of blockbuster shows lent by governments with whom our own government was involved in delicate negotiations were foreign policy ma-

neuvers that benefited everyone. . . . by taking these exhibitions, we were
adding our voices to those of the government's diplomatic advocates. Sometimes, however, the use to which others would put us is less palatable. A
science museum that is offered an exhibit supporting the need to retain the
oil depletion allowance, for instance, should seriously question its involvement in the political arena.[1]

It is vital that the public relations person be aware of any advocacy
implications in the museum's public programs and that the programs
be evaluated from the perspective of how they relate to the museum's
purpose.

Collection Policies

In recent years the public has expressed strong and effective opposi-
tion to the deaccessioning by museums of collection artifacts. The
problem has been exacerbated when museums have failed to disclose
plans to deaccession major holdings only to have their actions later
publicized by the media and by special interest groups who suspect
that the museum wished to cover up its plans. For this reason the
public relations person should be certain that the museum has a collections management policy that remains sensitive to the institution's
public responsibilities.

Marie Malaro, assistant general counsel for the Smithsonian Institution, notes that a collections policy serves most importantly "as a
public statement of the museum's professional standards . . . with increased pressure on museums to account publicly for their decisions
and with renewed emphasis on the fiduciary obligations of trustees, a
museum may well find that the formulation of such a policy is not just a
prudent step, but an imperative one." Under some legal interpretations,
a museum as a charitable trust has certain obligations to the public.
"These obligations require that the trustees of the museum establish
policies concerning the acquisition of collection items, the disposal of
such items and the records that must be kept of such transactions,"
according to Malaro.[2]

Furthermore, a museum's publics are likely to believe that it does
not own its collections in the same way that a manufacturer owns its
inventory. In a sense, the public entrusts museums with the responsibility to preserve the treasures of its heritage. When artifacts that are
important to some publics are deaccessioned, the museum can be regarded as having violated that trust. Nevertheless, rising operating

costs are causing even major museums to produce revenue by selling collection items.

Sometimes disclosure of sensitive information about a collection is avoided because museum staffs fear ridicule by their peers. A museum's failure to release information may later backfire, however, if the media unearth the story and blow it out of proportion. The accidental accessioning of forgeries is a case in point. The decision not to release information about the forgeries, although seeming to protect the museum's prestige, may actually threaten it. Sooner or later media sleuths may discover the omission and will view their find as a big story partly from their sense that an attempt was made to conceal it. In addition, visitors may feel that the museum was attempting to delude them into regarding a collection artifact as something that it is not.

By releasing even information that is somewhat embarrassing, the museum will ultimately benefit. It will better succeed in maintaining its credibility with the media and its publics and will not have missed an important opportunity to express its point of view. It is sometimes even possible to have fun with a difficult story. An art museum once staged a preview opening of an exhibit of its forgeries complete with museum staff and friends posing as celebrities. In the media's coverage the novel appeal of the fraudulent celebrities at the gala affair far out-weighed any criticism of the museum for owning forgeries.

The protection of one's collections can also become a matter for public concern. Citizen groups can be aroused to action when the public believes that the museum is endangering a treasured artifact. When one art museum had planned to build a new stairway, citizens voiced concern that the construction would crack the wall on which an important mural was painted. The well-publicized criticism was so persuasive that the museum had no choice but to forgo its plans. It is the place of public relations to be certain the museum brings to bear on its problems a perspective that indicates awareness of public responsibilities and of the need to preserve goodwill.

Sensitive Situations

When the media cover sensitive situations, the public relations person should handle all calls and should answer questions fully and truthfully, making sure he or she represents the museum's position on the matter. Interviews should be set up promptly for reporters who ask to talk with museum people who are central to the story. However, matters involving problems with museum personnel or questions of ethical behavior on the part of the museum should be handled with caution, and legal counsel is advisable prior to release of any information or statement to the media.

Clearly, a "no comment" in response to a media query about a sensitive incident will damage the museum's credibility with the media and the public, will result in a story that omits the museum's position, and will increase the possibility that the incident will be treated inaccurately and sensationally. Although museums differ in what they consider to be proprietary information, common sense and good judgment should prevail in releasing information that the public has a right to know.

Crisis Communication

Shootings, fires, explosions, tornadoes, activists' demonstrations, and nearly all other types of emergencies or crises can beset a museum. Because the media monitor radio channels used by emergency vehicles, they arrive on the scene of trouble very quickly and expect the same kind of help from the museum that the museum expects from them when it wants to place a story.

To be sure that you will be prepared to deal effectively with a crisis, develop emergency plans and procedures.

1. Determine who the official museum spokespeople are in times of emergency, and the order in which they should be called to the museum if an emergency occurs during non-business hours. They are usually the public relations person, the executive director and the head of security, but others may be designated by these individuals. Opening and staffing the telephone switchboard is an important priority.

2. Guidelines for procedures at times of crisis should be distributed to all employees. They should indicate priorities for contacting key museum personnel and should list home and office telephone numbers. The executive director should be the first person to be contacted, followed by the public relations director and the switchboard operator. It is critical that all staff who have contact with the public be kept informed if the crisis occurs during visiting hours.

3. Construct a list of crises that might be most likely to occur at the museum. Note the first steps to be taken in each situation. For example, if an explosion injured several visitors, securing medical treatment would be the first priority. If there is continuing peril, such as a radioactive leak at a science museum, evacuation of the area might come first. If there are fatalities, do not release names of victims until families have been notified. This task is usually performed by police officers.

4. Establish with museum security, interpretation, ticket and switchboard personnel, and all other individuals in contact with visitors, the nature of their respective responsibilities at the time of a crisis. Although museum employees should not attempt to prevent reporters from talking with anyone, one or more staff members should be designated to answer questions. The switchboard operator should be instructed either to transfer calls to particular telephone lines or to answer questions using prepared statements. People handling telephone inquiries should be kept informed. The public relations person should also designate a museum staff member to stay with reporters.

5. Do not hide the facts if they are known, but avoid giving speculative answers to questions. All information should be verified before it is released and should have direct bearing on the situation. Delay discussing the extent of damage to specific artifacts until there has been time for the damage to be properly assessed. Do not estimate monetary loss or speculate as to the cause of an emergency. Do not offer the media any exclusive interviews or show any favoritism. Do permit reporters and photographers to tour damaged areas that are judged safe by authorities. The media should be accompanied by a museum representative on such occasions. Be patient and expect to repeat the same information many times for different reporters.

6. Be prepared to turn over to the media museum offices that have telephones and typewriters if the crisis is prolonged.

7. As soon as more complete information becomes available, it should be released to the media and to museum employees. It may be appropriate to send a special bulletin from the museum to publics most affected by the crisis (for example, collection donors might be notified in the case of a destructive fire). Emphasize the positive aspects such as a good fire and security record and plans for recovery.

Rumors

The first step in responding to rumors is to determine exactly what is being said. If the allegation is true, it should be confirmed and explained by a source with high credibility, usually the executive director. If it is not true, try to determine where the misinformation originated. Many rumors are prompted by delays in announcing changes that affect employees. Mistaken assumptions can be counteracted only with the correct information. It should be provided privately first to any persons who may have been damaged by the rumor and then to all employees, perhaps in a bulletin from the executive director. The best way to prevent rumors is to keep people as fully informed as possible on subjects with which they are personally involved.

The Rewards

Public relations is one of the most satisfying positions in museum management. For those who do not require being in the limelight, there is pleasure in being part of a smooth functioning team that is moving the museum toward its goals. There is perhaps less a sense of personal satisfaction from completing specific projects than there is a sense that you play a key role in charting a course that will help every museum department succeed. There are few other positions in museum management that offer a greater opportunity to make a difference in the museum's overall success.

Appendix

Appendix

THE EDISON INSTITUTE
Henry Ford Museum
& Greenfield Village

VISITOR INFORMATION SHEET

The Edison Institute is an independent, nonprofit, educational institution whose programs and activities are centered at Henry Ford Museum and Greenfield Village. The institute is supported primarily by admissions, revenues from visitor services and contributions, and is not connected with the Ford Motor Company or the Ford Foundation. The museum and village are open year-round, with the exception of Thanksgiving, Christmas and New Year's days.

HOURS

Museum — 9:00 A.M. to 5:00 P.M. daily
Village — 9:00 A.M. to 5:00 P.M. daily

ADMISSION
(Separate admissions are charged for the museum and village. Prices are subject to change.)

Museum — adults, $7.00; children 6 through 12, $3.50; children under 6, free; senior citizens, $5.50; group rates available
Village — adults, $7.00; children 6 through 12, $3.50; children under 6, free; senior citizens, $5.50; group rates available
Note: June 12 through Labor Day — adults, $8.00; children 6 through 12, $4.00; children under 6, free; senior citizens, $6.50; group rates available
Combination — A two-day unlimited admission ticket to the museum and village is available from June 12 through Labor Day: adults, $15.00; children 6 through 12, $7.50; senior citizens, $12.00

VILLAGE RIDES
(Additional charge, prices subject to change.)

Carriage Tours: mid-March through December (sleighs, weather permitting); narrated; $3.00
Suwanee Steamboat: daily, May through September; 75¢
Model T: daily, summer months; 75¢
Steam Train: April through September; adults, $1.50; children, $1.00
Carousel: May through September; 75¢

WHERE TO EAT
(Not all eating facilities operate daily.)

Museum — Heritage Hall: accessible to both museum and village visitors; first-floor cafeteria service; plate lunches, salads, sandwiches
Corner Cupboard: hot dogs, light refreshments
Village — Riverfront Restaurant at Suwanee Park: indoor; air-conditioned; cafeteria style; hot and cold sandwiches, salad plates, beer and wine
Eagle Tavern: indoor; air-conditioned; served lunches, snacks (full-service bar available)
Main Street Lunch Stand: outdoor; hamburgers, hot dogs, light refreshments
Covered Bridge Lunch Stand: outdoor; chicken, fish, hot dogs

BOOKS & SOUVENIRS

Visitors may shop for books, souvenirs, museum and village handcrafted objects and selected items from the Henry Ford Museum reproductions program at a number of locations. Income is used to further the institute's ongoing educational programs.

HOW TO FIND US

From eastbound I-94: Exit left lane to northbound Southfield (M-39); go 3 miles.
From westbound I-94: Exit right lane to northbound Oakwood; go 2 miles.
From northbound I-75: Exit right lane to northbound Southfield (M-39); go 8 miles.
From eastbound I-96: Exit left lane to I-696; go 15 miles and exit right lane to southbound Southfield (M-39); go 11 miles.
From Detroit Metropolitan Airport: Follow eastbound I-94; exit left lane to northbound Southfield (M-39); go 3 miles.
Amtrak connections to Detroit.

1. *A general fact sheet*

ADVANCE ON BRICK HOTEL OPENING

*Winterthur in Odessa adds third public facility
with the opening Sunday, May 24, 1981, of the
Brick Hotel Gallery of American Art containing
the Sewell C. Biggs Collection of nineteenth-century
paintings, furniture, and silver.*

FACTS

WINTERTHUR
MUSEUM AND GARDENS
WINTERTHUR, DELAWARE
19735

January 26, 1981

Site:
: The Brick Hotel is a restored 1822 building that once did serve as a hotel.

Collection:
: The Sewell C. Biggs Collection of nineteenth-century American paintings and Delaware Valley furniture and silver.

Opening:
: Sunday, May 24, 1981, as part of the fourth annual Corbit-Sharp House Festival, 1 - 4:30 p.m. Craft demonstrations, colonial cookery by students from St. Andrews School in Middletown, Delaware, entertainment, and tours. Adults $4.00; children 6-16 $2.00.

Winterthur in Odessa:
: Includes Corbit-Sharp House (1772), built by a wealthy Quaker tanner and furnished with many Corbit family pieces, and Wilson-Warner House (1769), containing many Delaware-made eighteenth and nineteenth-century pieces.

Tours:
: Regular tours of the Brick Hotel as part of Winterthur in Odessa begin Tuesday, May 26, 1981. Hours: Tues.-Sat. 10-4:30; Sun. 1-4:30. Closed Mons., January 1, July 4, Thanksgiving, and December 24 and 25. Prices as of May 26: adults $2.00 per building or $5.00 combination of all three; students over 12, senior citizens, and groups $1.50 or $3.75.

Donors:
: The late H. Rodney Sharp, of Sussex County, Delaware, restored the exterior of the Hotel and gave the building to Winterthur in 1966. Sewell C. Biggs, of Middletown, Delaware, donor of the collection. Heritage Conservation and Recreation Service of the U.S. Department of the Interior, a $130,400 matching grant-in-aid through the Delaware Division of Historical and Cultural Affairs. Kresge Foundation, $75,000 challenge grant for interior restoration. New Castle County Department of Community Development and Housing, $20,000 for removal of architectural barriers.

Odessa background:
: Formerly an important grain-shipping port on the Appoquinimink Creek, Odessa has retained its nineteenth-century atmosphere. Located on Route 13 halfway between Wilmington and Dover, Delaware.

CONTACT:
: Catherine Wheeler or Janice Clark, Public Relations Office, Winterthur, Delaware 19735 (302) 656-8591.

2. A fact sheet for a specific occasion

Henry Ford Museum
& Greenfield Village

Operated by:
The Edison Institute
Dearborn, Michigan 48121
(313) 271-1620

We hope your trip to Henry Ford Museum and Greenfield Village has been enjoyable.

In our continuing effort to provide our visitors with a worthwhile experience, we survey them on a regular basis during the year. Please spend a few minutes completing the enclosed form at your first opportunity and returning it to us in the postage-paid envelope provided. Only a small percentage of our visitors are chosen (at random) to participate in our surveys, so your response is important.

As a token of our appreciation for your help, we will send you a free souvenir upon receipt of your questionnaire. Thank you very much.

Sincerely,

J. Robert Dawson
Vice-President, Public Affairs
Henry Ford Museum & Greenfield Village

Enclosures

a nonprofit, educational institution

3. A visitor survey questionnaire with cover letter

1982 VISITOR QUESTIONNAIRE
Henry Ford Museum & Greenfield Village

Please
do not write
in this column

Please circle or fill in the appropriate answers. Thank you!

1. What day did you   ? _____ _____
                           MONTH   DAY   (1-4)

2. What is your home zip code? ___ ___ ___ ___ ___
   (if other than U.S. or Canada, indicate country)   (5-9)

3. Approximately how far (one way) is that from Dearborn?

0-50	miles	1.
51-100	"	2.
101-130	"	3.
151-200	"	4.
201-250	"	5.
Over 250	"	6.

   _____(10)

4. Have you ever visited here before? Yes 1. No 2.   _____(11)

   If yes, in what year was your last visit?   19___ ___   (12-13)

   If this year, how many times this year?   ___ ___   (14-15)

5. How many nights away from home did you spend on this trip?   Nights: ___ ___ (16-17)

6. Where did you stay the night before you visited? The night of your visit?

	NIGHT BEFORE	NIGHT OF
At home	☐ 1.	☐ 1.
Nearby hotel/motel (Detroit)	☐ 2.	☐ 2.
Nearby campground	☐ 3.	☐ 3.
Nearby friend or relative	☐ 4.	☐ 4.
Hotel/motel/campground, friend or relative more than 30 miles away.	☐ 5.	☐ 5.

   _____(18)_____(19)

7. How old is the head of your family or group on this visit?

18-24	1.
25-34	2.
35-44	3.
45-54	4.
55-64	5.
65+	6.

   _____(20)

8. How many people are with you today?   ___ ___ ___   (21-23)

9. In your immediate party, is there anyone: (Check all that apply)

Under 6	_____	(24)
6-11	_____	(25)
12-17	_____	(26)
18-24	_____	(27)
25-34	_____	(28)
35-44	_____	(29)
45-54	_____	(30)
55-64	_____	(31)
65+	_____	(32)

10. Which best describes the group you visited with?

Just our family	1.
Just with friends	2.
With family & friends	3.
By myself	4.

    _____(33)

11. Sex

Male	1.
Female	2.

    _____(34)

3. A visitor survey questionnaire with cover letter

Please
do not write
in this column

12. Is the head of your household:

Employed full time 1.   ____(35)
Employed part time 2.
Retired 3.
Student 4.
Housewife 5.
Unemployed 6.
Military 7.

13. Which best describes your total yearly family income?

Under $10,000 1.   ____(36)
$10,000-14,000 2.
$15,000-19,000 3.
$20,000-24,000 4.
$25,000-29,000 5.
$30,000-34,000 6.
$35,000 and over 7.

14. How many hours did you spend seeing each?

The Museum _____   ____(37)
The Village _____   ____(38)

15. What did you enjoy most about this visit?

_____   ____(39) ____(40)
_____
_____   ____(41) ____(42)

16. What did you enjoy least about this visit?

_____   ____(43) ____(44)
_____
_____   ____(45) ____(46)

17. Was the Museum and/or Village different from what you expected?

Yes 1.   ____(47)
No 2.

If yes, how was it different?

_____   ____(48) ____(49)
_____
_____   ____(50) ____(51)

18. Please rate each of these aspects on the following scale:

	EXCELLENT	GOOD	AVERAGE	FAIR	POOR	
1. The number of things to see	5 ☐	4 ☐	3 ☐	2 ☐	1 ☐	____(52)
2. Merchandise/shopping	5 ☐	4 ☐	3 ☐	2 ☐	1 ☐	____(53)
3. Employees	5 ☐	4 ☐	3 ☐	2 ☐	1 ☐	____(54)
4. The number of things to do	5 ☐	4 ☐	3 ☐	2 ☐	1 ☐	____(55)
5. Restaurants/food	5 ☐	4 ☐	3 ☐	2 ☐	1 ☐	____(56)
6. Adult enjoyment	5 ☐	4 ☐	3 ☐	2 ☐	1 ☐	____(57)
7. Teenagers' enjoyment	5 ☐	4 ☐	3 ☐	2 ☐	1 ☐	____(58)
8. Children's enjoyment	5 ☐	4 ☐	3 ☐	2 ☐	1 ☐	____(59)
9. Village admission fee	5 ☐	4 ☐	3 ☐	2 ☐	1 ☐	____(60)
10. Museum admission fee	5 ☐	4 ☐	3 ☐	2 ☐	1 ☐	____(61)
11. The rides	5 ☐	4 ☐	3 ☐	2 ☐	1 ☐	____(62)

3. A visitor survey questionnaire with cover letter

Please
do not write
in this column

19. How soon do you think you would be likely to revisit?

This summer	1.	_____ (63)
Later this year	2.	
Next year	3.	
In a couple of years	4.	
Probably never	5.	

20. Did you know about the Museum and Village before you left home.

Yes	1.	_____ (64)
No	2.	

21. Did anyone recommend you visit or not visit?

Yes, visit	1.	_____ (65)
Don't visit	2.	
No recommendation	3.	

22. Why did you decide to visit?

_____   _____ (66) _____ (67)

_____   _____ (68) _____ (69)

23. Have you seen or heard any advertising about the Museum and Village recently?

Yes	1.	_____ (70)
No	2.	

If yes, what was it about?

_____   _____ (71) _____ (72)

_____   _____ (73) _____ (74)

24. How appealing do you feel each of these aspects of the Museum and Village are?

	APPEALING		UNAPPEALING		LIKED	
	VERY	SOMEWHAT	VERY	SOMEWHAT	*BEST	
1. All the buildings	4 ☐	3 ☐	2 ☐	1 ☐	☐ 1.	_____ (75)
2. The famous Americans represented	4 ☐	3 ☐	2 ☐	1 ☐	☐ 2.	_____ (76)
3. The cars, trains, and planes	4 ☐	3 ☐	2 ☐	1 ☐	☐ 3.	_____ (77)
4. Operating shops	4 ☐	3 ☐	2 ☐	1 ☐	☐ 4.	_____ (78)
5. Craft demonstrations	4 ☐	3 ☐	2 ☐	1 ☐	☐ 5.	_____ (79)
6. The rides, train, boat	4 ☐	3 ☐	2 ☐	1 ☐	☐ 6.	_____ (80)
7. Furnishings, glassware	4 ☐	3 ☐	2 ☐	1 ☐	☐ 7.	_____ (81)
8. Tours	4 ☐	3 ☐	2 ☐	1 ☐	☐ 8.	_____ (82)

*CHECK WHICH YOU LIKED THE BEST   _____ (83)

Thank you very much for your help. To receive your complimentary souvenir, please print your name and address below, and return the completed questionnaire in the self-addressed, postage-paid envelope.

NAME _____ ADDRESS _____

CITY _____ STATE _____ ZIP CODE _____

SU82

3. *A visitor survey questionnaire with cover letter*

196

PROOFREADERS' MARKS

OPERATIONAL SIGNS

ℐ	Delete
◡	Close up; delete space
ℐ	Delete and close up
#	Insert space
eq #	Make space between words equal; make leading between lines equal
hr #	Insert hair space
ls	Letterspace
¶	Begin new paragraph
no ¶	Run paragraphs together
□	Move type one em from left or right
⏋	Move right
⌐	Move left
⏋⌐	Center
⊓	Move up
⊔	Move down
=	Straighten type; align horizontally
‖	Align vertically
tr	Transpose
(sp)	Spell out
stet	Let it stand
⌄	Push down type

TYPOGRAPHICAL SIGNS

lc	Lowercase capital letter
cap	Capitalize lowercase letter
sc	Set in small capitals
ital	Set in italic type
rom	Set in roman type
bf	Set in boldface type
wf	Wrong font; set in correct type
X	Reset broken letter
⊙	Reverse (type upside down)

PUNCTUATION MARKS

⌃	Insert comma
⌄	Insert apostrophe (or single quotation mark)
⟨⟨ ⟩⟩	Insert quotation marks
⊙	Insert period
(int)?	Insert question mark
;|	Insert semicolon
:|	Insert colon
|=|	Insert hyphen
¦M	Insert em dash
¦N	Insert en dash

4. *Proofreaders' marks.* Source: A Manual of Style, *12th Edition, p. 72, The University of Chicago Press,* © 1969 by The University of Chicago.

THE EDISON INSTITUTE
Henry Ford Museum
& Greenfield Village

Events Calendar

Office of Public Relations, P.O. Box 1970, Dearborn, Michigan 48121, (313) 271-1620

Nov. 8 - Nov. 21

ACTIVITIES AND EVENTS (First listing)

Nov. 19

FAMILY THANKSGIVING GATHERING
The rich traditions of the first Thanksgiving
are explored in this holiday program that includes special crafts. FRIDAY EVENING
6:00 - 10:00 p.m. Admission $5.00 per person. ADVANCED REGISTRATION REQUIRED AND
LIMITED.
PLACE: GREENFIELD VILLAGE.

Nov. 20

SATURDAY EVENING CONCERT - CLARINO & CANTO
Henry and Victoria Meredith perform music
for voice and early trumpet. 8:00 p.m. Admission $3.
PLACE: HENRY FORD MUSEUM THEATER.

Through Dec. 3

FORD TOUR
A 45 minute tour stressing Henry Ford's
preservation efforts and a look at the man as historian and educator.
PLACE: GREENFIELD VILLAGE-TOWN HALL. NO ADDITIONAL CHARGE BEYOND VILLAGE ADMISSION.

Through Dec. 3

EDISON TOUR
A 45 minute tour focusing on Thomas Alva Edison
the man and his influence on the world of invention and technological change that thrust
America into the modern era.
PLACE: GREENFIELD VILLAGE-TOWN HALL. NO ADDITIONAL CHARGE BEYOND VILLAGE ADMISSION.

Through Dec. 3

DOMESTIC LIFE
A 45 minute tour showing the domestic modern-
ization of shelter, family, food and clothing. Shown through comparisons of homes from
the 17th C. to the late 19th C.
PLACE: GREENFIELD VILLAGE-TOWN HALL. NO ADDITIONAL CHARGE BEYOND VILLAGE ADMISSION.

ACTIVITIES AND EVENTS (Listed in previous calendar)

5. A calendar

198

Through Nov. 13
Fridays and Saturdays
Thursdays, Nov. 4 & 11   THE BAT
                                          A comedy thriller set in a summer home that
seems to be haunted. The audience is given clues to help solve the mystery. Admission
$4.75. Curtain 8:30 p.m.
PLACE: HENRY FORD MUSEUM THEATER.

     Same dates   DINNER/THEATER
                                         Dinner at Heritage Hall followed by a
performance of "The Bat." Reservations required. Optional cocktails at 6:30 p.m.
Dinner at 7 p.m. Cost $16.50.
PLACE: HERITAGE HALL AND HENRY FORD MUSEUM THEATER.

     Continuing   FROM FIELD TO TABLE
                                         A half-hour tour and demonstration of a selected
group of kitchen implements and agricultural devices to explain changes in how food was
obtained, prepared and preserved from the later 18th to the early 20th century.
PLACE: HENRY FORD MUSEUM. NO ADDITIONAL CHARGE BEYOND MUSEUM ADMISSION.

     Continuing   STEAM ENGINES IN ACTION
                                         A tour of the power and machinery collection
with demonstrations of several steam powered machines and selected steam engines.
PLACE: HENRY FORD MUSEUM. NO ADDITIONAL CHARGE BEYOND MUSEUM ADMISSION.

     Continuing   FROM CANDLE TO LIGHT BULB
                                         A demonstration of six different kinds of
lighting devices and a continuous demonstration of candle molding.
PLACE: HENRY FORD MUSEUM. NO ADDITIONAL CHARGE BEYOND MUSEUM ADMISSION.

               * * * * * * * * * * * * * *

HENRY FORD MUSEUM is a 12 acre museum with major collections in Transportation, Power,
     Agriculture, Lighting, Communications and Home Arts. Museum hours are 9 a.m. to
     5 p.m. daily.

GREENFIELD VILLAGE is an open-air museum separate from but adjacent to Henry Ford
     Museum. Historic buildings tell the story of America's transformation from an
     agricultural society to an industrial society. Village hours are 9 a.m. to
     5 p.m. daily.

ADMISSIONS for the village and museum are separate. Adults, $7; children 6-12, $3.50;
     senior citizens over 62, $5.50; children under six and Members of Museum and
     Village free.

                              - 30 -

          HENRY FORD MUSEUM AND GREENFIELD VILLAGE ARE PART OF THE EDISON
          INSTITUTE, A NONPROFIT EDUCATIONAL INSTITUTION.

101582 RM PRM, E2, E3, A4, M2, O1, O2, O3, O1A, I1, OC1, OC2, CAL (814)

                              199

Henry Ford Museum & Greenfield Village
FillerStuff
OCTOBER

Henry Ford Museum and Greenfield Village are incorporated as The Edison Institute, a nonprofit, educational institution.

It's no secret that Ford and Edison enlightened the world. Hope you find our "stuff" enlightening.

Office of Public Relations, Greenfield Village and Henry Ford Museum, Dearborn, Michigan, 48121 (313) 271-1620.

Automated Elbow Grease

The rotary washing machine was patented long before such machines were electric. Hamilton Erastus Smith gained a patent for a device which used a hand crank, causing a perforated cylinder within a wooden shell to revolve, turning and washing clothes at the same time. The many fascinations of early domestic living are part of the lure at Henry Ford Museum in Dearborn, Mich., which houses a wide array of household helpers in its collections, including a c.1860 "Standard Perfection" rocker type washing machine and a c.1899 "Boss" washer.

****

Magazine Misses Mark

The Literary Digest, a prominent publication at the turn of the century, proudly proclaimed in its October, 1899, issue that the horseless carriage would never become as popular as the bicycle. Anyone who strolls through the Transportation Collection of Henry Ford Museum, Dearborn, Mich., with its exhibit of some 180 automobiles, 40 bicycles, 22 motorcycles, 80 horse-drawn vehicles, 12 locomotives and 20 aircraft can discover the rapid and popular growth of that "unlikely mode of transportation."

****

Noah Counting of the Future

On October 16, 1758, Noah Webster began his 85 years on earth. As time passed the teacher, patriot, journalist, lecturer, lawyer, legislator and author managed to make a

- more -

6. A filler release

200

mark for himself few men can match. Webster is most remembered for his American Dictionary of the American Language, a work which took him 20 years to complete. The home where Webster completed his famous volume is now part of the collection of historic structures which make up Greenfield Village, Dearborn, Mich.

****

Tin Lizzie Launched

The Tin Lizzie, officially called the Ford Model T, began its illustrious career on October 1, 1908. Designed by Henry Ford for the common man, the Lizzie was undisputed queen of the highways for 20 years. Henry Ford Museum, Dearborn, Mich., offers both one of the first Model Ts and the 15 millionth model as part of its extensive transportation collection.

****

Hear, Hear

Dr. Lee DeForest became the father of the radio industry on October 25, 1906, when he filed his patent for a three-element vacuum radio tube. The tube, with a filament and two plate electrodes, made it possible to amplify sound, making radio broadcasts feasible. An example of the 1906 audion tube, as it was finally called, is on exhibit in the Communications Collection of Henry Ford Museum, Dearborn, Mich.

****

A Pneu Idea

While the name never caught on, John S. Thurman of St. Louis, Mo., presented the world with a good invention when he introduced his "Pneumatic carpet renovator" on October 3, 1899. Thurman's appliance was one of the earliest motor-driven vacuum cleaners. Examples of hand- and electric-powered cleaners, including a 1908 Hoover and a c.1910 Eureka Model 1, are a small part of the vast Home Arts Collection on exhibit in Henry Ford Museum, Dearborn, Mich.

-30-

HENRY FORD MUSEUM AND GREENFIELD VILLAGE ARE PART OF THE EDISON
INSTITUTE, A NONPROFIT EDUCATIONAL INSTITUTION.

083181 DEW PRM, E2, A4, M2, O1, O2, O3, O1A, OC1, OC2, ATM, ATE, E3, TW1, I1 (1232)

Williamsburg Can Be Fast Method To Learn History

By RICK SYLVAIN
Knight-Ridder Newspapers

WILLIAMSBURG, Va. — With all due respect to Sister Thomas (Mad Dog) Anine — my old high school history teacher — this beats any American History class you ever taught.

Remember all those chapters you force-fed us? History here is living, breathing, easygoing — and there's no test in the end.

George Washington and Thomas Jefferson could walk down Duke of Gloucester Street and not notice anything amiss. It's all just as they left it.

You spoke of the good old days. Well, Colonial Williamsburg makes no illusions about the way we were. Life in 18th-century America was hardship and drudgery.

Duke of Gloucester Street was a summer-long dust storm. Carriages jounced up and down its length, a measured mile. Whether you were headed for the Capitol to watch Patrick Henry rail against Britain's stamp tax or pointed in the opposite direction, to the College of William and Mary, where Jefferson studied, it was a bone-jarring ride. In winter, Duke of Gloucester was a river of mud.

Justice was uncompromising in those days. A guilty verdict usually meant the gallows. Taxpayers weren't about to fund a prison term in the gaol. Miscreants spent the night on a bed of straw and were hanging by their necks by daybreak. Petty criminals faced humiliation in the pillories and stocks.

Road-weary travelers at the Raleigh Tavern slept on a rope bed next to a big pitch-lined water bucket in case of fire. They brought their own sheets in a saddlebag. Bed linen was never changed unless someone soiled it. George Washington probably slept here, but he hated himself in the morning.

This small tidewater city was its capital. It was here where the ideals of a new nation were shaped.

I've always considered Williamsburg a sort of lived-in Greenfield Village. Outwardly, they bear an uncanny resemblance. Meticulously kept houses, shops and buildings line shady streets. There are greens and gardens by the acre. Horse-drawn carriages jingle past. Costumed hosts and hostesses are there interpreting history and artisans recreate ancient trades.

The rub is that Williamsburg was Williamsburg 200 years ago. History wasn't moved here; it was written here in the houses, shops, taverns, public buildings and dependencies of the historic area. Most are lived in today. Nearly 90 of the 18th- and early 19th-century buildings are original, on their original sites.

So history-minded are the homeowners that they keep things like mailboxes and air conditioners unobtrusive. You won't find a metal lawn chair in the place.

Today's visitors to Williamsburg can immerse themselves in the past; Williamsburg is arguably the finest living portrait of colonial America we have. Fall is an excellent time to visit, when color floods the town and the plantation-studded countryside, yet temperatures remain warm. Crowds aren't that diminished; schoolchildren begin coming in their colonial school buses.

This was a fairly sleepy tidewater town until 1926, when John D. Rockefeller Jr. poured $68 million into its restoration. He and his wife resided in Bassett Hall, a lavishly furnished 18th-century homestead on Francis Street surrounded by rolling woodlands.

A good entree to Williamsburg is the main Information Center. A film is shown daily from 8:45 a.m. to 6:05 p.m. and they can supply maps and brochures.

Far from a poverty pocket, Williamsburg was a fashionable address. At one time it was Britain's wealthiest colony.

Reflecting that elegance are the two buildings most popular with tourists, the Governor's Palace and the Capitol.

Visitors to the Palace are greeted by a footman in livery and taken through the mansion as if calling on Baron de Botetourt himself, one of seven royal governors to live here. A stirring speech is given by Botetout's clerk of council in an antechamber.

7. A sample feature story

A possible feature...

Who: Greenfield Village

What: Old Car Festival

When: September 11 and 12, 1982

Where: Greenfield Village Activities Field and Green

Why: To show automobiles dating from 1925 and <u>before</u>,
                in operation. To illustrate early development
                of automobiles.

How: More than 300 cars in prime running condition,
                featured in colorful displays, parades, and
                contests.

                Riding of turn-of-the-century bicycles by
                The Wheelmen.

                For the first time at Old Car Festival:

                    Exhibit of early gas pumps and other gas
                    station paraphernalia.

                    Judging of commercial vehicles.

                    Early motorcycles.

                    Exhibit on the early history of Oldsmobile,
                    marking 85th anniversary this year of that
                    automaker.

Your coverage is invited. For assistance, please call Jan Sherbin,
(313) 271-1620, ext. 360.

Contact: Office of Public Relations, (313) 271-1620
THE EDISON INSTITUTE
An independent, nonprofit, educational institution whose programs and activities are centered at
Henry Ford Museum & Greenfield Village

8. *A possible feature release*

THE EDISON INSTITUTE
Henry Ford Museum
& Greenfield Village

P.O. Box 1970   Dearborn, Michigan 48121
(313) 271-1620

DEARBORN, Mich. — Henry Ford Museum and Greenfield Village form the most visited indoor-outdoor history museum complex in North America. The museums located on a 260 acre site, complement each other in telling the story of America's transformation from a traditional rural society to a modern industrial society.

Founded by Henry Ford in 1929 and operated by the non-profit Edison Institute, the museum and village are not connected with or supported by the Ford Motor Company or the Ford Foundation.

Officially opened Oct. 21, 1929 on the 50th anniversary of Thomas Edison's invention of the incandescent light bulb, the complex includes a restoration of Edison's Menlo Park Laboratory. This group of buildings, moved from New Jersey, was the site of many famous inventions by Edison and his associates including the light bulb, the carbon telephone transmitter and the phonograph. It was one of the world's first research and development laboratories.

The village and museum exhibit buildings and objects covering over 300 years of history, but the greatest concentration is in the period from 1800 to 1950 when sweeping changes helped shape life in America as it is known today.

Highlights of Greenfield Village include the Wright Cycle Shop where Orville and Wilbur Wright planned and made parts for the first successful airplane; Henry Ford's birthplace, a typical 19th century Midwest farmhouse where the famous industrialist lived until early manhood; Noah Webster's house where the famous journalist and lexicographer finished his innovative dictionary; the Logan County Courthouse where Abraham Lincoln was a circuit riding attorney; and several steam-operated "industries" including a gristmill, printing shop and sawmill. A major project over the next few years at the village will be the reactivation of the Armington and Sims Machine Shop to show the operation of a 19th century machine shop and foundry.

While the village shows the setting and the processes by which the nation became industrialized, the museum shows the tools and products of that industrialization. It contains major collections in transportation, lighting and communications, power and shop machinery, agriculture, and the domestic and decorative arts.

Highlights in the Museum include the 600 ton Lima "Allegheny" coal-burning locomotive; an 1896 Duryea Motor Wagon, the first manufactured American automobile; Richard Byrd's 1925 Fokker Trimotor, first to fly over the North Pole; a 1938 Massey-Harris combine, one of the first to be self-propelled; an 1855 Corliss Conversion steam engine, possibly the oldest surviving Corliss engine; a collection of hundreds of light bulbs showing the search for a long burning filament; numerous examples of presses, radios, telephones, telegraphs and office machines; cooking implements; stoves and numerous early sewing machines.

The museum also has outstanding collections of fine furniture, silver, ceramics, glassware, and musical instruments.

In addition to the collections in the museum and village, The Edison Institute operates educational programs for adults, children and school groups.

Admission to the village and museum are separate. In the summer admission to the village is $8 for adults, $4 for children 6-12, and $6.50 for senior citizens 62 and older. The admission to the museum all year and to the village except in summer is $7 for adults, $3.50 for children 6-12 and $5.50 for senior citizens. Children under six are always admitted free. Hours are 9:00 a.m. to 5:00 p.m. daily.

9. A general backgrounder

204

THE EDISON INSTITUTE
Henry Ford Museum
& Greenfield Village

News

Office of Public Relations, P.O. Box 1970, Dearborn, Michigan 48121, (313) 271-1620

HENRY FORD MUSEUM AND GREENFIELD VILLAGE

BICYCLE COLLECTION

DEARBORN, Mich. -- Exhibited in Henry Ford Museum are machines that illustrate every stage in the evolution of the bicycle. In adjacent Greenfield Village is the original Wright brothers bicycle shop, where they did aircraft research and constructed their first airplane.

The first form of personal transportation to be widely available, the bicycle had its beginnings in Germany in 1818 when Baron Karl von Drais developed a device that could be ridden by straddling a wood backbone while thrusting against the ground with one's feet in a skating motion. Produced in small numbers, these crude machines, called hobby horses, are seldom seen today. The Museum's C 1818 hobby horse is embellished with a carved bird head at the front and heart-shaped cut-outs in the solid wood wheels.

It was not until 1863 in the Paris, France workshop of Pierre Michaux that cranks were added to the front wheel of a hobby horse, creating a bicycle that could be balanced and ridden without touching the ground. The Museum's C 1870 Pickering is a particularly fine example of the craftsmanship and attention to detail that was lavished on American boneshakers, most of which were built by carriage makers.

In England in the early 1870s, a bicycle with large front and small rear wheels was created to increase the speed and distance attained through each pedal revolution. It caught on quickly and was in common use by cyclists from 1880 to 1890. Because it was the most widely used type of bicycle, it was referred to as the

- MORE -

10. *A backgrounder on a specific subject*

205

"ordinary" to distinguish it from a group of uniquely designed bicycles called "safeties."

An 1878 British Singer #2 is the earliest ordinary in the Museum exhibit. It has wood spoke wheels, iron tires and a heavy solid frame. An 1884 Columbia Light Roadster is the same model as one ridden across America and around the world in 1884 and 1885 by Thomas Stevens of Denver.

Foremost among American bicycle innovations on exhibit is the Star, one of a group of bicycles described as safeties that were designed to prevent the hapless rider from taking a header over the handlebar, which was a constant risk when riding the ordinary. The Museum's 1886 Star Light Roadster has the large wheel in the rear and the small wheel in the front, making it impossible for the machine to pitch forward.

Other high-wheel safeties exhibited include an 1880 Singer Xtraordinary, which positioned the rider toward the rear of the bicycle and was driven through a series of levers; an 1885 Kangaroo, which utilizes chains and sprockets to accommodate a low riding position; and an 1888 Springfield Roadster, which positions the rider's weight toward the back of the bicycle and is driven through a ratchet mechanism.

With the application of chains and sprockets, a large wheel became unnecessary with the result that a bicycle similar to today's, with equally sized front and rear wheels, evolved. The Museum's 1889 Columbia Light Roadster was one of the first bicycles of this type to be popularized by an American manufacturer.

The collection further illustrates the evolution of the bicycle with such examples as an 1896 Punnett Companion, whose two riders were seated side-by-side; an 1897 Bamboo Safety, with frame made from bamboo stalks; an 1897 Chilion, with a hickory wood frame; an 1897 Rambler tandem, on which the lady was seated at the front but both handlebars steered and a 1900 Tribune Blue Streak that was raced by Barney Oldfield.

- MORE -

10. *A backgrounder on a specific subject*

Among the favorites with visitors are an <u>1885 Rudge Rotary</u> adult tricycle, the first commercially successful adult machine designed for women; an <u>1896 Orient "Oriten"</u> promotional bicycle for ten riders and a nostalgia-evoking <u>1951 Schwinn Black Phantom</u>.

An exhibit case displays a miniature <u>1869 Topliff & Ely</u> boneshaker built for General Tom Thumb and early bicycle accessories and memorabilia.

Altogether the 52 bicycles and tricycles exhibited at the Museum Interpretive Center, the Museum Transportation Collection and the Wright Cycle Shop constitute the nation's most comprehensive museum presentation on cycling history.

- 30 -

HENRY FORD MUSEUM AND GREENFIELD VILLAGE ARE INCORPORATED AS THE EDISON INSTITUTE, A NON-PROFIT EDUCATIONAL INSTITUTION.

052280 GDA

THE EDISON INSTITUTE
Henry Ford Museum & Greenfield Village
Nº 404
20900 Oakwood Boulevard • Dearborn, Michigan 48121 • (313) 271-1620

PHOTOGRAPHIC ORDER/LETTER OF AGREEMENT

Permission is hereby requested for photographs of the following items from the Edison Institute collections. Permission is granted in accordance with the conditions listed on the verso of this sheet. These conditions are approved and agreed to by the applicant. ANY VIOLATION OF THESE CONDITIONS MAY RESULT IN DENIAL OF FURTHER SERVICE AND/OR LEGAL ACTION.

Please complete the following items and forward the statement, along with your check made payable to "The Edison Institute," to Archives/Library, The Edison Institute, Henry Ford Museum & Greenfield Village, Dearborn, Michigan 48121.

IDENTIFICATION:

Name/Company: _____ Telephone: (____)_____

Address: _____
                    Street   City   State   Zip

REQUEST:

The following photographs are needed by _____
                                                                        Date

Neg. No.	Acc. No.	Description/Subject	Size/Type	Cost

Subtotal: _____
Postage & Handling: _____
4% Sales Tax (Mich. residents/businesses only): _____
TOTAL: _____

THESE PHOTOGRAPHS ARE TO BE USED FOR:

☐ Book/Periodical: _____
                                                    Title

_____
Name of Publisher   Date of Publication

☐ Film: _____
                    Project/Title   Date of Release

☐ Other: _____

Upon receipt of the FOUR completed order forms, your order will be processed. The conditions that appear on the verso of this form, including providing The Edison Institute with one complimentary file copy of any published work as stated in Condition #3, are approved and agreed to by:

_____ on _____
Applicant's Signature   Title   Date

PERMISSION AUTHORIZED BY: _____
                                                                                            Date

NOTICE: WARNING CONCERNING COPYRIGHT RESTRICTIONS

The copyright law of the United States (Title 17, U.S. Code) governs the making of photocopies or other reproductions of copyrighted material. Under certain conditions specified in the law, libraries and archives are authorized to furnish a photocopy or other reproduction. One of these specified conditions is that the photocopy or reproduction is not to be "used for any purpose other than private study, scholarship, or research." If a user makes a request for, or later uses, a photocopy or reproduction for purposes in excess of "fair use," that user may be liable for copyright infringement. This institution reserves the right to refuse to accept a copying order if, in its judgment, fulfillment of the order would involve violation of the copyright law.

(Aug. 1981)   Archives/Collections

11. Photographic order/letter of agreement

Society of
American Travel Writers
JUNE 12, 1979
DEARBORN/DETROIT

Thursday, June 7

9 a.m.-10 p.m.	Registration, throughout the day, Dearborn Inn.
6:00-8:00 p.m.	Welcome buffet, Dearborn Inn.
9:45 p.m.	Buses depart Dearborn Inn for Hyatt Regency. Reserved seats at db's for "Soupy Sales" show. Host Hyatt Regency.
11:45 p.m.	Buses depart Hyatt Regency for Dearborn Inn. Shuttle bus will be used until 2:00 a.m. for those who linger.

Friday, June 8

8:30 a.m.	Breakfast at Dearborn Inn sponsored by Dearborn Chamber of Commerce.
10:15 a.m.	Buses depart Dearborn Inn for Henry Ford Museum. Guided tour.
12:45 p.m.	Buses depart Henry Ford Museum for Dearborn Inn—cocktail reception and lunch.
2:45 p.m.	Buses depart for Ford Motor Co. Rouge Plant Tour.
4:00 p.m.	Buses from Rouge Plant to Greenfield Village.
4:15 p.m.	Guided tours Greenfield Village.
6:00 p.m.	Picnic dinner, carriages, riverboat, train operating. Menlo Park Laboratory, Sarah Jordan Boarding House, Saltbox House, Cotswold Cottage, Burbank and Webster houses remain open.
8:45 p.m.	Buses depart Greenfield Village for Dearborn Inn.
9:30 p.m.	Hospitality Suite opens, Dearborn Inn. (check lobby information board)

Saturday, June 9

8:15 a.m.	Buses depart Dearborn Inn for Hyatt Regency.
8:30 a.m.	Breakfast hosted by Hyatt Regency.
9:30 a.m.	SATW Central States and Canadian business meetings—Hyatt Regency.
9:30 a.m.	Travel by people mover to Fairlane Town Center for those not attending business sessions.
10:30 a.m.	General session—Speaker Robert Holland, deputy director, U.S. Dept. of Transportation.
11:30 a.m.	Half hour tour of Hyatt Regency complex.
12:00 noon	Buses depart Hyatt Regency for Fair Lane Mansion.
12:45 p.m.	Lunch and tour hosted by U. of M. at Fair Lane Mansion.
3:15 p.m.	Buses depart for Dearborn Inn.
3:15 p.m.	Buses depart for those wishing to visit Fairlane Town Center.
4:30 p.m.	Buses depart Fairlane Town Center for Dearborn Inn.
6:00 p.m.	Buses depart for Meadow Brook Hall.
7:00 p.m.	Candlelight reception and dinner hosted at and by Meadow Brook Hall.
10:00 p.m.	Buses return to Dearborn Inn.
11:00 p.m.	Hospitality Suite opens.

Sunday, June 10

8:30 a.m.	Breakfast at Dearborn Inn.
9:30-10:45 a.m.	Check out of Dearborn Inn (see information sheet in convention packet).
10:45 a.m.	Depart for tour of Cranbrook House and Gardens.

12. Travel writers' conference program

209

12:00 noon	Brunch hosted by Cranbrook House and Gardens.
1:15 p.m.	(A) Buses depart to Detroit for those attending Post-Convention activities.
	(B) Buses depart for Dearborn Inn. Airport service will be provided from Dearborn Inn when needed. (See information sheet in convention packet.)
1:30-2:30 p.m.	Check in Detroit Plaza. Society of American Travel Writers program participants will be pre-registered. Metropolitan Detroit Convention and Visitors Bureau and Detroit Plaza staff will greet SATW members in lobby.
3:00-5:30 p.m.	Philip A. Hart Plaza-German Ethnic Festival. SATW members will assemble in hotel lobby to be escorted to Festival area.

SPECIAL NOTE

	DETROIT PLAZA REPRESENTATIVES WILL BE AVAILABLE FROM 1:30-2:45 P.M. AND 4:15-6:00 P.M. IN THE LOBBY TO ESCORT SATW MEMBERS ON TOURS OF THE HOTEL AND RENAISSANCE CENTER, **ON REQUEST**.
6:30-8:00 p.m.	Reception and welcome at the Manoogian Mansion, official residence of Detroit's Mayor, the Hon. Coleman A. Young. Buses will depart from Plaza main entrance.
8:15-10:30 p.m.	Radisson Cadillac Hotel-Reception and dinner.
10:45-1:30 a.m.	Detroit Plaza-Metropolitan Detroit Convention and Visitors Bureau Hospitality Suite open for Nite Caps.

Monday, June 11

8:15 a.m.	Depart from Detroit Plaza main entrance via bus to Eastern (Farmers) Market area.
8:45 a.m.	Push Cart Cafe-Breakfast hosted by Metropolitan Detroit Convention and Visitors Bureau and Southeast Michigan Travel and Tourist Association.
10:00 a.m.	Walking Tour-Eastern Market. Buses depart from Push Cart Cafe at 10:50 a.m.
11:00 a.m.	Guided tour of Belle Isle attractions; Nature Center, Children's Zoo and Safari, Conservatory and other features.
1:00 p.m.	Dossin Great Lakes Museum Luncheon hosted by Great Lakes Maritime Institute and Detroit Historical Society.
2:30 p.m.	Reception and tour of Windsor area hosted by Tourist and Convention Bureau of Windsor and Essex County.
6:15 p.m.	Depart from Detroit Plaza by bus for Pontchartrain Hotel to attend P'Jazz featuring Ray Charles, hosted by Hotel Pontchartrain and C.A. Muer Corporation.
8:15 p.m.	Informal walking tour of Greektown hosted by Americal Development Corporation and area merchants. Return to Plaza whenever convenient.

Tuesday, June 12

8:30 a.m.	Depart from Detroit Plaza for bus tour of Downtown and New Center area.
9:45 a.m.	Detroit Institute of Arts—"Brunch with Bach," hosted by Detroit Renaissance, Inc.
11:00 a.m.	Walking tour of Cultural Center; Art Institute, Historical Museum, Main Library and Science Museum. Buses depart Art Institute at 12:50 p.m.
1:00 p.m.	Royal Eagle, Indian Village—Luncheon hosted by North Central Airlines.
2:45 p.m.	Return to Detroit Plaza Hotel. Program concludes.

12. Travel writers' conference program

MAIL THIS REGISTRATION FORM BY WEDNESDAY, APRIL 11

REGISTRATION DEADLINE MONDAY, APRIL 16

ACTIVES AND ASSOCIATES REGISTRATION
SOCIETY OF AMERICAN TRAVEL WRITERS
GREENFIELD VILLAGE CONFERENCE & DETROIT POST-CONFERENCE
June 7 to June 12, 1979

IMPORTANT: Please note, registration for both the
Dearborn Conference and the Detroit
post-conference is by this sheet.

GREENFIELD VILLAGE JUNE 7 to JUNE 10

Please guarantee a _____ single
_____ double room accommodation at the Dearborn Inn

Expected arrival time _____ date _____   I will be driving _____
Flying into Detroit _____

(We encourage you to arrive early June 7 if you
would like additional time at Greenfield Village
and Henry Ford Museum)

Expected departure time _____ date _____

DETROIT POST-CONFERENCE JUNE 10 to JUNE 12

Please guarantee a _____ single
_____ double at the Plaza Hotel in Renaissance Center

Expected departure time _____ date _____

IMPORTANT: PLEASE NOTE:

WESTERN CHAPTER – We suggest you check special air rates. For example in April United
offers a 25% discount off regular week night rates. If you can stay
in Detroit two extra days, you can use the 7 day super saver week
night rates of $186.00 from Seattle, $189.00 from Los Angeles and
$197.00 from San Francisco.

CHICAGO AREA   – If available I would be interested in a discounted group package on
Amtrak departing Chicago June 7 returning from Detroit June 10 _____.

Name, and name of person accompanying you, if any _____

Address _____ _____ Telephone days _____
City, State, Zip _____ _____

13. *Travel writers' conference registration form*

THE EDISON INSTITUTE
Henry Ford Museum
& Greenfield Village

P.O. Box 1970   Dearborn, Michigan 48121
(313) 271-1620

IT'S OUR 50TH ANNIVERSARY

AND WE'VE GOT

50 STORIES (AND LOTS MORE) FOR YOU!

JOINT CONFERENCE CENTRAL STATES, WESTERN AND CANADIAN CHAPTERS

SOCIETY OF AMERICAN TRAVEL WRITERS

REGISTRATION DEADLINE MONDAY, APRIL 16

June 7

Registration beginning 8:00 p.m.

Dearborn Inn

(Come early on June 7 if you want more time in
Greenfield Village and Henry Ford Museum)

June 10

2:30 p.m. start of Detroit post-conference program

June 12, 2:30 p.m., conferences conclude

The Edison Institute • Dearborn, Michigan 48121 • Phone (313) 271-1620

14. First direct mail about travel writers' conference

Here's half the stories: (Each host attraction has several more)

(1)   Reasonably priced Georgian elegance at America's oldest airport hotel, the Dearborn Inn.

    (2)   Sleep in Patrick Henry's house for $40 a night, or Oliver Wolcott's, Walt Whitman's or Barbara Fritchie's - all reproduction homes managed by the Dearborn Inn.

(3)   Greenfield Village and Henry Ford Museum, the world's largest indoor-outdoor collection of Americana and the nation's most visited private historical museums, celebrate their 50th anniversary.

    (4)   Henry Ford Museum's innovative new $2.4 million Hall of Technology, the largest reinstallation in an existing museum ever attempted, will be completed June 1.

    (5)   Thomas Alva Edison's Menlo Park Laboratory in Greenfield Village is a major travel attraction for visitors from throughout the world on this 100th anniversary of the most famous invention he made there, the first practical incandescent lamp.

    (6)   Greenfield Village and Henry Ford Museum, the nation's most popular private historical museums, are going all out to celebrate their 50th anniversary and the 100th anniversary of electric light, making this summer the best time to plan a visit.

(7)   The people mover offers a free ride on a transportation innovation connecting one of America's newest and most spectacular hotels, the Hyatt Regency Dearborn, with one of the nation's largest multi-level shopping complexes, Fairlane Town Center.

    (8)   There is free family fun touring the world's largest industrial complex where raw ore comes in and finished automobiles are driven out -- the Ford Motor Company Rouge Plant.

    (9)   Dearborn, a city of unique travel attractions, and the hometown of Henry Ford, is celebrating its 50th anniversary this summer.

    (10) Vacationers in Dearborn can eat in a converted pool at Henry Ford's 56-room Scottish baronial mansion, Fair Lane, and tour the richly decorated home on Sundays.

(11) Over the entertainment rooms door of the 100-room Meadow Brook Hall is the inscription "Welcome the coming -- speed the departing guest." Relatively unknown nationally, Meadow Brook Hall celebrates its 50th anniversary this year by continuing to give visitors a fascinating look at one of America's great mansions.

    (12) Candlelight dinner in a Christopher Wren Georgian dining room is a memorable dining experience available at Meadow Brook Hall.

14. First direct mail about travel writers' conference

(13) Cranbrook is a 300-acre oasis of culture and beauty with the Eliel Saarinen House, the Academy of Art Museum, the Greek Theater, the Institute of Science natural history museum, planetarium and observatory, Cranbrook House by Albert Kahn and 40 acres of gardens, pine walks, cascades and sculptures by such famous artists as Carl Milles, Michael Hall and Marshall Fredericks.

(14) The world's tallest hotel, the 1,400-room Detroit Plaza, centerpiece of the new Detroit Renaissance Center, the largest privately financed urban development in the world.

(15) Two years after Renaissance Center -- trolley rides, river-front parks, family fun in downtown Detroit.

(16) Detroit's famous Eastern Market, an ethnic potpourri that brings Old World charm to the Motor City.

(17) Beautiful Belle Isle, America's largest city island park -- the nation's first publicly owned aquarium, beaches, outdoor concerts, children's zoo, conservatory, new nature center, walking, biking, horseback riding, golfing, sailing, canoeing.

(18) The Dossin Great Lakes Museum on Belle Isle -- a vantage point from which to watch flag ships from 26 countries passing by on the Detroit River, the world's busiest inland waterway.

(19) Passport-free international shopping, spectacular public parks and gardens, cultural and entertainment events and fine restaurants are across a bridge or through a tunnel from Detroit to friendly Windsor, Ontario, Canada, the only place where one can be south of the United States in Canada.

(20) The outdoor P'Jazz tradition at the Pontchartrain Hotel, Detroiters' summer salute to the jazz greats.

(21) Greektown, an enchanting enclave where belly dancing and baklava reign supreme.

(22) Detroiters representing 20 nationalities produce the first and largest series of summer ethnic festivals in America.

(23) "Brunch with Bach," a medley for ear and palate at the nation's fourth-largest art museum, the Detroit Institute of Arts.

(24) Detroit's Cultural Center, its library with major map, genealogy and automotive collections, historical museum where visitors walk the streets of old Detroit, children's museum with its unique "Silverbolt" sculptured horse, the new $6 million science center and planetarium, the International Institute and Wayne State University home of the Hilberry Classic Theater, enrich the lives of visitors and Detroiters every day of the year.

(25) Indian Village, a Detroit district of historic homes in the grand manner.

See you June 7th!

G. Donald Adams
SATW Associate Member

14. *First direct mail about travel writers' conference*

THE EDISON INSTITUTE
Henry Ford Museum
& Greenfield Village

P.O. Box 1970 Dearborn, Michigan 48121
(313) 271-1620

101!

That's the number registered so far for the SATW conference that begins in Dearborn June 8.

There is room for more. Each day new story opportunities are being set aside in waiting! But we must give our host hotels the absolute number of rooms required by May 1. If you have not registered, please do so today.

Martin Hintz reports that Robert Holland, deputy director of the U.S. Department of Transportation in charge of public and consumer affairs will speak following our Saturday morning business meeting, on energy, mass transit, and administration policies affecting tourism. Also there will be interesting presentations by representatives from sites interested in hosting future meetings.

Please come!

See you June 8,

G. Donald Adams, Manager
Print Media Services
Office of Public Relations

encl.

am

15. *Second direct mail about travel writers' conference*

Not wanting you to miss out

on a good thing!

I've enclosed information 'on the new Henry Ford Museum Hall
of Technology that was distributed at the recent SATW conference.

Although it appears that a good and productive time was
enjoyed by all, it would have been even better if you could have
been here. If you can work a visit to us into your travel schedule
this year, please let me know.

Sincerely yours,

G. Donald Adams, Manager
Print Media Services
Office of Public Relations

encl.
am

16. Letter to writers who did not attend conference

Notes

Preface

1. Alan Rosenthal, "Museums jump into the marketing game," *Advertising Age*, September 27, 1982, p. M2.

Introduction

1. Frances A. Koestler, *Planning and Setting Objectives* (New York: National Communications Council for Human Services, Public Relations Society of America, 1977). p. 7.

2. "Goals for Museums and the Museum Profession," *Museum News*. October 1980, p. 68.

3. "Suggested Qualifications for Museum Positions," *Museum News*. October 1980, p. 36.

4. Thomas W. Leavitt, "From the President," *Museum News*, September/October 1982, p. 13.

Chapter 1

1. A. Westley Rowland, *Handbook of Institutional Advancement* (San Francisco: Jossey-Bass, 1977), p. 140.

2. "Suggested Qualifications for Museum Positions," *Museum News*, October 1980, p. 30.

3. Philip Lesly, *Public Relations Handbook*, 2nd ed. (Englewood Cliffs: Prentice-Hall, 1978), p. 287.

4. "Suggested Qualifications for Museum Positions," *Museum News*, October 1980, p. 28. The 1980 AAM report on its position qualification study described an ability to communicate knowledge relevant to the collections as a requirement for the position of curator.

5. It is also important for the curator to understand the policy according to which the museum authorizes or disallows use of its collections by the media.

6. Mary Ellen Munley and Frances Beth Kent, "Consulting Checklist," *Museum News*, May/June 1980, p. 68.

7. "Communication Forum," *Channels*, September 1978.

Chapter 2

1. Charles R. McClure, "The Planning Process: Strategies for Action," *College and Research Libraries*, November 1978, p. 459.

2. "How to Plan Public Relations Programs," *Publicity Craft* (New York: Public Relations Aids, 1982), p. 2.

3. Larry Morrison, "Public Relations and Public Image," *Museum News*, January/February 1979, p. 32.

4. Alice McHugh, "Strategic Planning for Museums," *Museum News*, July/August 1980, p. 25.

5. Morrison, "Public Relations and Public Image," p. 34.

6. Raymond P. Ewing, "Issues," *Public Relations Journal*, June 1980, p. 14.

7. Morrison, "Public Relations and Public Image," p. 33.

8. Ewing, "Issues," p. 15.

9. Philip Lesly, *Public Relations Handbook*, 2nd ed. (Englewood Cliffs: Prentice-Hall, 1978), p. 365.

10. Ewing, "Issues," pp. 15, 16.

Chapter 3

1. Philip Lesly, *Public Relations Handbook*, 2nd ed. (Englewood Cliffs: Prentice-Hall, 1978), p. 162.

2. A. Westley Rowland, Handbook of Institutional Advancement (San Francisco: Jossey-Bass, 1977), pp. 132, 133.

3. Rowland, *Handbook*, p. 136.

4. Rowland, *Handbook*, p. 130.

5. Rowland, *Handbook*, p. 136.

6. Nelson Graburn, "The Museum and the Visitor Experience," *Roundtable Reports* (Museum Education Roundtable), fall 1977, p. 1.

7. Graburn, "Museum, and Experience," p. 3.

8. Graburn, "Museum and Experience," p. 4.

Chapter 4

1. Rowland, *Handbook of Institutional Advancement* (San Francisco: Jossey-Bass, 1977), p. 154.

2. Scott M. Cutlip and Allen H. Center, *Effective Public Relations*, 5th ed. (Englewood Cliffs: Prentice-Hall, 1978), p. 488.

3. Alvin Toffler, *The Culture Consumer* (New York: Random House, 1964), pp. 122, 123.

4. Toffler, *The Culture Consumer*, p. 179.

5. "Newsgram," *U.S. News & World Report*, February 16, 1981, p. 12.

6. Cutlip and Center, *Effective Public Relations*, p. 489.

7. Rowland, *Handbook*, pp. 159, 160.

8. Lawrence L. Reger, "From the Director," *Museum News*, October 1980, p. 8.

9. Raymond F. Pisney, "Squeezing the Buffalo" (Paper presented at the American Association for State and Local History seminar on the interpretation of history, Dearborn, Michigan, November 18, 1980), p. 59.

10. Edwin McDowell, "Corporations as the New Medicis," *Saturday Review*, December 1980, p. 47.
11. Pisney, "Squeezing the Buffalo," pp. 61, 62.
12. Rowland, *Handbook*, p. 367.

Chapter 6

1. Charles Honaker, "News Releases Revisited," *Public Relations Journal*, April 1981, p. 25.
2. Philip Lesly, *How We Discommunicate* (New York: AMACOM, 1979), p. 133.
3. Gabe Thurston, *The TV News Handbook* (New York: Fowler and Wells, 1980), p. 8.

Chapter 7

1. Daniel Hurley and Jill Tobias, "On the Air: The Cincinnati Historical Society puts local history on commercial television," *History News*, September 1982, p. 20.
2. A 1981 Federal Communication Commission deregulation of radio, which at this writing is under appeal before the U.S. Court of Appeals in Washington, has resulted in some stations eliminating or reducing the use of public service material and with others keeping their usage at previous levels. According to the November 8, 1982, issue of *Broadcasting Magazine*, the FCC has announced that similar television deregulation is due for commission action soon.
3. *TV Public Service Announcements: What Do Stations Want?* (New York: Planned Communication Services, 1980).
4. *TV Public Service Announcements.*
5. Walter J. Klein, *The Sponsored Film* (New York: Hastings House, 1976), p. xiii.

Chapter 8

1. Scott M. Cutlip and Allen H. Center, *Effective Public Relations*, 5th ed. (Englewood Cliffs: Prentice-Hall, 1978), p. 197.
2. Julie Noel Gilbert, "Coming to Terms with the Tax Man," *Museum News*, September/October 1982, p. 23.
3. At this writing, the United States Internal Revenue Service is considering whether revenue from an item bearing the museum's name that is sold in its shops is taxable.

Chapter 9

1. Bruce H. Evans, "The Museum as Advocate," *Museum News*, March/April 1980, p. 26.
2. Marie Malaro, "Collections Management Policies," *Museum News*, November/December 1979, pp. 57, 58.

Sources of Further Information

DIRECTORIES

Media General

American Society of Journalists and Authors Directory. American Society of Journalists and Authors, 1501 Broadway, Suite 1907, New York, N.Y. 10036.

Ayer Directory of Publications. IMS Press, 426 Pennsylvania Ave., Fort Washington, Pa. 19034.

Bacon's Publicity Checker. Bacon Publishing Co., 14 E. Jackson Blvd., Chicago, Ill. 60604.

Broadcasting Yearbook. Broadcasting Publications, 1735 DeSales, NW, Washington, D.C. 20036.

Burrelle's Special Groups Media Directories Series. 75 E. Northfield Ave., Livingston, N.J. 07039. (Black, Hispanic, Women's media).

Cable Contacts Yearbook. Larimi Communications Associates, Ltd., 151 E. 50th St., New York, N.Y. 10022.

Cable TV Publicity Outlets Nationwide. Box 327, Washington Depot, Conn. 06794.

Editor & Publisher Yearbook. Editor & Publisher, 850 Third Ave., New York, N.Y. 10022.

Family Page Directory, Box 327, Washington Depot, Conn. 06794.

The FINDERBINDER. Gary Beals Advertising & Public Relations, 4141 Fairmount Ave., San Diego, Calif. 92105. Comprehensive and continuously updated listings of media personnel in cities.

Gebbie Press All-in-One Directory, Box 1000, New Paltz, N.Y. 12561.

Media News Keys, 150 Fifth Ave., New York, N.Y. 10011.

News Bureaus in the United States (1977). R. Weiner, Inc., 888 Seventh Ave., New York, N.Y. 10019.

New York Publicity Outlets, Box 327, Washington Depot, Conn. 06794.

New York Travel Writers Association Roster, free from Frances Shemanski, P.O. Box 113, Baychester Station, The Bronx, N.Y. 10469.

Richard Weiner's Media Directories, Public Relations Publishing Co., 888 Seventh Ave., New York, N.Y. 10106.
Sourcebook, Gary Beals Advertising & Public Relations, 4141 Fairmount Ave., San Diego, Calif. 92105.
Standard Periodical Directory (1979). Oxbridge, Inc., 183 Madison Ave., New York, N.Y. 10016.
Standard Rate & Data. 5201 Old Orchard Rd., Skokie, Ill. 60076. (Listing of advertising media)
Syndicated Columnists (1979). R. Weiner, Inc., 888 Seventh Ave., New York, N.Y. 10009.
Talk Show Directory. National Research Bureau, 310 S. Michigan, Chicago, Ill. 60604.
TV Publicity Outlets Nationwide, Box 327, Washington Depot, Conn. 06794.
TV/Radio Contacts. Larimi, Inc., 151 E. Fiftieth St., New York, N.Y. 10022.
Working Press of the Nation. National Research Bureau, Burlington, Iowa 52601.
Writers Market. Writers Digest Books, 9933 Alliance Rd., Cincinnati, Ohio 45242.

Travel Writers' Associations

Midwest Travel Writers Association Roster. Ms. Nancy Kennedy, Ford Times, P.O. Box 1899, Dearborn, Mich. 48121.
Society of American Travel Writers Membership Directory. Society of American Travel Writers, 1120 Connecticut Ave., NW, Suite 940, Washington, D.C. 20036.

PERIODICALS

Leads on Stories under Development by the Media

Contacts. Larimi Communication Associates, Ltd., 151 E. Fiftieth St., New York, N.Y. 10022.
PR Aids Party Line, 330 W. 34th St., New York, N.Y. 10001.
Freelancer's Newsletter, 307 Westlake Dr., Austin, Tex. 78746.
Travelwriter Market Newsletter, Room 1745, Plaza Hotel, New York, N.Y. 10019. (Includes some story leads but is most helpful in identifying the most productive travel writers)

For the Museum Professional

Aviso newsletter, *Museum Magazine*, and *Update* museum public relations and communications newsletter. American Association of Museums, Suite 428, 1055 Thomas Jefferson St., NW, Washington, D.C. 20007.
Historic Preservation and *Preservation News.* The National Trust for Historic Preservation, 1785 Massachusetts Ave., NW, Washington, D.C. 20036.
History News and technical leaflets on museum management. American Association for State and Local History, 708 Berry Rd., Nashville, Tenn. 37204.

For the Public Relations Professional

Broadcasting Magazine, Broadcasting Publications, Inc., 1735 DeSales St., NW, Washington, D.C. 20036.

Channels. Public Relations Society of America, 845 Third Ave., New York, N.Y. 10022. (Monthly newsletter for nonprofit field.)

Columbia Journalism Review, 700 Journalism Building, Columbia University, New York, N.Y. 10027.

Editor & Publisher, 575 Lexington Ave., New York, N.Y. 10022.

Impact, 203 N. Wabash Ave., Suite 1804, Chicago, Ill. 60601. (Emphasizes communication techniques)

Publicity Craft, PR Aids, 330 West 34th St., New York, N.Y. 10001.

Public Opinion Quarterly, 52 Vanderbilt Ave., New York, N.Y. 10014.

Public Relations Journal. Public Relations Society of America, 845 Third Ave., New York, N.Y. 10022.

Public Relations News, 127 E. Eightieth St., New York, N.Y. 10021.

Public Relations Quarterly, 44 W. Market St., Rhinebeck, N.Y. 12572.

Public Relations Review, 7338 Baltimore Blvd., Suite 101A, College Park, Md. 20740.

Publicist, 221 Park Ave. South, New York, N.Y. 10003.

Social Science Monitor, 7100 Baltimore Blvd., Suite 500, College Park, Md. 20740.

PHOTO SYNDICATES

Associated Press News Photos, 50 Rockefeller Plaza, New York, N.Y. 10017.

Globe Photos, Inc., 404 Park Ave. South, New York, N.Y. 10016.

Newspaper Enterprise Association, 230 Park Ave., New York, N.Y. 10017.

UPI Newspictures, 220 E. Forty-second St., New York, N.Y. 10017.

Wide World Photos, Inc., 50 Rockefeller Plaza, New York, N.Y. 10020.

PROFESSIONAL ASSOCIATIONS

American Association of Museums, Suite 428, 1055 Thomas Jefferson St., NW, Washington, D.C. 20007. A museum public relations code of ethics has been drafted by the American Association of Museums Standing Professional Committee on Public Relations and Communications Management and is expected to be ratified in 1983. Copies will be available from AAM.

American Association of Museums, Professional Committee on Public Relations and Communications, Suite 428, 1055 Thomas Jefferson Street, NW, Washington, D.C. 20007.

American Association for State and Local History, 708 Berry Rd., Nashville, Tenn. 37204.

Association of College, University, and Community Arts Administrators, P.O. Box 2137, Madison, Wisc. 53701.

Association for Living Historical Farms and Agricultural Museums, John

Schlebecker, Museum of American History, Suite 5035, Smithsonian Institution, Washington, D.C. 20560.

Council for Advancement and Support of Education, 11 Dupont Circle, Washington, D.C., 20036.

International Association of Business Communicators, 870 Market St., San Francisco, Calif. 94102.

International Council of Museums, Suite 428, 1055 Thomas Jefferson St., NW, Washington, D.C. 20007.

Public Relations Society of America, Inc., 845 Third Ave., New York, N.Y. 10022.

Women Executives in Public Relations, c/o Phyllis Berlowe, Doremus & Co., 120 Broadway, New York, N.Y. 10271.

Women in Communications, Inc., Box 9561, Austin, Texas 78766.

(Where applicable, press club membership is recommended.)

REFERENCE BOOKS

Alderson, William T., and Low, Shirley Payne. *Interpretation of Historic Sites.* Nashville: American Association for State and Local History, 1976. (708 Berry Rd., Nashville, Tenn. 37204.)

Alexander, Edward P. *Museums in Motion.* Nashville: American Association for State and Local History, 1979.

Bates, Don. *Communicating & Moneymaking.* New York: Heladon Press, 1979.

Benn, Alec. *The 23 Most Common Mistakes in PR.* New York: AMACOM, 1982.

Black, Sam and Sharpe, Melvin. *Practical Public Relations: Common-Sense Guidelines for Business and Professional People.* Englewood Cliffs: Prentice-Hall, 1983.

Breen, G. *Do It Yourself Marketing Research.* New York: McGraw-Hill, 1982.

Cutlip, Scott M., and Center, Allan H. *Effective Public Relations,* 6th ed. Englewood Cliffs: Prentice-Hall, 1982.

Douglis, Philip. *Pictures for Organizations: How and Why They Work As Communication.* Chicago: Ragan Communications Inc., 1982.

Fine, Seymore. *Marketing of Ideas and Social Issues.* New York: Praeger, 1981.

Hall, Mark W. *Broadcast Journalism.* 2nd ed. New York: Hastings House, 1978.

Hilliard, Robert L. *Writing for Television and Radio.* 3rd ed. New York: Hastings House, 1976.

Kotler, Philip. *Marketing for Nonprofit Organizations.* Englewood Cliffs: Prentice-Hall, 1975.

Lee, Sherman E. *On Understanding Art Museums.* Englewood Cliffs: Prentice-Hall, 1975.

Lerbinger, Otto. *Designs for Persuasive Communication.* Englewood Cliffs: Prentice-Hall, 1972.

Lesly, Philip. *How We Discommunicate.* New York: AMACOM, 1979.

PRSA Code of Professional Standards

Declaration of Principles

Members of the Public Relations Society of America base their professional principles on the fundamental value and dignity of the individual, holding that the free exercise of human rights, especially freedom of speech, freedom of assembly and freedom of the press, is essential to the practice of public relations.

In serving the interests of clients and employers, we dedicate ourselves to the goals of better communication, understanding and cooperation among the diverse individuals, groups and institutions of society, and of equal opportunity of employment in the public relations profession.

We pledge:

To conduct ourselves professionally, with truth, accuracy, fairness and responsibility to the public;

To improve our individual competence and advance the knowledge and proficiency of the profession through continuing research and education;

And to adhere to the articles of the Code of Professional Standards for the Practice of Public Relations as adopted by the governing Assembly of the Society.

Code of Professional Standards For the Practice of Public Relations

These articles have been adopted by the Public Relations Society of America to promote and maintain high standards of public service and ethical conduct among its members.

1. A member shall deal fairly with clients or employers, past and present, with fellow practitioners and the general public.

2. A member shall conduct his or her professional life in accord with the public interest.

3. A member shall adhere to truth and accuracy and to generally accepted standards of good taste.

4. A member shall not represent conflicting or competing interests without the express consent of those involved, given after a full disclosure of the facts; nor place himself or herself in a position where the member's interest is or may be in conflict with a duty to a client, or others, without a full disclosure of such interests to all involved.

5. A member shall safeguard the confidences of both present and former clients or employers and shall not accept retainers or employment which may involve the disclosure or use of these confidences to the disadvantage or prejudice of such clients or employers.

6. A member shall not engage in any practice which tends to corrupt the integrity of channels of communication or the processes of government.

7. A member shall not intentionally communicate false or misleading information and is obligated to use care to avoid communication of false or misleading information.

8. A member shall be prepared to identify publicly the name of the client or employer on whose behalf any public communication is made.

9. A member shall not make use of any individual or organization purporting to serve or represent an announced cause, or purporting to be independent or unbiased, but actually serving an undisclosed special or private interest of a member, client or employer.

10. A member shall not intentionally injure the professional reputation or practice of another practitioner. However, if a member has evidence that another member has been guilty of unethical, illegal or unfair practices, including those in violation of this Code, the member shall present the information promptly to the proper authorities of the Society for action in accordance with the procedure set forth in Article XII of the Bylaws.

11. A member called as a witness in a proceeding for the enforcement of this Code shall be bound to appear, unless excused for sufficient reason by the Judicial Panel.

12. A member, in performing services for a client or employer, shall not accept fees, commissions or any other valuable consideration from anyone other than the client or employer in connection with those services without the express consent of the client or employer, given after a full disclosure of the facts.

13. A member shall not guarantee the achievement of specified results beyond the member's direct control.

14. A member shall, as soon as possible, sever relations with any organization or individual if such relationship requires conduct contrary to the articles of this Code.

Public Relations Society of America

This Code, adopted by the PRSA Assembly and effective January 1, 1978, replaces a similar Code of Professional Standards for the Practice of Public Relations previously in force since 1954 and strengthened by revisions in 1959, 1963 and 1977.

Lesly, Philip. *Public Relations Handbook.* 3rd ed. Englewood Cliffs: Prentice-Hall, 1983.

Mokwa, Michael P.; Dawson. William M.; and Prieve, E. Arthur. *Marketing the Arts.* New York: Praeger, 1980.

Museum Ethics. Washington D.C.: American Association of Museums, 1978.

Nakamoto, Kent, and Levin, Kati. *Marketing the Arts: A Selected Bibliography.* Madison: Association of College, University, and Community Arts Administrators, 1981.

Newsom, Doug, and Scott, Alan. *This Is PR: The Realities of Public Relations.* Belmont: Wadsworth, 1981.

Nolte, Lawrence W., and Wilcox, Dennis L. *Fundamentals of Public Relations.* New York: Pergamon, 1979.

Preservation: Toward an Ethic in the 1980s. Washington, D.C.: The Preservation Press, 1980.

Public Relations Guides for Nonprofit Organizations. New York: Foundation for Public Relations. (Planning, Publicity, Volunteers, Special Events, Measuring and Evaluating, and Standards to Strengthen PR.)

Public Relations Society of America Public Relations Bibliography. New York: Public Relations Society of America, 1983.

Sanford, Bruce. *Synopsis of the Law of Libel and the Right of Privacy.* New York: World Almanac, 1981.

Simon, Morton. *Public Relations Law.* New York: Foundation for Public Relations, 1969.

Stempl and Westley. *Research Methods in Mass Communications.* Englewood Cliffs: Prentice-Hall, 1981.

Stonecipher, Harry W. *Editorial and Persuasive Writing.* New York: Hastings House, 1979.

Tarver, J. *Effective Speech Writing.* Richmond, Va.: Speech Writing Institute, 1982.

Thurston, Gabe. *The TV News Handbook.* New York: Fowler and Wells, 1980.

Toffler, Alvin. *The Culture Consumer.* New York: Random House, 1964.

Toffler, Alvin. *Future Shock.* New York: Random House, 1970.

Udell and Laczniak. *Marketing in an Age of Change.* New York: Wiley, 1981.

Westley, A. Rowland. *Handbook of Institutional Advancement.* San Francisco: Jossey-Bass, 1977.

Yankelovich, Daniel. *New Rules.* New York: Random House, 1981.

Yarrington, Roger. *Community Relations Handbook.* New York: Longman, Inc., 1983.

Zuckman, Harvey, and Gaynes, Martin J. *Mass Communication Law in a Nutshell.* St. Paul: West, 1977.

Museum Public Relations

Anderson, John, and Sperberg, Diana. *Public Media Manual for Museums.*

Austin: Texas Association of Museums, 1979. (P.O. Box 13353, Austin, Tex. 78711)

Bellow, Corinne, ed. *Public View*. International Council of Museums/American Association of Museums, 1981. 1055 Thomas Jefferson St., NW, Washington, D.C. 20007.

Publications

Alderson, William T., ed. *Marking and Correcting Copy for Your Printer*. Technical Leaflet No. 51. Nashville: American Association for State and Local History, 1969.

The Chicago Manual of Style. 13th ed. Chicago: University of Chicago Press, 1982.

Click, J. W., and Baird, Russell N. *Magazine Editing and Production*. Dubuque: William C. Brown, 1974.

Craig, James. *Production for the Graphic Designer*. New York: Watson-Guptill, 1974.

Derby, Charlotte S. *Reaching Your Public: The Historical Society Newsletter*. Technical Leaflet No. 39. Nashville: American Association for State and Local History, 1967.

Felt, Thomas E. *Researching, Writing, and Publishing Local History*. 2nd ed. Nashville: American Association for State and Local History, 1981.

How to Plan Printing. Boston: S. D. Warren, 1978.

Jones, Gerre. *How to Prepare Professional Design Brochures*. New York: McGraw-Hill, 1976.

Lawson, Alexander. *Printing Types: An Introduction*. Boston: Beacon Press, 1976.

Skillin, Marjorie E., and Gay, Robert M. *Words into Type*. 4th ed. Englewood Cliffs: Prentice-Hall, 1979.

Strunk, William, Jr., and White, E. B. *The Elements of Style*. 3rd ed. New York: Macmillan, 1979.

Walklet, John J., Jr. *Publishing in the Historical Society*. Technical Leaflet No. 34. Nashville: American Association for State and Local History, 1966.

White, Jan V. *Editing by Design*. New York: R. R. Bowker, 1974.

Journalistic Style

The Associated Press Stylebook. The Associated Press, 50 Rockefeller Plaza, New York, N.Y. 10020.

Ayer Public Relations/Publicity Stylebook. Ayer Press, One Bala Ave., Bala Cynwyd, Penna. 19004.

Broadcast News Stylebook (1977). The Associated Press, 50 Rockefeller Plaza, New York, N.Y. 10020.

New York Times Manual of Style/Usage. New York: McGraw-Hill, 1977.

The UPI Stylebook. United Press International, 220 E. Forty-second St., New York, N.Y., 10017.

CLIPPING SERVICES

Luce Press Clippings, 420 Lexington Ave., New York, N.Y. 10017. (Print and broadcast)

Burrelle's Press Clipping Service, 75 E. Northfield Ave., Livingston, N.J. 07039.

DISTRIBUTION SERVICES

Film

Association Films, Inc., 866 Third Ave., New York, N.Y. 10022.

Modern Talking Pictures Service, International Bldg., 45 Rockefeller Plaza, New York, N.Y. 10111.

Planned Communications Services, Inc., 12 E. Forty-sixth St., New York, N.Y. 10017.

Print Media

Derus Media Service, 8 W. Hubbard St., Chicago, Ill. 60610.

North American Precis Syndicate, Inc., 201 E. Forty-second St., New York, N.Y. 10017.

Public Relations Aids, 221 Park Ave. South, New York, N.Y. 10003. (Regional and national distribution from computerized lists)

FEATURE SYNDICATES AND WIRES

AP Newsfeatures, 50 Rockefeller Plaza, New York, N.Y. 10020.

Chicago Tribune—New York News Syndicate, Inc., 220 E. Forty-second St., New York, N.Y. 10017.

Chicago Tribune—New York News Syndicate, Inc., Tribune Tower, Chicago, Ill. 60611.

Columbia Features, Inc., 36 W. Forty-fourth St., New York, N.Y. 10036.

Copley News Service, 350 Camino DelaReina, P.O. Box 190, San Diego, Calif. 92041.

Doubleday Syndicate, 245 Park Ave., New York, N.Y. 10017.

Enterprise Features, 230 Park Ave., New York, N.Y. 10017.

King Features Syndicate, 235 E. Forty-fifth St., New York, N.Y. 10017.

Knight News Wire, 321 W. Lafayette, Detroit, Mich. 48231.

Los Angeles Times Syndicate, Times Mirror Square, Los Angeles, Calif. 90053.

Newspaper Enterprise Association, 230 Park Ave., New York, N.Y. 10017.

New York Times Special Features, 229 W. Forty-third St., New York, N.Y. 10036.

North American Newspaper Alliance, Inc., 220 E. Forty-second St., New York, N.Y. 10017.

United Feature Syndicate, Inc., 220 E. Forty-second St., New York, N.Y. 10017.

United Press International, 220 E. Forty-second St., New York, N.Y. 10017.

NEWS/FEATURE WIRE SERVICES

Associated Press, 50 Rockefeller Plaza, New York, N.Y. 10020.
Reuters, 1700 Broadway, New York, N.Y. 10019.
United Press International, 220 E. Forty-second St., New York, N.Y. 10017.

NETWORK NEWS/FEATURES CONTACTS

ABC Radio, 1926 Broadway, New York, N.Y. 10023. (212) 887-4171.
Associated Press Radio, Managing Editor, 50 Rockefeller Plaza, New York, N.Y. 10020. (212) 621-1516.
Cable News Network, National Assignment Desk, 1050 Techwood Drive, NW, Atlanta, Ga. 30318. (404) 898-8511.
"CBS Evening News," Executive Producer, 524 W. 57th St., New York, N.Y. 10019. (212) 975-3691.
CBS Radio News, Executive Editor, 524 W. 57th St., New York, N.Y. 10019. (212) 975-3615.
"Good Morning America," ABC-TV, Seven W. 66th St., New York, N.Y. 10023. (212) 580-6100.
"Morning," CBS-TV, 524 W. 57th St., New York, N.Y. 10019. (212) 975-4472.
Mutual Radio News, Vice President, News, Special Programming, 1755 S. Jefferson Davis Highway, Arlington, Va. 22202. (703) 685-2000.
National Public Radio, Attn: News, 2025 M St., NW, Washington, D.C. 20036. (202) 822-2000.
"NBC Nightly News," Executive Producer, NBC-TV, 30 Rockefeller Plaza, Room 520, New York, N.Y. 10020. (212) 664-4971.
NBC Radio News, Assignment Editor, 30 Rockefeller Plaza, Room 505, New York, N.Y. 10020. (212) 664-5681.
RKO Radio Network, Features Editor, 1440 Broadway, New York, N.Y. 10018. (212) 575-6100.
"Sunday Morning," CBS-TV, 555 W. 57th St., New York, N.Y. 10019. (212) 975-8954.
"Today," NBC-TV, 30 Rockefeller Plaza, New York, N.Y. 10020. (212) 664-3236.
"World News Tonight," Executive Producer, Seven W. 66th St., New York, N.Y. 10023. (212) 887-4040.

TRAVEL RESEARCH INFORMATION

Bibliography of Tourism and Travel Research Studies. The Business Research Division, Graduate School of Business Administration, University of Colorado, Campus Box 420, Boulder, Colo. 80309.
1982 State & Metropolitan Area Data Book. United States Bureau of Census, Government Printing Office, Washington, D.C. 20402.

Travel Industry Association of America. 1899 L St., NW, Washington, D.C. 20036. (Newsletter, conferences)

Travel Tourism Executive Newsletter, 53 Church St., Stonington, Conn. 06378. (Reports on travel trends)

U.S. Travel Data Center, 1899 L St., NW, Washington, D.C. 20036.

WORKSHOPS AND SEMINARS

American Association of Museums/International Council of Museums, Suite 428, 1055 Thomas Jefferson St., NW, Washington, D.C. 20007.

American Association for State and Local History, 708 Berry Rd., Nashville, Tenn. 37204.

The Association of College, University, and Community Arts Administrators, P.O. Box 2137, Madison, Wisc. 53701.

Council for Advancement and Support of Education, Suite 400, 11 Dupont Circle, Washington, D.C. 20036.

George Washington University, Center for Professional Development, 2019 Cunningham Dr., Hampton, Va. 23666.

Museums Collaborative in conjunction with Columbia University Graduate School of Business and the State University of New York. Museums Collaborative, Inc., 15 Gramercy Park South, New York, N.Y. 10003.

New York University, Business and Management Programs, Room 1412, 310 Madison Ave., New York, N.Y. 10017.

The Professional Development Institute, Pace University, 331 Madison Ave., Room 603, New York, N.Y. 10017.

The Ragan Report Workshops, 407 S. Dearborn, Chicago, Ill. 60605.

Smithsonian Public Information and Publications Workshops, Office of Museum Programs, A & I Building, 2235, The Smithsonian Institution, Washington, D.C. 20560.

Society of American Travel Writers Travel Communications Workshops, 1120 Connecticut Ave., NW, Suite 940, Washington, D.C. 20036.

Index